Understanding Death

To my husband, Zsolt (1945–2010)

Understanding Death

*An Introduction to Ideas of Self and
the Afterlife in World Religions*

Angela Sumegi

WILEY Blackwell

This edition first published 2014
© 2014 Angela Sumegi

Registered Office
John Wiley & Sons Ltd, The Atrium, Southern Gate, Chichester, West Sussex, PO19 8SQ, UK

Editorial Offices
350 Main Street, Malden, MA 02148-5020, USA
9600 Garsington Road, Oxford, OX4 2DQ, UK
The Atrium, Southern Gate, Chichester, West Sussex, PO19 8SQ, UK

For details of our global editorial offices, for customer services, and for information about how to apply for permission to reuse the copyright material in this book please see our website at www.wiley.com/wiley-blackwell.

Library of Congress Cataloging-in-Publication Data

Sumegi, Angela, 1948–
  Understanding death : an introduction to ideas of self and the afterlife in world religions / Angela Sumegi.
      pages cm
  Includes bibliographical references and index.
  ISBN 978-1-4051-5370-6 (cloth) – ISBN 978-1-4051-5371-3 (pbk.)   1. Death—Religious aspects—Comparative studies.   2. Future life—Comparative studies.   I. Title.
  BL504.S86 2013
  202'.3–dc23

                                                                      2013015109

A catalogue record for this book is available from the British Library.

Cover image: A woman grieves at her father's funeral in the Van Vien Cemetery, Hanoi, Vietnam. Photo © Larry Towell / Magnum Photos
Cover design by Design Deluxe

Set in 10.5/13.5pt Palatino by Aptara Inc., New Delhi, India

V8F733FC4-E320-408E-BBDD-46E709E022B5_120419

Contents

Contents

Preface

The meaning of the word "death," like so many other important words in our vocabulary – life, self, mind, body, love, respect, dignity, honor, grief – differs from culture to culture, from past to present, and even from person to person within one community. The field of death studies, which encompasses academic research, popular literature on death and dying, as well as the teaching of courses on death in colleges and universities, has its roots in a modern North American movement spurred on by the now famous 1969 publication by Elizabeth Kübler-Ross of *On Death and Dying*. The movement has resulted in worldwide studies that investigate and theorize death and dying from numerous perspectives: historical, ethical, psychological, sociological, philosophical, theological, and literary. As an introduction to the views and practices of various religions regarding death and life after death, this book offers the opportunity for a comparative reading in the hope that the reader will gain insight from what Arvind Sharma calls "reciprocal illumination" – the idea that we may find greater understanding of one tradition in the light of others (Sharma, 2005).

One's first encounter with death may result in childhood puzzlement, shock, or a deep feeling of irrevocable loss. The experience is intimately related to thoughts and emotions that shape our identity and revolve around a sense of what we intuitively hold to be self or the essence of life. Almost always there are questions. What exactly happened? Why? What do we do now? The book begins with an exploration of the questions that death evokes and that religions aim to answer. Subsequent chapters take the reader through the main responses of several religious traditions. There are nine chapters including one on death in religions of antiquity and seven on living religions. This is not a book on world religions; discussions related to the general belief systems of each religion are oriented towards those aspects that inform perspectives on death. The emphasis in each chapter, therefore, towards history, philosophy, or ritual will vary in order to reflect what is important in understanding the meaning of death in that religion. Throughout, however, notions regarding the self or soul and its trajectory through life and death, as well as the goal or culmination of this journey, will be highlighted. Each chapter will also describe some of the death rituals related to the religion. The ways in which each tradition conceives of the "person" who lives and the "person" who dies will form the central theme and primary organizing principle for the book, whether the discussion relates to primal religious beliefs in many souls, the Biblical view of the person as a holistic body/breath entity, the Hindu concept of *atman* – the undying, immortal soul – or the Buddhist idea of "no-soul." Furthermore, self-conceptions are a crucial element in understanding the varied rituals of closure and farewell that are intrinsic to the way in which individuals and human societies deal with the end of life.

The book is organized so that each religion is treated as a discrete unit. It has been my experience that a thematic approach is useful in a classroom context when students are already familiar with the religions in question, otherwise the various texts and teachings are easily confused. I have also found that the interest of students in this subject is very much tied to their interest in the religions themselves. In other words, they want to know specifically what Judaism or Buddhism or Islam teaches about the process of dying, what are the beliefs regarding the afterlife in that tradition, and what rituals are performed for the dead. The conversations recorded at the end of each chapter are intended to provide the reader with a glimpse of the personal views of people who live and work in the scientific industrialized environment of North America. They come from all walks of life and from all parts of the world. The only criterion for the conversation was that the person be someone who identifies with his or her religion and actively engages with it. Throughout this book, it will become apparent that religion, as it is expressed in texts and canonical interpretations, is diverse and contradictory – how much more so when it is combined with the diverse and contradictory nature of individuals who engage with the textual tradition. Among the interviewees are converts, life-long adherents, devout believers, as well as those who doubt. The conversations are there to offer a personal counterpoint to the abstract concepts and principles discussed in the chapters, and to underscore for the reader that just as human beings live life in a multitude of ways, death is not merely a common event that happens to all; death is interpreted, constructed, one might even say lived, in equally various forms.

I hope that this book will draw the readers' attention to differences and similarities among religions, as well as to the varieties of expression that can be found within one religious tradition. I aim to highlight the manifold conceptions of self and world that inform the way humans interpret life and personal continuation beyond death, as well as our shared human struggle to discover the meaning of, or assign meaning to, the phenomenon of death – a struggle that is renewed with each personal encounter.

Note

As this book is intended for a general audience diacritical marks have not been used and non-English terminology has been kept to the minimum necessary. Unless otherwise stated, quotations are drawn from the following translations:

Doniger, Wendy. *The Rig Veda*. New York: Penguin Books, 1984.
Haleem, Abdel. *The Qur'an: A New Translation*. Oxford: Oxford University Press, 2004.

The New Oxford Annotated Bible, 3rd edition, New Revised Standard Version, ed. Michael D. Coogan. Oxford: Oxford University Press, 2001.
Olivelle, Patrick. *Upanisads*. Oxford: Oxford University Press, 1996.
Stoler-Miller, Barbara. *The Bhagavad-Gita*. New York: Bantam Books, 1986.

Reference and Further Reading

Sharma, Arvind. *Religious Studies and Comparative Methodology*. New York: State University of New York Press, 2005.

Acknowledgments

This book has been many years in the writing, and after the death of my husband in 2010, it likely would never have been completed but for the patience and understanding of the editorial and publishing team at Wiley Blackwell who gave me the time to recover myself and encouraged me not to abandon the project. I extend my deepest thanks to them all.

Over the years, many people have read the drafts, assisted me with research, and offered good editorial advice. Among those I would like to thank especially are Ryszard Cimek, Gilles Comeau, Claire Belanger, and Nalini Devdas. Finally, I would like to thank my students, whose questions and abiding interest in the subject provided me with the incentive to begin and the energy to finish this work.

1

Understanding Death

Life surrounds us. Wherever we find ourselves, we are conscious that countless other living things exist alongside us – animals, plants, insects, microbes, as well as strange combinations of not-quite-animal, not-quite-plant life, like sea anemones. Death surrounds us. From the mosquito unconsciously slapped on an arm to the daily news stories that are of passing notice, to a loved one whose loss brings prolonged grief and mourning. In general, however, we tend to think deeply of death only when it becomes part of our emotional experience, and even then, the business and busyness of life is like a river that carries us along past the numerous moments of other deaths until our own moment arrives. One feels helpless in the face of inevitable death – what can one do about it, really? It is easy, therefore, even in the midst of death to avoid contemplating death, to turn to life where we can have some kind of control, where we can do something about it. I invite you to consider this book as a space in which you can take the time to consider questions like: What is

Understanding Death: An Introduction to Ideas of Self and the Afterlife in World Religions,
First Edition. Angela Sumegi.
© 2014 Angela Sumegi. Published 2014 by Blackwell Publishing Ltd.

death? Who dies? Where do we go from here? Do we go anywhere? And, as you will discover, these questions are much the same as asking: What is life? Who lives? Are we going anywhere now? In the complex symbol system that is language, however, words like "life" or "love" or "death" are bound up with feelings, emotions, and ideas that are very complicated; those that surround death have a long and complex history – you might think of it as the history of becoming who and what we are. When we look at the sacred stories of various cultures and religious traditions that aim to explain death and how it came into the world, we find that at the same time they tell of how we became human, how we became mortal. Take, for example, the Biblical story of Adam and Eve. Their life in the Garden of Eden is one of innocence and joy in the presence of God. Without work or toil, they enjoy the fruit of all the trees, but tempted by the serpent, they disobey God's commands and eat of the forbidden fruit of the Tree of Knowledge of Good and Evil.

> Now the serpent was more crafty than any other wild animal the Lord God had made. He said to the woman, "Did God say, 'You shall not eat from any tree in the garden'?" The woman said to the serpent, "We may eat of the fruit of the trees in the garden; but God said, 'You shall not eat of the fruit of the tree that is in the middle of the garden, nor shall you touch it, or you shall die.'" But the serpent said to the woman, "You will not die; for God knows that when you eat of it your eyes will be opened, and you will be like God, knowing good and evil." So when the woman saw that the tree was good for food, and that it was a delight to the eyes, and that the tree was to be desired to make one wise, she took of its fruit and ate; and she also gave some to her husband who was with her, and he ate. Then the eyes of both were opened and they knew that they were naked; and they sewed fig leaves together and made loincloths for themselves. (Gen. 3:1–7)[1]

Due to this transgression, God banishes them from the Garden. They must make their way in the wilderness beyond, working hard for their food, the woman experiencing pain in childbirth, and eventually they must return to the earth from which God made them.

But this is not only a story of temptation, disobedience, punishment, and the suffering and death that are an inevitable part of the human condition, it is also a story that acknowledges human powers of reasoning and judgment, the attraction of wisdom, thirst for knowledge overcoming rules and regulations, and the responsibility and danger that come with the knowledge of good and evil. Ultimately, the story points to an understanding of humankind as partaking of divinity in that knowledge.

> Then the Lord God said, "See, the man has become like one of us, knowing good and evil; and now, he might reach out his hand and take also from the tree of life, and eat, and live forever" – therefore the Lord God sent him forth from the garden of Eden, to till the ground from which he was taken. He drove out the man; and at the east of the garden of Eden he placed the cherubim, and a sword flaming and turning to guard the way to the tree of life. (Gen. 3:22–24)

The immortality that was denied to humans in the Garden of Eden, eternal life in the presence of God becomes a primary goal of Biblical traditions. Stories such as this relate the mythic events of our past and tell us why we must die; they also look to the future and tell us where we go when this life is finished.

Throughout human history, there have been many who claimed to have made the journey, many who believed that they received a glimpse of that future; a life beyond life in a time beyond time and a place beyond place. One of the earliest literary accounts of what would be now called a "near-death experience" comes from the Greek philosopher Plato (427–347 BCE). It is the story of Er, a soldier who died in battle and returned to life on his funeral pyre:

> He [Er] said that when his soul departed, it made a journey in the company of many, and they came to a certain demonic place, where there were two openings in the earth next to one another, and, again, two in the heaven, above and opposite the others. Between them sat judges who, when they had passed judgment, told the just to continue their journey to the right and upward, through the heaven; and they

3

attached signs of the judgments in front of them. The unjust they told to continue their journey to the left and down, and they had behind them signs of everything they had done. And when he himself came forward, they said that he had to become a messenger to human beings of the things there, and they told him to listen and to look at everything in the place. (Bloom, 1968, pp. 297–298)

Such reports have inspired faith among some, disbelief or skepticism among others. In the last century, the personal accounts of those who have been declared dead or appeared dead but revived have received increasing attention both from the spiritually thirsty and from scholars who seek to analyze and understand the nature of these experiences. Carol Zaleski (2006) notes that in comparison with ancient and medieval stories of afterlife journeys, the theme of judgment and the fear of death as a prelude to hell have mostly disappeared from modern accounts, as they have from the following memoirs of another soldier who was also felled on the battlefield more than 2,000 years after Plato.

Return from the Dead

It is 1915 and 20-year-old Vaughan Ivan Milton Henshaw is a Canadian soldier on the frontlines of World War I. What follows is his personal account recorded by his granddaughter, Linda Henshaw.

On the first of September, it started to rain and the rain never stopped day and night and what were trenches turned into canals – the water waist deep. The dugouts were the same; we'd put stuff under our heads at night to keep our head and shoulders out of the water. We had no protection standing around in the rain, at night we'd sleep in the mud and rain. On November 6th the rain stopped and turned to sleet, great walls of sleet swept in on 20–25/hour winds. That was the day we were to leave for a 6 day so-called rest.

That was also the morning that Henshaw was scheduled to escort the colonel and the doctor on a morning inspection tour of the line. As they arrived at the front line, Henshaw noticed the presence of a sniper. He knocked the colonel into the mud and was hit by the sniper's fire. *"I was badly hit; the blood was running out of my nose and mouth. My left side was mostly blown away."* He has a chance to live if he is transported immediately to the hospital, but the wounded are only taken out at night due to the danger of enemy fire. Despite the danger, however, Henshaw's comrades decide to carry him out wrapped in a rubber sheet and lashed to a pole. They emerge from the trench carrying the makeshift stretcher, falling in shell holes and scrambling out, mud halfway to their knees: *"The air was torn to shreds* [from gun fire]." They finally make it to a protected knoll. Many years later, at a reunion, Henshaw learns from one who was there:

> *When we first saw you, your face was just as black as my shoe but in about a minute or two, suddenly your eyes closed and you turned as white as a sheet and one of the boys said, "he's gone," and I don't mind telling you many tears were shed over your doggone frame.*

But for Henshaw, something else was happening:

> *As for me, when that happened apparently that was when I thought I was being airlifted. I thought the boys had picked up the pole and started to carry me on. Instead in a split second I was in a great concourse of people stretching away as far as I could see to left and to the right. I call them people but later I discovered that they weren't people at all . . . However, what caught my attention almost immediately was a wall, like a blanket or sheet, a white covering of some sort and behind it was a bright light, the brightest light I ever could see. There was something about that light that was different from any ordinary light. It seemed to fill me full of the greatest desire to penetrate that sheet or whatever it was and see what that white beautiful bright light was all about. When I had a chance to look, I couldn't move my head or my hands or anything at all because of the people – later I thought they were not really people, they seemed more like objects or shapes, all black in long lines; they were moving forward as if they were on an escalator only there was no escalator – we were just drifting forward. I was so impatient I felt like brushing them all out of my way to get to that wall and see what that*

bright light was all about. I could hardly contain myself. Then I watched these black shapes; when they reached this so-called wall, they entered one by one. They just seemed to fade through. I could see them as far as about a foot and a half into the wall and then just barely make them out, and then they would dissolve. That went on all the while we were drifting forward. I don't know how long it was before I reached that transparent white wall. What it was made of, I don't know, but it was plain to be seen that those black figures weren't solid because they made no motion at all when they went through – if it had been any solid body passing through, there would be some commotion in the hole where they went through but that wall never moved. Finally it came pretty close to my line with only one line ahead of me, but even then I couldn't see how the line ahead of me could pass one by one through the same place in that wall without a ripple and yet not hold up my line or the lines behind. How that could be done, I couldn't understand. The line passed through one by one, and we were still drifting forward with no hesitation whatsoever and finally it came my turn. I was just ready to dive head first through that beautiful white wall, but when I attempted to do it, in one split second I found myself floating back to earth about 40 feet in the air. I saw my comrades standing off to one side talking. I saw the great walls of sleet blowing in making the puddles and ponds of water into foam. Then I saw a man lying in the mud and I thought "how pitiful! That poor fellow far miles from home lying there dead in the mud. What a place to die!" and by then I was getting a little closer and to my amazement I found I was looking at myself. I couldn't understand how I could be in two places at once – one dead and one seemingly alive. All the while I was drifting down and then presently I saw myself more plainly – but how can I see myself when my eyes are closed? And then a feeling of utter desolation swept over me so deadly that in the next second I was home and opened my eyes, and that feeling of utter desolation was so great that two tears were rolling down my cheeks, something that had never happened before in the wide world – my tear ducts had dried up long ago. Well, I heard one fellow cry out in a voice so full of excitement. In a loud, loud voice he yelled "He ain't dead yet."

Although the term near-death experience (NDE) would not appear in popular literature for another 60 years,[2] Vaughan Henshaw's experience is a classic example of this phenomenon. Moving through darkness, encountering other beings, visions of light, feelings of joy or excitement, a sense of dying, observing one's own body from a distance, and finally the return to the body and to life are all standard features of NDEs documented by researchers studying the experiences of people who were assumed or declared dead but later revived.[3] In this account, Henshaw, a soldier grounded in the physical realities of life and death, struggles to make sense of the immateriality of a world that, nevertheless, appears physically external to him. He is confounded by the fact that even while perceiving his own dead body, he is experiencing himself as alive. As we will see in future chapters, other cultures interpret similar experiences as an aspect of the dying process. For example, in Tibetan Buddhist literature, the newly dead experience themselves as existing in another "in-between" state that intersects with this world. They are, therefore, thought to be confused about what is happening to them and in need of help to understand that they are indeed dead, as well as guidance in learning how to negotiate this new reality.

According to a 1997 survey, over 15 million American adults claim to have had a near-death experience (Carr, 2006, p. 235). But what does that mean? Have these people encountered an objective reality beyond the hallucinations and psychological projections of a dying brain? Does this constitute proof of survival after death? Is this what happens to all of us when we die? Perhaps for those who have been profoundly affected and altered by their experience, for those who no longer fear death because of it, such questions, and their answers, do not matter; do not change the event or what it means to that individual. Nevertheless, in the face of spiritualist or transcendentalist interpretations, scientific researchers and theorists have proposed various explanations for the thousands of anecdotal descriptions that feature NDE. Most of these take a biological or psychological approach.

Thomas Carr provides the following breakdown of these differing interpretations. On the psychological side, NDEs manifest (a) an *emotional response* to the shock and trauma of death resulting in a state of depersonalization or detachment from the body; or (b) represent *fantasy and wish-fulfillment* in the face of the horror of death; or

(c) result from *mythological archetypes* buried in the brain that surface under extraordinary circumstances and are of evolutionary survival value in creating calm in the person facing death. On the biological side, NDEs can result from (a) *metabolic disturbance*, i.e. severe imbalances in the body arising in the process of dying or sickness, for example due to lack of oxygen or high fever; (b) *drug overload*, of anesthesia, for example, during surgery – many NDEs come from those who report what they heard and saw while undergoing surgery; (c) *endorphins*, a tranquillizing substance released by the brain during times of shock or exertion that results in feelings of calm and happiness, experienced for example by long-distance runners; (d) *limbic lobe seizure*, the seizing up of the area of the brain that controls mood and memory; (e) *visual cortex hyperactivity*, which explains the sensation of a bright light approached through darkness or a dark tunnel due to the hyperactivity of the area of the brain responsible for processing visual stimuli (Carr, 2006, pp. 235–236).

Scientific research concludes that NDE relates to the nature and functioning of the physical brain and its relation to the body and perception. Nevertheless, despite decades of study and many theories regarding the exact nature of the relationship between ourselves as creatures of body and creatures of thought or mind, most of us are still as mystified as Vaughan Henshaw was by the how and why of consciousness and its connection to bodies that live and die. This book does not propose any answer to those questions; I raise the issue of NDE here because it represents an enduring theme of return from the dead – underpinned by diverse human experiences and formalized in the death teachings of many religions.

Regardless of the narrative content, whether it comes from contemporary reports of NDE or medieval Christian accounts of visitations to hell or the reports of those the Tibetans call *delok* ("returned from the dead"), a crucial aspect of the narrative is that the person has returned to this world to act as a living witness to the experience of dying and the encounter with what lies beyond death. However, from another perspective, if death is defined as a state of no return, then perhaps such people have not died at all.

Debates and Definitions

Death from which there is no return would appear to be a different matter altogether. How do we know when *that* death takes place? What happens then? These are questions that raise many debates among scientists and theologians. In the past, the clues that indicated a state of death were related to the condition of the physical body. Does it move, breathe, or have a heartbeat? Does it emit heat? Is it in a state of decay? At a certain level of physical destruction, the condition of death is not ambiguous – whether we are talking about a goldfish floating belly up in a fish tank or distressing television pictures of victims of violence, there is no confusion as to who is living and who is dead. However, before decay or destruction is apparent, there are living states that can be mistaken for death. In Victorian times, the fear of being buried alive was so widespread that safety coffins were developed in which a bell was attached by a cord to the hand of the person who could ring it as an alarm upon awakening.

Although the final condition of death is not ambiguous, the moment when that which is alive becomes that which is dead is a lot vaguer, a lot more confusing and subject to error because death is both process and event. As an event, it marks the beginning of preparations to dispose of the body, the final physical separation from the living. The weightiness and mystery of death lie in that physical absence. In modern western cultures, prior to the technology that allows us to keep the body "alive," dying was understood, as it still is by most ordinary people today, to be a passage, a process, the ending of life, which both culminates in the event of death and transforms into the processes of burial, grieving, and remembrance. Mistakes were certainly made in the past, based on the traditional determination of death as the cessation of breath and heartbeat, but when developments in technology and expertise opened up a new frontier of possibilities, such as transplanting the organs of the dead to give life to others,[4] then the magnitude of the error of mistaking that which is alive for that which is dead became even greater, the interconnection between life and death more difficult to disentangle, more crucial to separate. The organ to be transplanted must be living but the person from whom it is taken must be declared legally dead, otherwise the procedure constitutes murder. You can see, then, how urgent the need would be for the medical establishment to identify more exactly when death had taken place, both for the one who waits for a life-giving transplant and for the one whose death allows for it.

Other technologies developed in the mid-twentieth century required not only a definition of death but a definition of life. Mechanical respirators and electronic pacemakers meant that the physical body could be kept functioning like a machine without any brain activity or apparent conscious activity – a boon for those who pray that a loved one will eventually awaken from a death-like coma, or for those who seek for an organ transplant to provide a chance at continued life, but an ethical dilemma of profound proportions for those who must consider the question of whether or not the costly machinery is merely animating a corpse. The decision to remove someone from life support depends on whether or not we consider "life" or "death" to be present, and if life is present, then is it the kind of life that is to be maintained? Is death always an evil to be suppressed at all cost? Is life always a value to be promoted at all cost?[5]

The first response to these dilemmas came from the Ad Hoc Committee of the Harvard Medical School. It should be noted that they did not set out to define death; as the chairman of the committee stated: "Only a very bold man, I think, would attempt to define death" (Bleich, 1996, p. 29). They proposed to define irreversible coma by establishing the characteristics of a permanently non-functioning brain. This would replace the traditional criteria of death as cessation of breath and heartbeat. A person could be declared dead if brain function was irreversibly lost even though heart–lung activity was present due to mechanical support. The confirmation that all brain activity had permanently ceased was assisted, though not determined, by the use of an electro-encephalograph (EEG). This became known as "brain death" and passed into popular culture in any number of hospital and medical television shows that dramatize the moment of death as a flat line on the EEG monitor – your grandmother passed away at 11:52 p.m. But is brain activity more definitive of life than respiration and blood circulation? Must all brain activity be permanently lost to declare death or only the higher-brain functions that support consciousness, sensation, and mental factors like thought? Is it life that we seek to define or human life? These questions remain unresolved; they continue to fuel religious, philosophical, and legal debates. In his book *Death, Dying, and the Biological Revolution*, Robert Veatch provides the following general definition: "Death means a complete change in the status of a living entity characterized by the irreversible loss of those characteristics that are essentially significant to it" (1976, p. 25). The question then is this: what is essentially significant to a human person, so much so that when it is lost – that is called death? Veatch suggests four possible answers.

1. Irreversible loss of the flow of vital fluids and functions such as blood circulation, heartbeat, and breathing – this refers to the traditional heart–lung definition of death. Since machines can maintain these functions for the body, then according to this definition, for however long heart–lung capacity is maintained, the person is alive.
2. Irreversible loss of soul – for many cultures, life-force is encompassed in the notion of soul; death results from the permanent departure of the soul. This definition would depend on being able to scientifically determine exactly what the soul consists of, where it leaves the body, and how one would know when it has left.
3. Loss of the capacity of the body to regulate its own vital activities due to the irreversible loss of whole brain functions, called "brain death." This definition is challenged by those who regard human life as more than simply body functions.
4. Loss of capacity for social function due to the irreversible loss of higher-brain functions. (1976, p. 30 ff.)

The last answer seeks to establish that what makes us human is our capacity for social interaction with our world, but this definition depends on our understanding of "capacity for social interaction." Simply because a person in a deep coma has no capacity for interaction that we can perceive, are we convinced that such a person is unaware of his or her environment at every level of consciousness? Is consciousness to be exactly equated with the physical activity of the brain?

What should be considered essentially significant to human life? Breath? Soul? Brain? Or the conscious ability to communicate and interact with one's environment? When does the loss that constitutes death take place and the process of dying become the event of death? That may appear to be a biological question, since we are accustomed to thinking of ourselves, at least in part, as biological organisms, but does it have a biological answer? Or, in the last analysis, is death a social construction, a condition that is so when we agree that it is so? What exactly is the relationship between mind and body?

In considering the body–mind relationship, Ornella Corazza refutes the dualism inherent in concepts of mind *and* body, a dualism that leads to confusion when body and mind appear to be separated as in near-death experiences. In her explanation of NDE, she draws on the work of Japanese philosophers and theorists who propose a vision of the human body as extended in space, and who explore what it means to be a body. According to this view, "Our use of tools creates a semi-definite body-space around us, while our visual and tactile perception extends this dimension still further until it reaches the immensity of space" (Corazza, 2008, p. 1). In other words, I not only have a body, I am my body, and "from within" my body-space is indefinite, and as vast as the universe. Still, the question remains: who or what is this "I," this "person" that has a body or is a body; that has a mind or is a mind? Who dies? This question was raised by Richard Zaner (1988) in his critique of the whole-brain criteria for death. According to Zaner, if we are to determine when the death of a person has taken place, surely there is a prior need to establish the meaning of "person" relative to the death that takes place. The debate turns on where we place the emphasis; emphasis on the loss of physical body functions underlies strictly defined biological definitions of death, emphasis on the loss of personhood underlies a "societal" or "ontological" approach that seeks to define death as the loss of what makes a person a person.

In her review of the issues, Margaret Lock (2004) points out that the biological approach is criticized because it presumes that a person is identified solely with the body; the societal approach is criticized because personhood is culturally constructed, therefore subject to varying interpretations, and could be easily manipulated according to the interests of the society without attention to the interests of the individual. However, Lock also highlights the fact that the body is equally a cultural construction when it is regarded as "precultural, an aggregation of natural facts amenable to rational experiment and manipulation" (Lock, 2004, p. 95). In other words, even the physical body is not simply a "given" fact understood in the same way by all peoples; different cultures conceive of the body and its meaning in different ways. For example, among the Wari' of the Western Brazilian rainforest, the word for flesh or body is the same as the word for custom or habit. They explain personality and behavior not with reference to mind but as located in the body. "Peoples' habits, eccentricities, and personality quirks are explained in phrases such as 'His flesh is like that' . . . or 'That's the way her body is'" (Conklin, 2004, p. 248). For the Wari', the body does not become a mere corpse or shell upon death. The dead body still retains the personal identity of the deceased, which is transformed through their funeral rites into the "body" of an ancestor. The Wari' believe that their dead ancestors live in an underworld beneath the rivers and lakes where there is no hunting or fishing because all animals have human forms there. However, to feed their children, the ancestors emerge from the water and return to life in the human world as peccaries (a type of wild pig) that are hunted as food for the community. The peccaries, then, are kin who are roasted and eaten by humans. This was symbolically reflected in the mortuary cannibalism practiced by pre-contact tribes. In a very formal, solemn, and sad ceremony the corpse was dismembered, roasted, and eaten by the relatives of the deceased. In the eating of their dead, the Wari' affirmed the relationship

13

between those who eat and those who are eaten. Through the ritual, the body of a human who was an eater of animals is transformed into the eternal spirit of an ancestor who appears in the form of a peccary to be slain and eaten. The funeral ritual then constituted "the dead person's first offering of self as food" (Conklin, 2004, p. 256). Regardless of the fact that many may regard such practices as barbaric or repulsive, it is a powerful reminder that human beings construct their worlds, their identities, and their bodies in many different ways.

Death and the Self

When asked, "Who are you?" in our society, most people will respond first by giving a name. At the same time, we know that the mere name is not definitive of who I am. That story involves many more people, places, events, thoughts, emotions, accomplishments, and so on, all of which underscores a sense of personal existence, a feeling of "me-ness" that, despite all description, remains undefined by the details of our lives. The story of "me" is also shaped by the way we understand words such as *self* or *identity*. In 1992, at the Fourth Mind and Life Conference held among representatives of Tibetan Buddhism led by the fourteenth Dalai Lama and western scientists and humanists, the philosopher Charles Taylor explained that the modern western way of describing the essential nature of oneself as a *self* rather than a "soul" or "intelligence" is related to the history of how we regard ourselves within the larger context of our existence. From Plato in the fourth century BCE to Descartes in the seventeenth century, philosophical notions of selfhood and identity have been contingent on the ways in which we reflect on being human and on our capacities for self-control and self-exploration. Taylor's conversation with the Dalai Lama appears in the proceedings of the conference narrated and edited by Francisco Varela under the title *Sleeping, Dreaming, and Dying* (Varela, 1997, pp. 11–21). According to Taylor, these attitudes to the self are crucial to the modern view of being human, but at the same time they exist in tension with each other. For Plato, self-control was a function of the capacity of human reason to understand the greater order of the universe and to align with it. For the fourth-century theologian Augustine, reason led to the discovery of one's innermost self as dependent on God. For Descartes, self-control meant that a human being had the capacity to control body and mind as one controls an instrument. In his review of the historical development of the self in the West, Taylor says,

> [W]e had these two spiritual directions: one, Plato turning outward, and the other, Augustine, turning inward, but still with the intention of reaching something beyond ourselves, which is God . . . Descartes reinterpreted human life as the way we concentrate on ourselves as instruments. We came to see our bodily existence as a mechanism we can use, and this happened in the great age when a mechanistic construct of the universe arose.
>
> The modern idea of self-control is very different from Plato, because the order of the universe is no longer important or relevant. It's not in control. I am no longer even turning inward to get beyond myself to God; instead I have a self-enclosed capacity to order my own thoughts and my own life, to use reason as an instrument to control and order my own life. (Varela, 1997, p. 13)

Self-control, however, has an inhibiting effect on the freedom implied in self-exploration and self-expression. Taylor finds the common source of the modern view of both self-control and self-exploration in "a conception of the human being that focuses on the human being in a self-enclosed way." He continues:

> Plato could not grasp the human being outside the relationship to the cosmos, and Augustine couldn't grasp the human being outside the relationship to God. But now we have a picture of the human being in which you may also believe in God, you may also want to relate to the cosmos, but you can grasp the human being in a self-enclosed fashion with these two capacities of self-control and self-exploration. It also has meant that perhaps the most central value in the moral and political life of the west is freedom, the freedom to be in control or the freedom to understand who one is and to be one's real self. (Varela, 1997, p. 15)

In our exploration of religious responses to death, we will find differing approaches to the discovery of "one's real self" – some seek to find and know the self, some seek to lose the self. From infancy, consciousness of our needs and desires influences our actions and responses to our environment. As one grows and becomes conscious of "myself" as the one who desires, then "I" becomes unquestionably present in all my conscious hours, whether waking or dreaming. Under some conditions, such as deep sleep or deep states of meditation, this sense of personal existence may disappear, only to return upon waking or coming out of meditation. The persistence of "self"-consciousness is a strong theme in Herman Hesse's novel *Siddhartha*, the story of a young Brahmin man who seeks to escape both life and death by escaping the self through meditation and ascetic practices.

> He waited with new thirst like a hunter at a chasm where the life-cycle ends, where there is an end to causes, where painless eternity begins.... He lost his Self a thousand times and for days on end he dwelt in non-being. But although the paths took him away from Self, in the end they always led back to it. Although Siddhartha fled from the Self a thousand times, dwelt in nothing, dwelt in animal and stone, the return was inevitable; the hour was inevitable when he would again find himself, in sunshine or in moonlight, in shadow or in rain, and was again Self and Siddhartha... (Hesse, 1957, pp. 16, 17)

The "me" that I am continues from birth to death and is a little-understood combination of material and immaterial factors, whose nature and relationship have been argued by philosophers, ancient and modern. The fact of death is a severe challenge to the common human awareness of personal existence. In life, the body constitutes an inescapable, recognizable form that situates a person in space and time. As near-death experiences attest, even if I wander far from my body in dreams or altered states of consciousness, paradoxically, the body that I perceive separate from me is still me, but who am I, where am I when my body no longer exists? Materialists, from ancient times, will answer, you are not; you are nowhere. Death is the end of personal existence and identity. In the contemporary scientific world, the Nobel prize-winning scientist Francis Crick does not mince words in his book *The Astonishing Hypothesis* when he says:

> The Astonishing Hypothesis is that "You," your joys and your sorrows, your memories and your ambitions, your sense of personal identity and free will, are in fact no more than the behaviour of a vast assembly of nerve cells and their associated molecules. (Crick, 1994)

For those who equate consciousness with brain activity, the other side of death is simply oblivion like a deep sleep from which one never wakes, but the idea that consciousness is not entirely physically determined has never lost its hold on human thought.

Descartes, following the ancient Greeks, concluded that the essential "me" is not the physical body but the immaterial soul or "thinking being," which, although intimately connected to the body, is an entirely different order of being whose continuity does not depend on the body. The question is – how can that which is immaterial be connected to that which is material? This is the so-called mind–body problem and, ever since Descartes, it has elicited various responses from philosophers, theologians, scientists, and psychologists. With regard to the continuity of the individual beyond death, such responses generally fall into three categories. There are those that support a wholly physical explanation for the sense of a persisting self. Their focus, like Francis Crick's, is on the function of the brain as the seat and source of consciousness. Then there are those who support a type of Cartesian dualism, according to which some immaterial aspect of a person, whether called consciousness or soul or mind, persists after departing the body upon death. This would include all religious traditions that propose the existence of an innermost self or soul that supports personal identity and experience during life and after death. Finally, there are those who seek the roots of the mind–body connection in a holistic approach to both the body and the mind. Scientists like Francisco Varela (1997) have drawn on eastern meditative systems and their philosophies to generate a new science of consciousness, to reconceive what it means to be a body, and to seek new answers to the problem of how subjective experience arises from physical processes. We may know, for example, that the physical occurrence of rapid eye movement indicates that a person is dreaming, but we still don't know how the subjective dream arises; the gap between immaterial consciousness and physical brain remains.

In the field of consciousness studies, Corazza's work on NDE aims to redefine or, more accurately, undefine the body so as to reveal it as "an indefinite entity, which is always changing and has no physical boundaries or delimitation such as the skin" (Corazza, 2008, p. 126). Nevertheless, despite such research, despite the teaching of philosophers, the experiences of meditators, and our own moments of unitary feelings, our ordinary experience is that I cannot be in two places at once, that in life, I am bound to my body, which is very much defined and will one day be destroyed. Although there are many living states that mimic the immobility and inactivity of death – sleep, hibernation, dormancy, coma, states of catatonia, deep states of meditation – nevertheless, the physical condition of death is unmistakable. Dead bodies rot, and it is this irreversible transformation that underlies our sense of the finitude of death. That which was, no longer is. For the most part, we accept this as a fact of life. Dead leaves are burned or turn to mulch; dead animals are cleared off the road by the sanitation department; the goldfish floating belly up in the bowl is flushed or buried. However, for the majority of human beings, evidence of the finitude of death in the decomposition of the physical is challenged by the feeling that "persons" are not constituted merely of material bodies and physical processes.

The idea of a fundamental duality underlying the complexities of human nature is common to societies past and present. In her linguistic analysis of soul discourse, Anna Wierzbicka (1989) suggests that soul concepts present in cultures around the world reflect a universal belief that the visible material body is only one aspect of a person, and that to be a person involves an immaterial counterpart, interpretations of which vary widely. She notes that regardless of the way in which the immaterial aspect is understood or analyzed – whether as soul, mind, heart, life-force, or consciousness – cross-culturally, the linguistic terms for "person" or "self" or "I" assume a relationship between the physical body and something other than the body. This "something other," when understood in terms of the spiritual or transcendent aspect of a person, becomes the basis of beliefs in a future beyond death. Just as we have rituals that mark birth, the beginning of our life's journey, or farewell parties that express sadness at separation, or good wishes at the start of a new adventure or phase in one's life, so humans have developed rituals that mark the transformation that death entails, both for the living and the dead. Just as, in this life, we imagine our future and then make preparations for it despite the fact that our future is not at all guaranteed, similarly, humans have considered it prudent to prepare for a future after death despite the undetermined nature of such a future. Death rituals signify that most undying of human characteristics – hope. Of course hope in the future depends on the strength of one's belief that one's actions now can bring about a desirable state in the future. This is the primary support of self-cultivation, social activism, and religious teaching on death and afterlife.

Ritual and Transformation

High on the Tibetan plateau, it is still possible to observe the ritual dismemberment of a corpse, which is then fed to the waiting vultures. The Tibetan Buddhist sky burial emphasizes the impermanent nature of the body and underscores concepts of universal compassion and responsibility for the well-being of all living things. On the other side of the world, until 1969, the Wari', as mentioned above, consumed and cremated their dead to respect the corpse, which should not be allowed to touch the cold, damp ground. Their practice reinforced their understanding that the ancestors care for them by becoming the animal flesh that they hunt and eat; it was their way to recognize the transformation that is death. In Varanasi, in India, at the edge of the Ganges River, corpses are burned on great

19

pyres of wood and their remains thrown into the river. Hindu cremation rites represent the understanding that upon death, the person's
higher self, the unborn, undying soul, has left the body to be reincarnated in another form, to enter into another birth, life after life,
until the final goal of liberation from any embodiment is achieved.
These rituals may be very different from the ones with which you
are familiar, but they all represent ways in which humans have disposed of their dead, ways in which they have interpreted the action
of removing the body from among the living. As we examine the
mortuary rituals of different religious traditions in the subsequent
chapters of this book, it will become clear that death rituals reveal,
perhaps more than any other type of ritual or custom, the ways in
which a particular group of people understand what it means to be
a person in life and in death.

Funeral practices and death rituals can be related to geographical, economic, social, and political concerns – the presence or absence
of wood for burning, the cost of burial or cremation, the need for
memorials that celebrate national heroes or commemorate private
loss. However, in this book, we will focus on death rituals as both
signifying and acknowledging the transformation that takes place
when a person shifts from a living to a dead status. Death rituals
are cultural constructions that tell us when this shift takes place,
where the person is located after death, and what kind of status they
have now attained. They reflect the values and beliefs of a community regarding the essence of personal existence and the meaning of
life and death. Beyond that, they highlight the intimately interconnected nature of the person as biological organism and as socially
constructed self. Death rituals not only indicate what a community
believes regarding self or soul and a person's future after death, but
also how a community regards the physical body and what kind of
transformation is enacted by death upon the body.

Despite the great variety of religious beliefs and teachings about
the meaning of death, all of which emphasize the continuity of the
person in some form or other, not everyone regards death as a gateway to a future or alternate existence. For many people death is simply oblivion, like a deep sleep, from which one does not awake – a

comforting thought because at least there is nothing to fear in oblivion. However, since death is a state of no return, doubts and questions linger. This is Shakespeare's point in the famous passage from *Hamlet*:

> To die, to sleep.
> To sleep, perchance to dream. Ay, there's the rub,
> For in that sleep of death what dreams may come
> When we have shuffled off this mortal coil
> Must give us pause. (3.1.72–76)

What dreams may come? The religious response to this question is what we will examine in the future chapters of this book. It may be good to bear in mind that all the stories we hold dear, whether Christian, Muslim, Buddhist, or Jewish narratives – of heaven and hell, of the first humans, of a great flood, of judgment and the afterlife, of spirit or soul – all have antecedents. These stories were old when they were new; they create the tapestry of religion, and in them we can find the threads that connect us individually with our common ancestral heritage as human beings. They are not the property of one culture or tradition; they may have been preserved by a particular culture, but they are our common human heritage. For some people, the religious narratives that they have been taught about death and life after death are true. Others "just don't know what happens." And there are those who would say – all your speculations and ideas about life after death are merely wishful thinking, just coping strategies for dealing with the reality of the loss that is death; there is no reason to believe the stories of religion – death is simply the end of life. This may be so; I do not have the personal experience to contradict it. However, let me suggest that there is more to learn from all the various propositions of myth and religion than the truths they claim. Because it is in contemplating these different ideas, teachings, and stories of death and future life – no matter how strange or alien some of them might seem – that one may come upon what is actually important for one's own life and death, if only to arrive at a deeper understanding of what it is that I don't know when I say – "I don't know."

Notes

1. All Biblical quotations throughout the book, except where otherwise stated, are taken from *The New Oxford Annotated Bible*, 3rd edition, New Revised Standard Version, ed. Michael D. Coogan (Oxford: Oxford University Press, 2001).
2. The term near-death experience (NDE) first appeared in Raymond Moody's book *Life after Life* (1975).
3. For a history of the research into NDE, see Corazza (2008).
4. The first successful kidney transplant took place in 1954 and the first successful heart transplant by the South African surgeon Dr. Christiaan Barnard in 1967.
5. For a full discussion of these and other ethical issues, see Beauchamp and Veatch (1996).

References and Further Reading

Beauchamp, Tom L. and Veatch, Robert M. (eds.) *Ethical Issues in Death and Dying*, 2nd edition. Upper Saddle River, NJ: Prentice Hall, 1996.

Bleich, J. David. "Establishing Criteria of Death." In Tom L. Beauchamp and Robert M. Veatch (eds.), *Ethical Issues in Death and Dying*, 2nd edition. Upper Saddle River, NJ: Prentice Hall, 1996, pp. 28–32.

Bloom, Allan. (Trans.) *The Republic of Plato*. New York: Basic Books, 1968.

Carr, Thomas K. *Introducing Death and Dying*. Upper Saddle River, NJ: Pearson Prentice Hall, 2006.

Conklin, Beth A. "'Thus Are Our Bodies, Thus Was Our Custom': Mortuary Cannibalism in an Amazonian Society." In Antonius C.G.M. Robben (ed.), *Death, Mourning, and Burial: A Cross-Cultural Reader*. Oxford: Blackwell, 2004, pp. 238–262.

Corazza, Ornella. *Near-Death Experiences: Exploring the Mind–Body Connection*. London: Routledge, 2008.

Crick, Francis. *The Astonishing Hypothesis*. New York: Scribner, 1994.

Hesse, Herman. *Siddhartha*. New York: New Directions Publishing Corporation, 1957.

Lock, Margaret. "Displacing Suffering: The Reconstruction of Death in North America and Japan." In Antonius C.G.M. Robben (ed.), *Death, Mourning, and Burial: A Cross-Cultural Reader*. Oxford: Blackwell, 2004, pp. 91–111.

Varela, Francisco J. (ed.) *Sleeping, Dreaming, and Dying: An Exploration of Consciousness with the Dalai Lama*. Boston: Wisdom Publications, 1997.

Veatch, Robert. *Death, Dying, and the Biological Revolution: Our Last Quest for Responsibility*. New Haven: Yale University Press, 1976.

Wierzbicka, Anna. "Soul and Mind: Linguistic Evidence for Ethnopsychology and Cultural History." *American Anthropologist*, 91 (1989): 41–58.

Zaleski, Carol. "NDEs as Symbolic Narratives." In Thomas K. Carr, *Introducing Death and Dying*. Upper Saddle River, NJ: Pearson Prentice Hall, 2006, pp. 260–268.

Zaner, Richard M. "Introduction." In Richard M. Zaner, *Death: Beyond the Whole-Brain Criteria*. Dordrecht: Kluwer Academic Publishers, 1988.

2

Primal Perspectives on Death

The religions of small-scale tribal peoples around the world are as diverse as the communities themselves. Nevertheless, despite great differences in beliefs, practices, social structures, and cosmologies, there are some elements that appear common to a primal worldview. Primal religious systems conceive of the universe as comprised of overlapping visible and invisible dimensions. The visible dimension is available to our ordinary senses; the invisible dimension is the world of spirit, which is, nonetheless, perceivable – in dreams by many people, and in waking life by some. Like the world they inhabit, human beings also possess visible and invisible dimensions – body and soul or souls. Further, primal religions generally involve some form of animism. In other words, due to the spirit dimension of the external universe, human beings interact with the elements of their environment as spirit persons – requiring courtesy and respect, capable of helping or harming an individual. The animistic perspective is often simplistically interpreted as "everything

Understanding Death: An Introduction to Ideas of Self and the Afterlife in World Religions, First Edition. Angela Sumegi.
© 2014 Angela Sumegi. Published 2014 by Blackwell Publishing Ltd.

is alive," but an animistic worldview does not necessarily ascribe life to non-living things. Nurit Bird-David's study of the Nayaka, a South Indian hunter-gatherer community, shows that they differentiate between ordinary non-personified aspects of their environment and the personalized spiritualized aspect (the *devaru*). A stone may be just an ordinary stone, but some event involving the stone might take place that would indicate that it is a stone spirit, a "stone *devaru*" (Bird-David, 1999, p. 75).

In her analysis of the Nayaka view of persons, Bird-David points to the emphasis on kinship as a constructing device. Persons are those who "we share with," who we relate to. In other words, persons are those in relationship with us (Bird-David, 1999, p. 73). She concludes that animism among the Nayaka signifies the objectification of sharing relationships between the Nayaka and their environment. "*As and when* and *because* they engage in and maintain relationships with other beings, they constitute them as kinds of person: they make them 'relatives' by sharing with them and thus make them persons" (Bird-David, 1999, p. 73). The status of the beings that constitute the Nayaka environment, then, as in human relations, depends on their involvement and interaction with others, and the interpretations placed on personal encounters.

Many, but not all, primal societies depend on specially trained people among them to communicate with the spirit world in order to resolve conflicts and ensure harmony between humans and non-humans, to negotiate the needs of humans when they conflict with the interests of other beings, and to protect the community from the harmful activities of evil spirits. Each group has its own name for such specialists, who are also frequently consulted for healing purposes. The Evenk people of Siberia call their spirit specialist "shaman," a word that has now become a generic term used by outsiders for practitioners who are assisted by the spirits and who use consciously induced and controlled states of consciousness ranging from trance and possession to dream or waking visions to enter into the spirit world and mediate on behalf of individuals or the community as a whole.

The worldviews of primal religions reflect, more or less, many of the following characteristics outlined by Vladimir Basilov (1999, pp. 25–29).

1. *Animation or spiritualization of the whole surrounding world in which human beings exist.* As noted above, however, we should be careful not to oversimplify the concept of animism. The elements of the external world may be regarded as imbued with spirit, or can be ordinary inanimate objects, or even change status. For example, Caroline Humphrey relates a story from the Daur Mongol tradition in which a man who had moved to a treeless stony place began to worship the one beautiful but ordinary tree growing there. Due to his ritual worship, the tree was subsequently thought to be possessed of an in-dwelling spirit (Humphrey, 1996, p. 59).
2. *Belief in mutual all-embracing connections in nature.* What might be termed "supernatural" is for many primal religions merely an extension of the "natural" environment. The seen and unseen worlds and their inhabitants belong to one universe and, therefore, interconnect and impinge on one another, influence and communicate with one another.
3. *No separation from the surrounding world.* Human beings are not regarded as superior to other forms of life. They belong to a web of interconnectivity and are intimately related to their environment, including the animals they hunt, the grain they eat, and the features of the landscape in which they live.
4. *The cosmos is accessible.* The most distant reaches beyond the stars or in the subterranean depths are accessible to the shamans and dreamers of a group. By means of their ability to travel to other spheres in the cosmos and communicate with the beings there, the ritual experts of a community maintain the harmony necessary for the well-being of the community and influence events on behalf of the group.
5. *Religion is a form of social consciousness.* Religious systems reflect the various origins, conditions, and needs of their societies. The

shaman serves the welfare of a particular group guarding them from malignant powers, and providing for communal health and prosperity.

Soul Theories of Primal Peoples

In many of the religions to be examined in this book, the word "soul" refers to the unseen innermost dimension of a person; however, in the context of primal religions, the use and understanding of this term is quite different from the monotheistic traditions of Christianity, Judaism, or Islam, and different also from the understanding of *atman* or soul in Indian religious traditions. The concept of soul in the major world religions refers to an aspect of the person that is metaphysical, entirely beyond the physical world. Further, the soul is understood as the unitary, undying essence of a person; whether one speaks of the Christian, Jewish, or Islamic idea of soul or the Hindu idea of *atman*, the soul is unitary in nature. By contrast, most primal religions speak of many souls associated with an individual, and although these soul theories can differ greatly from group to group, again, there are cross-cultural resemblances to be noted. Souls are described in terms of multiplicity, mobility, shape, as physically distinct from other entities, and vulnerable to attack, illness, or destruction.

The following words of a South American Guajiro elder recorded by Michel Perrin (1987, pp. 7–8) illustrates many of the characteristics of soul theory found among primal peoples.

> To each of us is attached a *soul*.
> It is like a bit of white cotton fluff,
> Like smoke.
> But no one can see it.
>
> Our *soul* leaves us only when we sleep
> Or when we are sick,
> When we have been pierced by the arrow of a *wanülü*.

Primal Perspectives on Death

Everything that happens in our dreams
Is what happens to our *soul* . . .

He is still alive,
He who dreams that a knife has been stuck in his chest,
But his *soul* is wounded.
Sickness is there.
Death is near.

When a Guajiro is sick,
It's as though his *soul* were a prisoner in Dream's abode.
It's there that the [helper] spirit of the shaman
Can find it and bring it back to the sick man.

When they die, the Guajiro become *yolujas*.
They go to Jepira, by the Milky Way,
The way of the dead Indians.
There is where their houses are.

It is the *souls* of the dead who come back to earth
By way of our dreams.
They are ones that are met by our *souls*
When we dream of the dead.

Here sometimes their shadows are seen.
They are the *yolujas*,
Shadows of the dead on earth.

When we die, then, our *soul* is not lost.
Only our bones are lost.
Our bones and our skin.
Our *soul* goes off, that is all.
What leaves is like our shadow,
Or like our silhouette, blurred hazy . . .

But we die twice,
Once here
And once in Jepira

From this passage we can understand that for the Guajiro, the soul is in some way visible, appearing like cotton fluff or as a hazy, smoke-like, shadow-like entity. It is separable from the body and can move about in dreams and interact with the spirits of the dead. It can be lost or injured. If a lost soul is found by the shaman then the sick person lives, but if not, the person dies. The soul of the dead one is called a *yoluja*. Although the *yoluja* have their own land beyond the Milky Way, called Jepira, they can also wander the earth making mischief for humans. Finally, the Guajiro soul survives after death but is not eternal; it eventually dies. This passage speaks of soul in the singular, but for many primal religious traditions a person can possess souls of many types.

The Nanai (called Golds by the Russians) who live in the Amur river basin identify at least three souls: the child's bird soul (related to the Nanai belief that all the souls of the clan, in the form of little birds, wait in a heavenly tree to be born), the soul of an adult in the shape of a small man, and a vaguely defined "body-soul" that inhabits the body and remains at the burial place after death (Smoljak, 1978, pp. 441 ff). Another Siberian group, the Ob Ugrians, speak of the "shadow soul" that haunts the burial place, the "life-force soul" that lives on the crown of the head, the "dreaming soul" that lives in the forest in the form of a wood-grouse, and a fourth soul related to reincarnation (Chernetsov, 1963). In traditional Tibetan culture, the idea of multiple souls is reflected in the belief that a person has five or six protective spirits that come to be associated with the child at birth and that reside in different parts of the body. These spirits are worshipped externally as separate beings and requested to protect and keep the person from harm but at the same time they are regarded as internal aspects of the person's life-force or soul (Samuel, 1993, pp. 186–188, 442).

The notion of separate souls inhabiting various parts of the body appears in cultures from the Arctic to the South China Sea. According to an early twentieth-century report on Inuit soul beliefs, the souls located in the larynx and on the left side of a person are tiny people the size of a sparrow; other souls the size of a finger joint reside in all the limbs of a person (Jakobsen, 1999, p. 80). Among the Rungus people of Borneo, the joints of the body each have their own soul whose activity in the spirit world results in the various aches and pains of the joints. Children's souls especially are thought to run about in the dream world, falling out of trees, scraping their knees, having foot-races, and being chased by spirit dogs, the result of which, not surprisingly, is that the person wakes up entirely sore and worn out from such spirit-world adventures (Appell and Appell, 1993, p. 17). The point I wish to make with these examples is one that I have made elsewhere, that is, with regard to primal religions:

> ... the quasi-material, multiple spirit-energies or "souls" of an individual, although intrinsically linked to the physical body, frequently behave like separate persons themselves, in that they communicate, transform, and possess agency to act independently. The shamanic world is one in which the various powers or capacities of a person – to live, to dream, to move this or that limb, to heal – are constituted as beings in themselves with their own powers and limitations. (Sumegi, 2013, p. 74)

In other words, souls, no less than human persons, belong to a world of beings and can interact with other beings. Upon death, the soul or souls are permanently separated from the body to begin a separate bodiless existence in the spirit world. The final destiny of souls, however, varies according to the tradition – souls can reincarnate in the clan or be transformed into ancestors, some stay around the grave with the body, others dwell in various locales in the spirit world; finally, some are lost and wander the earth.

Although the soul is described as unseen or ephemeral, nevertheless, there is a sense of materiality about it. Siberian peoples claim that the soul of the dead person can feel cold and hunger, even become drunk on too much liquor (Chernetsov, 1963). Among the Nanai, when a soul has been rescued from an evil spirit by the shaman, he first examines its physical characteristics to make sure that it is indeed the soul of the person he is treating (Smoljak, 1978, p. 441 ff.). Even though invisible to ordinary people, the soul is treated as a tangible entity with personal limitations such as carelessness and the inability to find its way home; so before leaving their fishing camp at the end of the summer, with everyone seated in the boat, it was a Nanai custom for the women to call out for the souls of the children to take their places in the boat, lest anyone get left behind (Smoljak, 1978, p. 441 ff.).

The physical characteristics of souls can have serious implications for their owners. A twelfth-century chronicle from the Saami tradition recounts a story in which the shaman's soul traveling across the ocean in the form of a whale encounters his adversary in the form of sharp poles at the bottom of the ocean that cut open the stomach of the spirit whale. According to the story, the shaman dies as a result of this accident in the spirit world (Hultkrantz, 1992, p. 139). Belief in the deadly results of actions in the spirit world continued into the twentieth century. The anthropologist Waldemar Bogoras reported the dream of a Chukchi man who had lost his entire family to disease.

> I had a dream. . . . I picked up a piece of wood from the ground, and suddenly I saw myself soaring upwards. Then I began moving to and fro, and struck with the stick upon the top of all the tents of my camp. I struck down all the tents, but in reality it was the souls of my wife and children who I struck down. Thus I killed all of mine with my own hand. (Bogoras, 1904–1909, p. 295)

The spirit and material worlds are thus conceived as integral to each other. Action in one is perforce manifest in the other. This dynamic is most commonly expressed in the conditions of illness as an effect in the material world directly caused by activity in the spirit world.

So among the Soyot of Siberia,

> If the wicked spirit dips the soul into hot water, the man, whose soul it is, suffers of fever. If it is submerged in cold water, the owner will have the shivers. If the spirit twists the hands and the legs of the soul, then the owner has pains in his limbs. (Diószegi, 1968, p. 294)

Visible and invisible worlds operate as interwoven dimensions of each other and human beings, therefore, live in a much vaster environment than can be ordinarily perceived.

Human souls, as we can see from these examples, are just as vulnerable to attack and injury as the physical body, and although the belief that the individual continues in the spirit world is prominent, it is not universal – the soul can also die. The Russian anthropologist Valerii Chernetsov studied the soul theories of the Ob Ugrians of western Siberia and reported that when a person dies, the grave-soul continues its shadow-like existence in the graveyard until the physical remains of the person are entirely disintegrated; at this point, the "person" undergoes a second death when the grave-soul is transformed into a beetle and, "after the third death in the form of this animal, the person finally disappears without trace" (Chernetsov, 1963, p. 7).

The idea that the soul declines from human status and transforms into an animal and dies a number of times after death is also found in other societies. The Krahó of Brazil believe that the soul dies many times, each time transforming into a smaller and smaller animal, eventually becoming a rock, or root, or tree stump (Child and Child, 1993, p. 174). In the religious systems of such indigenous peoples, one finds evidence of belief in a continuing soul but not necessarily an eternal soul. Indeed, not all communities would even agree that everyone has a soul. Among the tribal peoples of India, the Kol believe that a person gains a soul only upon marriage. Therefore, only the souls of married people have the opportunity to travel to the land of the ancestors and become an ancestor spirit. Small children are buried, not cremated, because they do not have souls (van Gennep, 2004, p. 221 n. 18). The nature of the soul in traditional tribal communities is so fundamentally different from the concept of soul as it is understood in any of the world's major religions that it seems almost misleading to use the same word to refer to these concepts. Perhaps another word like "spirit-power" or "spirit-energy" would give us a better idea of what primal religions mean when they speak of soul.

The Destiny of Souls

When we consider the fate of the soul, most religions provide us with both positive and negative destinies. The negative implies suffering as various conceptions of hell tell us, or total annihilation as in ancient Egyptian religion. The positive, which can be conceived of as salvation or liberation, generally implies victory over death in that one gains eternal life in the presence of God, as in the monotheistic traditions or, as in the eastern traditions of Hinduism and Buddhism, that one no longer participates in the cycle of birth and death. Further, the fate of the soul in the major world religions is linked to morally good or bad behavior in life. Primal religions, on the other hand, generally do not seek to overcome or escape death (in any ultimate sense). Death is understood as an aspect of the whole universe (seen and unseen) that encompasses human beings. Escape from the world is not envisioned – the dead merely change their dwelling place, and in many instances have the capacity to visit or wander about in the land of the living.

Primal religions exhibit characteristics of what religion theorist Jonathan Smith calls "locative" as opposed to "utopian" traditions (Smith, 1978, p. 101). Locative traditions are focused on place, boundaries, and the task of maintaining harmony in the cosmos. Utopian traditions emphasize transcendence, the "going beyond" this life and this world. Salvation, then, for primal religions is not a matter of resurrection or return to life but of finding one's way after death to the right place. Smith writes: "What is soteriological is for the dead to remain dead. If beings from the realm of the dead walk among the living, they are the objects of rituals of relocation, not celebration" (Smith, 1990, p. 124). We will examine now the place of the dead and the relations between the dead and the living among a group whose geography of the afterlife is among the most complex in primal religions, the Warao Indians of Venezuela, as reported in the ethnographic work of Johannes Wilbert (1993).

Afterlife among the Warao

The Warao, whose name means "boat-people," live in the region of the Orinoco Delta in eastern Venezuela. According to the ethnologist Johannes Wilbert, the geography of the supernatural world of the Warao Indians is extremely complex. Human beings live at the center of the earth, which is flat, saucer-shaped, and surrounded by water that reaches to the end of the world, the whole enclosed by a ring of mountains. At the center of the earth is the world axis that penetrates from the bottom of the underworld through the earth to the apex of the sky. It represents all the various pathways by means of which humans and gods communicate with each other and travel from place to place in the cosmos. Circling the base of the world axis under the surrounding ocean and supporting the earth floating on the ocean is the Snake of Being – a four-headed sea monster with deer horns on each head. At the horizon in the ten directions (cardinal and intercardinal points, zenith and nadir) are world mountains or world trees, where the gods of the directions live – known collectively as "Our Grandfathers." Among these, the god of the west, who takes the form of a scarlet macaw, rules over the underworld; unlike the others, he cannot travel throughout the cosmos but is confined to the dark world of death.

The gods of the directions are male but there are also "Our Grandmothers," the Mother of the Forest and Animals, patroness of master canoe-builders; and the Mother of the Moriche (the palm tree that provides the staple food of the Warao), patroness of women expert in the weaving of baskets and hammocks and of men who master the sacred trumpet (Wilbert, 1993, pp. 88–91). Many other deities control numerous pathways of the universe. They are divided into deities of the world of light and of the world of darkness. Only the Warao shamans know how to travel the cosmic pathways between the worlds.

Three types of shamans specialize in the negotiations and communications with the gods: the priest-shaman who is responsible for relations with the directional gods, the "Grandfathers"; the light-shaman who presides over the fertility of all things and communicates with the powers of light and life in the east; and the dark-shaman who deals with gods of the underworld who dwell in the west. Each of these religious practitioners can be benevolent or malevolent, they can kill and they can cure the sicknesses brought about by other shamans of their own type or by the powers of the deities with whom they communicate. In the Warao world, the gods are to be nourished by humans and humans seek to be protected by the gods. The gods of light are offered flour, honey, and tobacco but the spirits of the dark underworld require human flesh, blood, hearts, and livers, and it is the responsibility of the dark-shaman to see that they are fed (Wilbert, 1993, p. 114 ff.).

An immortal afterlife in the heaven of the Warao gods is guaranteed only to the shamans and those artisans and their spouses who follow the ritual and ethical demands of their profession and who are masters of their art – the expert canoe-builders, basket-weavers, hammock-makers, herbalists, and musicians; the souls of such people live eternally in the beautiful abodes of their patron gods. For example, the Warao master canoe-builder is one who approaches every stage of the canoe-building process with reverence, taking care to respect the numerous taboos involved. He begins his career as a novice with an extended period of sexual abstinence, fasting, and constant tobacco smoking. Finally, he enters into an initiatory trance-like vision in which he ascends to the zenith of the sky and is led by a black guide to a celestial bridge that stretches from the zenith to the mountain of the Mother of the Forest in the south-east. The bridge is formed by the body of a hissing, horned sky-serpent with its head at the zenith and its tail at the root of the mountain. Regardless of his fear, the novice must step on its head, shake its horns, and traverse the snake's body, either across it like a bridge or through it like a tunnel, exiting at the anus to make his way to the mountain of the Mother of the Forest, his patron deity. Should the snake swallow the novice, he would die. When the time comes for the master canoe-builder to die, if he has conscientiously kept to all the moral and ritual requirements of his profession, he will die confident that he has done nothing to offend the patron goddess and, therefore, will not be devoured by the sky-snake but pass over safely as he had done before during his initiation. After death, a black soul-guide conducts his soul to the zenith from where, after a few days of rest, he begins his journey to his final destination. It is felt that the soul at this point may feel sad at leaving the family, but that is the final test; he must go forward along the snake bridge without looking back once to earth. Finally, he enters the house of the Master Spirit of Canoe-Making:

> ...a rectangular windowless house that boasts but one arched entrance, which faces west. Nevertheless, its interior is bathed in a blaze of light and never darkens. He finds a bed and a table on which rests a bowl of water perfumed with incense. The roof of the house is beautifully decorated with six pairs of flowers at the four corners and at the centre of the long sides... Their perfume of tobacco smoke and incense is most agreeable to the arriving soul, who is given a similar house for his own use. In it he finds a complete new outfit, which he puts on after taking a bath in incensed water. He has reached his heaven in proximity to the patron deity he has served so diligently throughout his adult life. (Wilbert, 1993, p. 75)

Each type of shaman also has his own destiny (Wilbert, 1993, p. 94 ff.). The priest-shaman's soul travels on a winged golden horse looking like a shooting star, comet, or lightning across the sky. When he arrives at his destination he is given beautiful clothes, hat, shoes, a house furnished in gold and surrounded by a garden of white flowers. He lives in the company of his colleagues, delighting in the constant stream of the sweet tobacco smoke offered by the living.

The light-shaman's soul crosses a bridge made of tobacco smoke and bordered with flowers, and enters a white oval-shaped house made also of tobacco smoke. The souls of the light-shamans and their wives as well as the souls of basket-makers live on the same mountain. Now and then, through the floor of the house, the plumed head of a serpent emerges – the colored plumes on its head chime like bells and on the tip of its tongue is a glowing white ball. Like the sky-serpent for the canoe-builder, this snake would have already been encountered by the light-shaman during the initiatory visions of his profession.

The dark-shaman's soul will have made the journey to the Land of Death many times before, via a black house at the zenith – inside which is furniture made of human skin and bones and a crying child in a hammock made of dried blood. In the west, the dark-shaman's houses are built with iron posts and beams on top of a barren mountain.

> The soil is a blood-soaked black morass, and the air is heavy with the stench of putrifaction which serves the approaching soul as a guide. Also, big black flies fill the air and thickly cover every land surface.... Upon his arrival the soul is greeted by his patron god, who allows him to drink blood from the canoe and eat as much human flesh as he pleases, a food that was denied him in life. He is given a necklace of human rib bones ... and proceeds to occupy his personal dwelling in the joyful company of his fellow dark-shamans. Like them, he assumes a body that is half parrot and half human, with the tail of a monkey. (Wilbert, 1993, p. 98)

Any adult can aim to attain the heaven of their patron deity as long as they have become proficient in the work that they do within the group. Children, however, have no such opportunity. They, along with ordinary unskilled people, are sacrificed as food for the dark-shaman spirits who inhabit the underworld. Protection for children is, therefore, a constant concern. Such protection is associated with sago fertility festivals and shamanic rituals focused on petitioning the mythical Shiborori, the Bird of the Beautiful Plumage that is seen in the sky in the constellation known to us as the Southern Cross (Wilbert, 1993, p. 105).

Regarding the work of the dark-shamans and the fate of children and common people, the Warao myth recounts that in primordial time the underworld was connected to the earth through an umbilicus-like cord which ran from the underworld abode of the scarlet macaw in the west to the center of the sky, from where it hung down over the dancing stage in the village. At the end of the cord was a ball of light which penetrated the heads of sleeping people at night in order to drain their hearts of blood. Their life-blood flowed back through the artery to the underworld where the spirits could be nourished from it. The people did not die but were merely weakened and then recovered. However, in an act of human jealousy, this artery was severed and, ever since, the dark-shamans have used their magic arrows to kill people and carry their souls to the land of the dead where they provide the nourishment that the spirits need. No one is safe from the death arrows of the dark-shaman, but he can also cure those of his own community who have been stricken by the arrows of another dark-shaman, so there is a kind of balance. Nevertheless, the dark-shaman cannot refuse the spirits who come to him in his dreams and ask to be fed.

But, we can ask, why must this continue, why must the dark-shaman kill people? The Warao reply to a fieldworker's question about this is, "One cannot imagine what would happen if our dark-shamans were to stop providing nourishment for the spirits of the west . . . the world would probably come to an end. All children would die and so would the gods" (Wilbert, 1993, p. 99). In the Warao view, then, in order for life to continue, death must have its place in the universe. They have no word for living, only for dying – someone who is feeling unwell would say they are "somewhat dying" (*wabaia subuka*), someone who is quite sick is "dying" (*wabaia*), the corpse is "dead" (*waba*) and buried in a dugout canoe (*wa*), which represents the womb of the Mother of the Forest (Wilbert, 1993, p. 94). In other words, life is a process of dying and returning to the womb of life.

In the Warao world, continuity of the soul is assured for those who are initiated into the world of the spirits, i.e., the shamans, and for those whose specialized vocations are imbued with religious significance – they live on. For them, death is a doorway to another life. In the dark-shaman's work, however, other meanings of death are acknowledged – death as the final end of an individual, death as sacrifice, death as providing nourishment, death as the reinstatement of a primordial bond between the living and the dead. In the Warao system, death is never irrational or meaningless.

Rituals of Departure

Funerals in primal societies generally encompass a number of distinct rituals, sometimes separated by months or even years. These rituals involve, among others, rites related to separation and mourning, disposal of the body, the journey of the soul, reaffirmation of social bonds, protection against the dead, and purification of the pollution of death. The theme of marriage is also frequently represented in primal death rituals. For example, among the Kol people of India, the funeral includes a betrothal ceremony in which the deceased is united with the people of the land of the dead.

> Marriage songs are sung, there is dancing, and the woman who carries the pot [containing the bones of the deceased] leaps with joy. A marriage retinue with music, etc., goes to the village from which the deceased and his ancestors have originated. The pot containing the bones of the deceased is deposited in a small ditch, above which a stone is erected. On their return the participants must bathe. (van Gennep, 2004, p. 215)

We will look more closely now at the theme of marriage and the preservation of clan alliances that underpin rituals of departure of the Gurung people of Tapje village in northern Nepal, profiled by Stan Royal Mumford in his work *Himalayan Dialogue: Tibetan Lamas and Gurung Shamans in Nepal* (1989).

In the Gurung world, entry to the land of the ancestors is at the top of the Oble Dome, a massive rock dome in the Annapurna mountain range about a day's walk from the village. The path leading to the land of the ancestors is the white path of the gods. There are other paths that, if followed, would leave the soul confused and wandering – the red path of the mountain spirits, the black path of demons, or the yellow path of the subterranean water spirits. Finding the right path, however, is linked to clan alliances and the reciprocal relationships among the relatives of the deceased. The dead one cannot find the path unless a male from his maternal affinal relatives provides the white shroud that covers the corpse. This symbolizes a primordial marriage exchange between the underworld of the dead and the world above of humans. In the origin myth that is chanted at the funeral, the parents of a neglectful son warn him that: "If we die and you do not do the rites to receive our blessing, you will become poor. You will become small as a needle, thin as paper, weak as water" (Mumford, 1989, p. 184). According to the myth, the parents die and descend to the underworld (Khro-nasa) where they request the people to send a daughter to marry their son and to warn him that if he does not send offerings to receive their blessing, he will be cursed with poverty. The Khro-nasa people convey the message of the parents, and the son, who is already suffering from poverty due to the curse of his parents, accepts the girl, gathers up food from his relatives, and with the ritual assistance of the shaman takes it to his parents below:

> They were satisfied and gave him a gift: a bird of gold, turquoise, silver, copper, and iron. The son returned to the human world with the wealth-bearing bird. It was the blessing of the inheritance. He married the daughter of Khrō-nasa. Rain came down from above. Crops grew up from below into the human world. Animals increased. There was great wealth. The deceased parents found the path to the land of the gods. (Mumford, 1989, p. 184)

Two relationships are highlighted in the story: the marriage exchange signifying the clan alliances that result in social and cosmic harmony, and the food exchange signifying the harmonious relationship between the living and the dead. Should either of these relationships falter, poverty and illness would be the result. In the Gurung death rites, then, both exchanges are symbolized by the offering of the white shroud, and members of each side of the family have specific responsibilities to carry out in the funeral.

In the funeral procession to the cremation grounds, a long pole symbolizes the connection between the upper and lower worlds. It is hung with strips of colored cloth, fruit, cigarettes, and other things for the soul to take on its journey. A 7-meter-long white cloth is tied to the pole and carried on the heads of the women of the paternal affinal relatives, while their men carry the body wrapped in a white shroud. Other men point arrows at the corpse symbolically offering weapons to the deceased to take for his protection. The Gurung have two kinds of shaman: the Paju shaman who specializes in recalling the soul from the underworld and exorcising evil spirits, and the Ghyabre shaman who specializes in conducting the soul to the land of the ancestors. After the cremation the Paju shaman conducts a rite of exorcism to free the soul from any demonic agents that may try to capture the soul.

The series of subsequent rites overseen by the Ghyabre shaman may take place months later. A soul effigy is constructed by the women of the maternal affines: "a cone-shaped bamboo cage one metre high. The stick frame represents the bones of the deceased, and the white cloth covering it [the same shroud that covered the corpse] . . . is the outer flesh" (Mumford, 1989, pp. 182–183). Food offerings are set out in front of it and the names of the donors announced. The shaman journeys in his trance to the underworld to deliver the food offerings to the soul so that the deceased will be pleased and not take the wealth of the family with him. In a very emotional farewell ceremony, the shaman ties a cord from the soul effigy to a pigeon so that the soul may enter the pigeon, which then goes from person to person in the group eating from their hands and jumping up onto the laps of some, and finally shaking its feathers to indicate that it is pleased and will not take the wealth of the family. At the end, the pigeon is released to the sky. This exchange also releases the soul from the underworld and allows it to go on to the land of the gods and ancestors. The Paju shamans consider the Khro-nasa underworld to be an alternative dwelling place of the dead, but in the Ghyabre tradition, the soul only stays there for a while until it is rescued by the shaman and conducted to the land of the ancestors.

In the final journey of the soul, the shaman dances around the soul effigy, drumming and chanting the story of the path they will take. Through his chanting, drumming, and dancing, the shaman guides the soul to the Oble Dome along a path in the real world; he calls out the villages and landmarks that they pass, which all the participants recognize. All along the way, he encourages the soul to leave its home and family: "You no longer have the right to remain at the hearth. Your place is different now. Only alive ones can stay here. You are dead now, go!" (Mumford, 1989, p. 188). Wherever the soul passes, the spirits tell him to go further – the spirits of the doorstep that he crosses over, the spirits of the porch as he leaves the house, and as he proceeds along the trail, the spirits of the passing rivers, rocks, and soil tell him to keep going. Finally, they arrive at Oble Dome and climb to the top where they are greeted by the ancestors. The top of the Oble Dome is thought to be the entrance to the land of the ancestors called Sa Yi Gompa ("earth" gompa, dwelling place of the ancestors as distinct from "sky" gompa, dwelling place of the gods). The shaman tells the soul that he can now stay on here with his ancestors or take rebirth as a human. He also warns the soul not to be tempted to return to the world of the living, either to see his family or check on his property or even to see a show going on in the village, but to remain with the dead. The shaman, however, must return and must avoid being followed back to the land of the living, so he cleverly distracts the soul by saying, "Look there at how those cats and snakes are playing together!" (Mumford, 1989, pp. 190–191). And while the soul looks away, he turns into a vulture and flies off. Later the community takes the soul effigy out of the village and throws it into the river.

The Gurung death rites emphasize death as a moment for reconciliation and harmony. The relatives must come together and reaffirm their relationship to the deceased and, therefore, to each other. Their actions are not only socially and familially significant but underscore the bond between the world of the living and of the dead ancestors established in the primordial marriage myth. Morality is not entirely missing from Gurung afterlife theories; it is said that a person with many misdeeds would not be able to find the right path, even if the white shroud was offered, but for a successful journey to the land of the ancestors, greater emphasis is placed on the participation of the family members and the ritual guidance of the shaman.

A Conversation on Understanding Death

With Albert Dumont

Albert Dumont (Oshki Nodin) is a Canadian Algonquin elder born on the Kitigan Zibi First Nations reserve in the Outaouais region of Quebec; he is also a poet, a social activist, storyteller, and spiritual guide. Although most of his family is Christian, Albert tells me that it was due to the help of his ancestors that 25 years ago he was able to turn his life around and overcome alcohol addiction, and since then he has followed the "Red Road," the ancient spiritual way of the Algonquin. He holds an eagle feather while we speak to show that his words are true.

When I ask him to tell me about his views on death and dying, he speaks first of love and connection. "All must die," he says, "but we want to be connected again in the spirit world. We want to be surrounded with our loved ones and feast with them again." When Albert thinks of the Christian idea of heaven, even if it is a place of great joy and happiness, it appears too abstract to him. "I want to be me," he says, "if, in this life, it was my joy to walk through the mountains and forests until my legs ached, I want to know that joy again."

For Albert, our ancestors connect us from generation to generation; they are the link between life and death, and they speak through the forest. "The forest," he says, "is a place of great wisdom because the forest is a place the ancestors knew." Albert recounts a story of one of his walks deep into the forest where the sounds and sights of all man-made technology are left behind. "I stopped and made an offering of tobacco and asked the space around me to speak, to tell me something. There was a hollowed-out dead tree trunk still standing there. It had first sprung to life hundreds of years ago and was now dead. Suddenly a squirrel running from a fox ran to the tree for safety. I realized instantly that, like the squirrel, we are sometimes fearful of what would harm us in this dysfunctional world and as the squirrel ran to the tree for safety and refuge, so too can we go to the protective spirit of our ancestors for salvation." Albert reminds me that "we pray for the health of the land but we must think also of future generations hundreds of years to come, and pray to be present, to be there when they have need of us, for we will be the ancestors at that time and they, our descendants."

Not everyone is worthy of being with the ancestors in the spirit world. Albert recounts a vision-like dream that he had in which he was slowly making his way down a dark river in a canoe. On either side were dead dark trees, but in the distance was a light that he knew signified the place of the ancestors to which he was traveling. Now and again, there would be a voice calling to him, "Oshki Nodin, take me with you," and if it was a person that he knew to have a good heart, he would welcome him aboard the canoe, but if it was someone who had perpetuated hatred and greed in life, then he would ignore the call.

When I ask Albert how best one can prepare for death, he first points out the preciousness of life and tells me that we must never give up, "fight for every breath," but if death is truly present, then the place to go is into our memories. He says, "revisit the places and people you have known, offer forgiveness to those who need it, express your remorse for wrongs done and your gratitude for the gifts you have received, and most of all think how wonderful it was to live as a human being and now to enter the spirit world." This is how he prepares for his own death. Finally, Albert tells me that through the things of this physical world, the spirit world touches us, speaks to us; through our interactions with the natural world we hear the "whispers of the ancestors." And upon death, "one's spirit goes into the next world connected to the spirit of all the things of one's life, which bear witness to the life we lived." So for Albert, the spirit of the maple tree at his fasting site, the spirit of the fish that he catches for food, the sky and the earth – they will all speak for him in the world of the ancestors, and "encourage honor songs for me because of the way I lived my life."

References and Further Reading

Appell, George, and Appell, Linda. "To Converse with the Gods: Rungus Spirit Mediums." In Robert Winzeler (ed.), *The Seen and the Unseen: Shamanism, Mediumship and Possession in Borneo*. Williamsburg, VA: Borneo Research Council, 1993.

Basilov, Vladimir N. "Cosmos as Everyday Reality in Shamanism: An Attempt to Formulate a More Precise Definition of Shamanism." In Romano Mastromattei and Antonio Rigopoulos (eds.), *Shamanic Cosmos: From India to the North Pole Star*. Venice: Venetian Academy of Indian Studies, 1999, pp. 17–39.

Bird-David, Nurit. "'Animism' Revisited: Personhood, Environment, and Relational Epistomology." *Current Anthropology*, 40 (1999), supplement, pp. S67–S91.

Bogoras, Waldemar. *The Chukchee–Jesup North Pacific Expedition*, Vol. 7. New York: G.E. Stechert, 1904–1909.

Chernetsov, V.N. "Concepts of the Soul among the Ob Ugrians." In Henry N. Michael (ed.), *Studies in Siberian Shamanism*. Toronto: University of Toronto Press, 1963, pp. 3–45.

Child, Alice B. and Child, Irvin L. *Religion and Magic in the Life of Traditional Peoples.* Upper Saddle River, NJ: Prentice Hall, 1993.

Diószegi, Vilmos. *Tracing Shamans in Siberia: The Story of an Ethnographical Research Expedition.* Oosterhout: Anthropological Publications, 1968.

Hultkrantz, Ake. "Aspects of Saami (Lapp) Shamanism." In Mihaly Hoppal and Juha Pentikainen (eds.), *Northern Religions and Shamanism*, Vol. 3. Budapest: Ethnologica Uralica, 1992.

Humphrey, Caroline. *Shamans and Elders: Experience, Knowledge and Power among the Daur Mongols.* Oxford: Clarendon Press, 1996.

Jakobsen, Merete Demant. *Shamanism: Traditional and Contemporary Approaches to the Mastery of Spirits and Healing.* New York: Berghahn Books, 1999.

Mumford, Stan Royal. *Himalayan Dialogue: Tibetan Lamas and Gurung Shamans in Nepal.* Madison: University of Wisconsin Press, 1989.

Perrin, Michel. *The Way of the Dead Indians.* Austin: University of Texas Press, 1987.

Samuel, Geoffrey. *Civilized Shamans: Buddhism in Tibetan Societies.* Washington, DC: Smithsonian Institution Press, 1993.

Smith, Jonathan Z. *Drudgery Divine: On the Comparison of Early Christianities and the Religions of Late Antiquity.* London: School of Oriental and African Studies, University of London, 1990.

Smith, Jonathan Z. *Map is not Territory: Studies in the History of Religions.* Leiden: Brill, 1978.

Smoljak, A.V. "Some Notions of the Human Soul among the Nanais." In Vilmos Dioszegi and Mihaly Hoppal, *Shamanism in Siberia.* Budapest: Akademiai Kiado, 1978.

Sumegi, Angela. "On Souls and Subtle Bodies: A Comparison of Buddhist and Shamanic Perspectives." In Geoffrey Samuel and Jay Johnston (eds.), *Religion and the Subtle Body in Asia and the West: Between Mind and Body.* London: Routledge, 2013, pp. 69–82.

van Gennep, Arnold. "The Rites of Passage." In Antonius C.G.M. Robben (ed.), *Death, Mourning, and Burial: A Cross-Cultural Reader.* Oxford: Blackwell, 2004, pp. 213–223.

Wilbert, Johannes. *Mystic Endowment: Religious Ethnography of the Warao Indians.* Cambridge, MA: Harvard University Press, 1993.

3

Death in the Ancient World

Did humans always bury their dead or have ideas about a life beyond death? Archaeological findings give clues but no definitive answers to this question. The remains of the dead tell us that human-like primates lived millions of years ago but archaeologists are divided in their interpretations of what constitutes evidence of intentional burials or mortuary practices. Some scholars would date the earliest burials between 30,000 and 50,000 years ago, while others claim that burials took place thousands of years before that (Kellehear, 2007, pp. 22–23). We cannot know very much about what our collective prehistoric ancestors believed or thought about death, and the graves of early humans are subject to much conjecture. Some details, however, such as the presence of food or tools like hand axes, awls, and scrapers in Neanderthal graves (*c.* 200,000–30,000 BCE), might indicate that such practical things were being "sent along" with the

Understanding Death: An Introduction to Ideas of Self and the Afterlife in World Religions,
First Edition. Angela Sumegi.
© 2014 Angela Sumegi. Published 2014 by Blackwell Publishing Ltd.

person – but why? Did early humans think that the person embarked on a journey after death requiring physical food and necessary tools, or are the grave goods there primarily for symbolic or sentimental reasons?

Possible signs of less practical offerings have also been found. The presence of pollen from many different types of flowers surrounding Neanderthal remains at the Shanidar caves in Iraq suggests to some that the ritual of laying flowers on a grave goes back a very long time; others argue that the pollen could equally be the result of the activity of a little rodent that stores flowers in its burrows found in the vicinity (Sommer, 1999). Perhaps the most we can be sure of is that the treatment of the dead implies that early humans assigned some significance to death. The nature of that significance becomes clearer as we draw closer to our own time and archaeologists are able to study not merely bones and bits of broken flint, but coffins and tombs, paintings, hieroglyphs, and inscriptions.

In the evolution of the use and manufacture of tools, and of human interaction with the environment, the Neolithic age (7000–3000 BCE) represents a major movement from hunting and foraging to agriculture as a source of food, a movement that contributed to the settled lifestyle of farmers as distinct from roaming hunters. Along with agriculture came the domestication of animals, the need for greater social organization, the need to protect the crops from raiders, and the development of larger and larger political units. This period sees the beginnings of the great empires of the ancient world built around the most important requirement of an agrarian society – water. Along the banks of the great rivers of the Nile, the Tigris and Euphrates, the Indus, and the Yellow River flourished the civilizations of ancient Egypt, Mesopotamia, India, and China; and as human beings' expertise in technology developed in complexity, so the ordering of life and death became more complex and more elaborate. In this chapter, as a background to the perspectives found in Judaism, Christianity, and Islam, we will look at three ancient Middle Eastern religious approaches to death and afterlife – Egyptian, Mesopotamian, and Persian.

Egypt

Ancient Egyptians not only looked to the Nile to provide water for their crops, they also depended on the annual flooding of the river to revitalize the fertility of the earth and make it ready to receive the new seed. The theme of the renewal of life that features so strongly in Egyptian death rituals echoes the annual life-giving action of the Nile, the cycle of the seasons, the death and rebirth of the sun each night and day, all bearing evidence of the triumph of life over death. More than any other ancient culture, because of the magnificence of the pyramid tombs, the mystery of the so-called Book of the Dead, and the technology of embalming, Egyptian culture has been associated with an extraordinary emphasis on the rituals surrounding death. Yet the evidence points not to a preoccupation with death but to a vital concern with life – eternal life. As Egyptologist John Taylor notes, the houses of the living were built of perishable mud-brick and wood and, like them, Egyptians regarded this life as transient and passing; but the tombs for the dead were built of stone to last through the ages and, like them, the Egyptians believed that life could be renewed as an eternal blessing (Taylor, 2001, p. 12). The preoccupation with ensuring that the dead person would be restored to full capacity led to an elaborate and sophisticated death culture related to the rituals of negotiation that could bring a person through the darkness of death into the light of life. Although there are similarities with the Judeo-Christian-Islamic traditions in the belief in resurrection and the hope for eternal life after death, the Egyptian view of the deceased's return to life is quite different from the monotheistic belief in resurrection and eternal life at the end of time. According to Jon Davies (1999), the Egyptian belief system did not include any idea of a cataclysmic end of the world scenario towards which human history is moving. In ancient Egypt, an individual, innocent of wrong-doing, with the right resources, carrying out the proper rituals, could count on an immediate future in which life itself was reassembled and revitalized, transformed from ordinary life into divine eternal life. To understand how this revitalization took place and how Egyptians viewed the journey and the destiny beyond death, we must first examine their understanding of the person who makes that journey beyond death.

Egyptian Soul Theory

In Egyptian thought, the person was a complex combination of four material and immaterial aspects: the physical body with a focus on the heart; immaterial entities (souls) called *ba* and *ka*; the name of the person; and the shade or shadow (Taylor, 2001, pp. 16–24). With regard to the body, the Egyptians differentiated between the living body (*khet*), the corpse (*khat*), and the body prepared and transfigured through rituals and mummification for eternal life (*sah*). The divine nature of the *sah* is emphasized in texts that identify the parts of the body with various deities:

> My hair is Nun; my face is Ra; my eyes are Hathor; my ears are Wepwawet; my nose is She who presides over her lotus leaf; my lips are Anubis; my molars are Selkis; my incisors are Isis the goddess; my arms are the Ram, the Lord of Mendes . . . (Taylor, 2001, p. 17)

Like other ancient cultures, the Egyptians believed that the heart, not the brain, was the seat of the mind and all that made a person good or evil. In the mummification process they attempted to preserve the heart within the body because, after death, the heart remained the focus of innocence or guilt, according to which a person was restored to eternal life or annihilated forever. The "weighing of the heart" will be explained further when we examine the myth of Osiris.

With regard to the immaterial aspects of a person, the *ka* soul was considered to be the person's life-force related to the capacity for action and to the capacity for regeneration and reproduction. It comes into existence with the person at birth and appears as an exact likeness of the person, like a spirit double. After death, the *ka* continued to reside in the mummified body within the burial chamber, and because life-force requires food and drink for sustenance, then it was to the *ka* that offerings of food and drink were made as sustenance for the next life. The offerings were made in front of a statue of the person set up in an outer chamber as a temporary physical residence for the *ka* so that it could leave the body in the sealed burial chamber and be present in the statue to receive the offerings.

Another immaterial entity, the *ba*, was a kind of spirit essence, possessed not only by persons but also by objects. With regard to persons, the animating *ba* soul departed the body upon death, leaving behind a lifeless corpse. It was depicted as a human-headed bird signifying capacity for free and unhindered movement and indicating its ability to travel far from the body and the tomb. The *ba*, however, never completely abandoned the body and returned each night to its "home." Pyramid tombs frequently provided a shaft and exit hole for the *ba* to come and go. For the Egyptians, the body was not dispensable; eternal life required that the *ba*, whose departure signified death, be reunited with the physical form of the body in its transformed, mummified state, and that the body continue to be nourished by food and drink offered to the *ka*.

The individual's name was another important aspect of their personhood signifying uniqueness and individuality in the world. The name was regarded not merely as an identifying factor but as a site of personal power, prosperity, and well-being. The one whose name was written, remembered, and spoken lived on after death. Taylor notes the prominence that the Egyptians gave to preserving the name of the person both in the public parts of the tomb and in the sealed burial chambers (Taylor, 2001, p. 23). Finally, the shadow or shade was another aspect of the body in life that followed the person after death and was to be protected from harm. The function of the shadow is not very well understood. It was depicted as a dark figure of the person, said to possess great speed, and although it was mobile, it remained near the tomb and the body.

This description of the various components of a person, like Egyptian views of the afterlife, should not be taken as a definitive or cohesive system. It represents a complex vision of personhood played out in overlapping and multifaceted concepts. What is important to note is that in death no element of what was important to the living person was abandoned. There was no idea that the body disintegrates and the soul goes on to an eternal life – the body was regarded as the home of all the other aspects of the person and it was to be maintained for all eternity.

Jon Davies writes:

> The Egyptians feared chaos in this world and the next: the whole purpose of their spells and rituals was to deny the chaos implicit in death and to preserve continuity at the time of death so that its divisive and dis-membering consequences could be pre-empted. Death was an opportunity to reassemble life, with all of the threatening elements removed . . . (1999, p. 29)

Transforming the Body

The cornerstone of the Egyptian transformation from death to eternal life was the practice of mummification or embalming – the artificial preservation of the body. This was a highly ritualized process carried out by embalming priests who were associated with the jackal-headed god Anubis. It began with the ritual washing of the corpse, which not only delayed the onset of decay but more importantly symbolized purification and rebirth.[1] After that came the extraction of internal organs, then the drying out of the corpse with natron, a naturally occurring chemical compound of salts. The desiccated corpse would then be packed with sweet-smelling resins and linen packages of salts to reproduce the shape of the body, anointed with oils and perfumes, and finally wrapped in strips of linen accompanied by ritual incantations and amulets to assist the deceased in successfully overcoming death. The history of embalming in Egypt extends from *c.* 3500 BCE to *c.* 200 CE. Over that period of time, embalming techniques changed and developed. Attempts during the Old Kingdom (*c.* 2686–2160 BCE) to preserve the body in a life-like and naturalistic fashion gave way to more symbolic representations of the transfigured body (*sah*) wrapped in a cocoon of linen with the head covered by an idealized mask of painted cartonnage.[2] Egyptian mummification reached the height of sophistication in the elaborate cosmetic treatments and decorations of the 21st Dynasty (*c.* 1069–945 BCE). According to Taylor, "The skin of male mummies was painted red, that of female bodies yellow . . . Thinning hair was eked out by extensions, and artificial eyes of glass or stone were inserted into the eye-sockets. Repairs were even made to the skin, where damage had occurred" (Taylor, 2001, p. 87).

Among all the rituals of transformation, the most important was the "Opening of the Mouth" (Taylor, 2001, pp. 190–191). Originally, this was a ritual in which the mouth and eyes of the dead one's statue were touched with different types of tools used in the making of the statue in order to empower the image with properties of the living. It was the final act of creation through which the image became a suitable support for the person's animating *ka* spirit and could receive the offerings of food and drink made to it. Eventually, "Opening the Mouth" was adapted from a statue-consecrating ritual to become the most important rite to be performed on the mummified body itself at the entrance to the tomb – the final act in the restoration of life to the dead body. Accompanied by incantations and liturgy, special priests would touch the mouth of the mummy with various objects including sculptor's tools like a chisel and adze, thereby revivifying the person's sense faculties that had been destroyed in death. According to one New Kingdom (*c.* 1550–1069 BCE) text:

> You come to life a second time . . .
> You thrive on water, you breathe air,
> You drink as your heart desires.
> Your eyes are given you to see,
> Your ears to hear what is spoken;
> Your mouth speaks, your feet walk,
> Your hands, your arms have motion.
> Your flesh is firm, your muscles are smooth,
> You delight in all your limbs;
> You count your members: all there, sound,
> There is no fault in what is yours. (Taylor, 2001, p. 35)

A perfected and divinized form of life arising out of death was a possibility, not a surety, but when that possibility was realized then the person attained to the status of *akh*. This was an aspect of the personality that came into being after death, thought by some to result from the union of the *ba* and the *ka*. It signified the transfiguration of the person into a living being of light and was associated with the stars (Ikram, 2003, pp. 30–31). As an *akh*, the person was capable of exercising spiritual "effectiveness" or influence over the lives of others. This state was the goal of the funerary rituals and texts, which were collectively called *sakhu*, "that which makes [a person] *akh*" (Taylor, 2001, p. 32). Letters to the dead, written mostly on pottery bowls that would likely have held food offerings, indicate the power accorded to the dead. They tell us that the living petitioned dead relatives to intercede for them in the hereafter, to remove sickness or other troubles in this life; but not all letters were supplicant. Sometimes the living wrote to castigate the deceased for their unfortunate circumstances, as this husband wrote to his dead wife:

> What evil thing have I done to you that I should come into this wretched state in which I am? What have I done to you? What you have done is that you have laid hands on me, although I had done nothing evil to you . . . (Taylor, 2001, p. 44)

As in many other cultures, the dead could help or harm the living.

Egyptian Afterlife

Our knowledge of Egyptian attitudes to death comes from archaeological excavations of pyramid tombs, from examination of mummified corpses, and especially from the spells and incantations written on sheets of papyrus, or inscribed on pyramid walls and on coffins. Egyptologists trace the development of these funerary texts and other mortuary practices in three main stages corresponding to the broad periods of political stability and cultural growth in Egyptian history known as the Old Kingdom (*c.* 2686–2160 BCE), the Middle Kingdom (*c.* 2055–1650 BCE), and the New Kingdom (*c.* 1550–1069 BCE) (Shaw, 2002).[3]

The earliest stage is represented by the *Pyramid texts,* which date to the period of the Old Kingdom. These are spells or "utterances" inscribed primarily on the walls of pyramid tombs built for kings and queens, possibly indicating that at this time the notion of eternal life in a divinized body was reserved for the ruling class and other nobility. It should be remembered that Egyptian religion in general was a complex and frequently confusing pantheon of deities and practices resulting from the interaction and amalgamation of the tribes that settled along the length of the Nile. The Egyptian approach to death was marked by an equally complex amalgamation of myths, beliefs, and practices that do not comprise a consistent system but reveal a wide range of ideas relating to the defeat of death and the continuation of individual life. Views on the final destination of the transfigured dead changed over the centuries. The Pyramid texts suggest three possible destinations for a dead ruler: to live eternally among the heaven-dwelling gods associated with the stars of the northern sky; to live with the sun god and join him in his cyclical journey across the sky; or to dwell eternally in the underworld kingdom of the Lord and Judge of the dead, Osiris. Afterlife in the kingdom of Osiris received much greater emphasis in a later period, but the Egyptian denial of the finality of death is apparent even at this early stage. A well-known utterance of the Pyramid texts states "O King, you have not departed dead, you have departed alive" (Faulkner, 1969, p. 40). Such denial, however, should not be understood as a simplistic negation of the fact of death but as an orientation towards the notion that the chaos of death could not overrule the order of life. The myth of Osiris (see below) showed how death could be reordered and rearranged so as to reconstitute life; not ordinary life, but transfigured, divine life.

The next stage in funerary texts is represented by the *Coffin texts,* which take their name from inscriptions dating to the Middle Kingdom that were carved onto the wooden coffins of commoners, as well as elsewhere, such as on the tomb walls or mummy masks. The Coffin texts emphasized an afterlife in the kingdom of Osiris. They included many of the spells from the older Pyramid texts but others were added, and it would seem that during the Middle Kingdom, eternal life became an opportunity not only limited to the privileged ruling class but available to all those who could afford to prepare themselves properly – to have the body mummified, to procure the right spells, to have the statue built for the *ka* soul – all who could make the right arrangements for death could have a chance at eternal life in the kingdom of Osiris.

In popular western imagination, the book that came to epitomize the Egyptian approach to death and afterlife was a translation of the Ani Papyrus, a text held by the British Museum, by E.A. Wallis Budge published in the late nineteenth century as the *Book of the Dead*. This was a collection of about 200 incantations, which the Egyptians called *Spells for Going Forth by Day* (Taylor, 2001). They represent the third stage of funerary text development and date to approximately the fifteenth century BCE. They were written on sheets of papyrus with accompanying illustrations to be placed with the dead, and reflect the Egyptian hope that the person would be able to "go forth by day," renewed in life, unbound from the darkness and lifelessness of death. Prominent among the spells that appear in the *Book of the Dead* is the theme of the soul standing in judgment before Osiris and his 42 judges; an indication that a good afterlife is not automatic but subject to judgment, the basis of which turns out to be moral behavior in this life.

The Story of Osiris

Osiris, Lord of the underworld, is one of the most prominent deities of ancient Egyptian religion. In his story that comes down to us from Greek and Egyptian sources, we find the idea of resurrection and the happy land beyond death that subsequently continued to be played out in many different ways in various religious traditions. Osiris was regarded as the first mythical king of the Egyptians who introduced them to agriculture. He is depicted wrapped in white mummy bandages wearing a white crown and his flesh colored black or green, colors that identify him with the black alluvial soil left behind by the annual flooding of the Nile and the regeneration of life inherent in the agricultural cycle of seeding and harvest. In the myth, Osiris' jealous brother Seth plots to kill him and is successful. Seth has a beautiful chest made exactly according to the dimensions of Osiris' body and at a great feast to which Osiris is invited Seth offers the chest to whomever it fits. Following the rest of the party, Osiris climbs inside and is trapped. The casket is thrown into the River Nile and is carried away. Osiris' sister-wife, the goddess Isis, goes searching for his body. After many adventures, Isis finds the coffin and the body, but she is discovered by Seth who destroys the body of Osiris by cutting it up and scattering the pieces. Isis and her sister Nepthys search for and recover the dismembered pieces, all but the phallus, which had been eaten by a fish and symbolically remained behind to ensure the fertility brought to Egypt by the Nile. Isis makes a substitute phallus from clay and the sisters reassemble the dead Osiris and bring him back to life. In the form of a great hawk, Isis mates with her husband and later gives birth to Horus, the sun god, Osiris' hawk-headed son, who eventually defeats his wicked uncle in battle and assumes the throne. In life, Egyptian pharaohs were identified with Horus, and in death with Osiris, the resurrected lord of the dead, judge and king of the underworld. The story of Osiris' death and resurrection serves as the origin myth of the Egyptian funeral cult and the practice of mummification.

In the resurrection of Osiris, Egyptians saw the possibility of their own return to life from the dead, the possibility of becoming like Osiris. In the *Book of the Dead*, the dead person is frequently referred to as Osiris N (where N stands for the name of the deceased). Some of the earliest mummies from Hierakonapolis and Adaima in southern Egypt show signs of deliberate dismemberment and restoration with the head placed on the chest clasped in the hands, calling to mind the myth of Osiris' dismemberment and a Pyramid text that says:

> Oho! Oho! Arise, O King!
> Take your head,
> Gather your bones,
> Gather your limbs . . .
> . . . Rise up, O King, for you shall not perish! (Ikram, 2003, p. 51)

In ancient Egyptian thought, death was the beginning of a journey through a series of tests and trials culminating in the judgment of Osiris. Salima Ikram notes that the *Book of the Dead* differs from earlier mortuary texts in its emphasis on judgment and morality (Ikram, 2003, p. 43). At the end of the journey, the soul is conducted into the hall of judgment by Anubis, the jackal-headed guide of the dead and guardian of the cemetery.[4] In Osiris' judgment hall, the person must make a confession and give up his heart to be weighed in the balance. The confession made in front of 42 judges is very different from what we might think of as a confession whereby one declares one's sins and requests forgiveness. This was a negative confession, a profession of innocence and purity, a justification as to why the person deserves to be admitted to Osiris' kingdom. The person was required to greet each judge by name and deny a specific sin:

> O Far-strider who came forth from Heliopolis, I have done no falsehood.
>> O Fire-embracer who came forth from Kheraha, I have not robbed.
>> O Dangerous One who came forth from Rosetjau, I have not killed men.
>> ... I have not stolen the god's offerings ... I have not killed a sacred bull ... I am not wealthy except with my own property ... I have not reviled God. (Taylor, 2001, p. 37)

The person's heart would then be weighed in a scale against the feather of righteousness and Truth – the feather represents Maat, the goddess of truth and order. If goodness had made it equally light, the person is welcomed into Osiris' kingdom, called the Field of Reeds; if it was heavy with sin, then the person is overtaken by a terrifying second death, devoured by "the Eater of the Dead," the crocodile-headed Ammit. This was the fear of the ancient Egyptians. Death could be negotiated with the help of rituals and spells, but the second death was absolute, total annihilation.

The ancient Egyptian view of death and afterlife presents us with certain themes that appear in later monotheistic religions – hope for the resurrection of the dead, eternal life in a perfect kingdom, and a strong belief that the fortunate continuation of the person after death is related to purity of conduct and good behavior in life.

Mesopotamia

The Egyptian hope of reclaiming life after death and enjoying eternal future happiness stands in stark contrast to Mesopotamian views of the same period, which are much more pessimistic regarding the fate of the dead, and indeed, regarding the entire relationship between humans and gods. From the Babylonian "Poem of the Righteous Sufferer" (*c.* 1500 BCE) we read:

> Who knows the will of the gods in heaven?
> Who understands the plans of the underworld gods?
> Where have mortals learned the way of a god?
> He who was alive yesterday is dead today.
> One moment people are singing in exaltation,
> Another they groan like professional mourners.
> My god has not come to the rescue in taking me by the hand,
> Nor has my goddess shown pity on me by going at my side.
> (Davies, 1999, pp. 49–50)

The Mesopotamian gods appear capricious, petty, and concerned with their own affairs. Humans are portrayed as having been created to serve the gods through their work and their worship. In the epic of *Atrahasis* (*c.* 1700 BCE), the lesser gods, wearied by 3,600 years of labor – digging out the channels for the rivers and piling up the great mountains to create the earth – revolt against their task and take their complaint to Ellil, father and counselor of the gods. It is decided that another type of creature (humankind) should be created to do their work: "Let the womb-goddess create offspring, and let man bear the load of the gods!" (Dalley, 2000, pp. 14–15). And so it was done, but humans multiplied and filled the earth with their noise, so much so that the father of the gods was sleepless from the clamor. In anger, he sent disease and famine to decrease the population, and finally, in an effort to destroy all of humankind, the great flood. As in all ancient flood stories, the destruction is not total – like the Biblical Noah, Utnapishtim and his wife survive and are granted immortality by the gods, but this is an exception. The gloomy underworld was the destiny of all the ghostly dead, low or highborn.[5] Jon Davies points out that in the Mesopotamian context, there is no "salvation":

> By existential definition, and because it suits the gods, humans are mortal: they die. They die in order to avoid provoking (merely by being alive) the gods, rather than because they have sinned, collectively or individually. They cannot achieve immortality, because their death is a necessary part of the ontology *of the gods*. (Davies, 1999, p. 53)

The purpose of human life, then, is to serve the gods, and death is built into humans by the gods for their own purposes. The overall feeling in Mesopotamian literature is that humankind struggles alone at the mercy of unreliable, all-powerful gods, and death brings only death:

> You have toiled without cease, what have you got?
> Through toil you are wearing yourself out,
> You are filling your body with grief,
> You are bringing forward the end of your days.
> Mankind which is like a reed in the cane-break, is snapped off. . . .
> No one can see death.
> But savage death snaps off mankind.
> Suddenly there is nothing.
> The prisoner and the dead are alike . . .
> They [the gods] established life and death . . .
> Death they fixed to have no ending. (Lambert, 1980, p. 55)

Death in the Ancient World

Gilgamesh and the Search for Immortality

The famous Mesopotamian epic (*c.* 2150 BCE) of Gilgamesh, ruler of the city of Uruk, tells the story of a semi-divine hero-king who seeks fame in the company of his beloved friend, Enkidu. Gilgamesh and Enkidu set out to kill Huwawa, a great forest monster, and in so doing to secure for themselves a name and reputation that will live forever in song and story. They defeat the monster but Gilgamesh angers the goddess Ishtar by spurning her advances and she sends a sickness to strike down his companion. In contrast to the Egyptian denial of the finality of death, the death of Enkidu throws Gilgamesh into the depths of grief and fear:

> Enkidu my friend whom I love so much, who experienced
> every hardship with me –
> The fate of mortals conquered him!
> For six days and seven nights I wept over him . . .
> I was frightened . . .
> I am afraid of death . . .
> Enkidu my friend whom I love has turned to clay.
> Am I not like him? Must I lie down too,
> Never to rise, ever again? (Dalley, 2000, pp. 103–104)

Fearful of death and no longer satisfied with the biological immortality that comes with children or the cultural immortality of having a name that lives on, Gilgamesh wishes to be immortal like the gods. So he roams the world in search of the secret of immortality. On his travels he meets a practical alewife who tries to show him the futility of his heroic search and who speaks to him about the simple pleasures of domestic life:

> Gilgamesh, where do you roam?
> You will not find the eternal life you seek.
> When the gods created mankind,
> They appointed death for mankind,

Kept eternal life in their own hands.
So, Gilgamesh, let your stomach be full,
Day and night enjoy yourself in every way,
Every day arrange for pleasures.
Day and night, dance and play,
Wear fresh clothes.
Keep your head washed, bathe in water,
Appreciate the child who holds your hand,
Let your wife enjoy herself in your lap.
This is the work [of the living]. (Dalley, 2000, p. 150)

But Gilgamesh is not to be dissuaded; he consults Utnapishtim, the survivor of the great flood, who has been granted immortality by the gods. In the Mesopotamian flood story, which is echoed in the Biblical story of Noah and the ark, it is Utnapishtim who builds the ark and saves mankind from utter destruction. He eventually tells Gilgamesh about a thorny plant at the bottom of the ocean that rejuvenates life. With great effort, Gilgamesh retrieves it and gives it the name "An old man grows into a young man." Gilgamesh is joyful with the thought that he will become again the young man that he once was, but on the journey home, due to a moment of carelessness, the plant is carried off by a snake. Gilgamesh is left empty-handed to return home and lament his loss. This epic emphasizes that a glorious death for a Mesopotamian hero was death on the battlefield, memorialized in song and story; and that the only immortality men could hope to gain was be found in the achievements of life – Gilgamesh finds solace in the great city of Uruk whose walls and towers would remain as a monument to his name. In the Mesopotamian view, then, this life is the arena for all action, enjoyment, and posterity, whether public or private.

The Spirits of the Dead in Mesopotamian Culture

Funerary rituals and the cult of the dead were as much a part of Mesopotamian culture as Egyptian but the purpose and focus were quite different. In Mesopotamian myth, the gods made man to labor for them by mixing the blood of a minor god with clay:

> Then one god should be slaughtered . . .
> Nintu shall mix clay with his flesh and his blood.
> Then a god and a man will be mixed together in the clay . . .
> Let a ghost come into existence from the god's flesh . . .
> And let the ghost exist so as not to forget (the slain god).
> (Dalley, 2000, p. 15)

Upon death the bones returned to the earth/clay of which they were made and the ghost remained in memory of the god that was slain to create man. There is no idea here of an eternal essence or soul belonging to a human; the ghost came into existence only at death and was simply the spiritualized aspect of the dead person that could receive offerings, be called upon to assist the family, or, if angered or neglected, bring harm to them. In this, we see a much simpler approach to the make-up of the psycho-physical personality compared with the Egyptian view. While Egyptian rituals were intended to transform death and bring about a happy future life, the Mesopotamian death cult, like their relationship with the gods, was driven by fear and appeasement. Fear of the dead whose ghost, if not properly buried and treated, could inflict harm on the living, but if treated properly could be of assistance to the family. Family members provided food and drink offerings to appease the ghost and to make sure that it did not become unhappy or lost – a "strange ghost." Proper burial was very important because the tomb was the entrance to the place below, the land of the dead. The shrouded body would be placed directly in the earth or a tomb or cave. It would never be burned or left unburied. The responsibility of the family to appease the spirits of the dead was underscored by the location of domed tombs under the houses with staircases leading down into them (Davies, 1999, p. 56). In contrast to the possibilities open to the Egyptians of life in the celestial realm of the sun god or in Osiris' paradise where the grain grows 10 feet high, the Mesopotamian underworld held no such promise. It was a gloomy place where the dead continued to render service to the gods as they had in life. Before he dies, Enkidu shares with his friend Gilgamesh a depressing vision of the destiny of all mankind:

> On the road where travelling is one way only,
> To the house where those who stay are deprived of light,
> Where dust is their food, and clay their bread.
> They are clothed, like birds, with feathers,
> And they see no light, and they dwell in darkness.
> (Dalley, 2000, p. 89)

The afterlife held no hope for the Mesopotamians. Immortality lay only in the continuing glory of one's name and achievements in this life. The capricious and unreliable nature of the Mesopotamian gods, the cult of the dead, and the hopelessness of death would, however, be challenged by the rise of monotheism.

Persia

Of all the great founders of world religions, the historical reconstruction of the life of the Persian prophet Zarathustra, more familiar to us in the Greek form Zoroaster, is the most difficult. The central Zoroastrian scripture, the *Avesta*, gives no information that would determine when Zoroaster lived. Zoroastrian tradition maintains that he lived sometime between the seventh and sixth centuries BCE. Linguistic analysis of the *Avesta*, whose language is close to the earliest Indian scripture, the *Rig Veda*, suggests a date sometime around 1500 BCE. Classical Greek sources place his birth prior to 6000 BCE, and numerous other dates for Zoroaster's life have been proposed, both ancient and modern (Nigosian, 1993). The conflicting evidence is reflected in the choices of two recent Zoroastrian scholars – Mary Boyce (2001) chooses a date of 1500 BCE, but S.A. Nigosian, noting difficulties with all sources and methods, prefers to let the traditional Zoroastrian dates of seventh to sixth centuries BCE stand. In the history of the Middle East, the fifth and sixth centuries BCE saw the rise of the Persian Achaemenid Empire that ruled over the Mesopotamian region until it broke up under the invasion of Alexander the Great in the fourth century BCE. Zoroastrianism became prominent under the rulers of the Persian Empire from the time of their first king, Cyrus II (559–530 BCE). In conquering Mesopotamia, the Persians brought to the polytheistic, pluralistic religious culture of the region yet another approach to death and the journey beyond.

Zoroaster and the Evil of Death

Whether Zoroastrianism is essentially dualistic or monotheistic in nature continues to be a subject of scholarly debate. Although Zoroastrians believe in the supremacy of the one Lord, the uncreated all-good Ahura Mazda (Wise Lord) who upholds the cosmic principle of order (*asha*), they also believe in the existence of his equally uncreated evil twin, Angra Mainyu (also known as Ahriman). All goodness, joy, light, and life in the world belong to the domain of Ahura Mazda; all evil, pain, and death were brought about by Ahriman. Human beings stand between the two, their ethical choices bringing them under the dominion of one or the other. Humans are bedeviled by the legions of demons in the service of Ahriman, but they are also surrounded and supported by the angels of Ahura Mazda. Death is not considered natural to humans; it was part of the chaos and evil brought into the world by Ahriman. However, human beings are created by Ahura Mazda, created in goodness and of concern to him; therefore all have the potential to be brought to eternal life by him, having earned it either through their virtue or through purification.

On a cosmic level, all of existence is moving towards the end of time, the moment of the final battle between good and evil when evil will be utterly overthrown and human life and existence will again be perfect as it was created. In Zoroastrian teaching, cosmic history is divided into three times: the time of "Creation," when all is brought into existence, perfect and pure, by Ahura Mazda; the time of "Mixture," when Ahriman attacks the perfect creation and permeates it with every physical and moral evil; and the time of

"Separation," the time of the great battle, when evil is separated from good and Ahura Mazda's creation is once again perfect and pure. On an individual level, the great drama of good versus evil is played out in every moral choice that a person makes, for good or for ill. By making morally good choices, humans assist in the cosmic struggle against evil as well as determine their fate after death. Humans are assisted in their life choices through the good offices of a powerful class of beings called the Fravashi. Every person or divinity or created thing in the universe has its own Fravashi, a higher spiritual double that, for humans, serves as conscience, moral guide, and benefactor. It is the divine voice that warns of evil, protects, chastises, or praises the individual. The purity and goodness of the Fravashi are never affected by the person's thoughts or deeds and a person prospers by supplicating and honoring them throughout life. Upon death, the person's soul continues on to face its fate, and the Fravashi departs to live on in the celestial realm. The Fravashi of the dead can still communicate with the living so the descendants of the deceased make offerings to the Fravashi on the death anniversary and on other special days. It is believed that by so doing the soul of the deceased can be helped to rise from a lower to a higher state (Nigosian, 1993, pp. 83–84).

Salvation for All

Upon death each person faces immediate judgment for the choices they have made and the way in which they have lived life. For three days after death, the soul remains with the body, prevailed upon by both good angels and evil spirits, existing in a state of joy or pain depending on past deeds and thoughts. On the fourth day after death, the soul begins its journey to the Chinvat Bridge that crosses over the fires of hell to paradise on the other side. This is the place of judgment where the soul's thoughts, words, and deeds are weighed in the balance. If virtue prevails, then, as the virtuous soul crosses the bridge, it meets with a fragrant breeze and a beautiful young girl, the spiritual form of its own good conscience, who leads the soul across the wide bridge to paradise. By contrast, for the evil soul, the bridge becomes razor thin, a horrible smell rises up, and the soul is met by an ugly old hag, the form of its own evil thoughts, words, and deeds, who clutches the soul and drags it down to the abyss below. In paradise, the soul lives in a state of bliss, light, fragrance, and beauty. Hell is a state of misery, darkness, disgusting stench, and great suffering. Those whose good and evil deeds are equally balanced go to *hamestagan*, a shadowy, in-between place reminiscent of the Mesopotamian underworld where they dwell until the final judgment, experiencing neither joy nor misery.

Traditionally, the body was neither cremated, as that would be polluting to the fire, which is sacred to the Zoroastrians, nor buried, since the corpse, regarded as a magnet for evil forces, would pollute the sacred earth. The dead body was subject to numerous taboos, and all that it had come in contact with had to be purified. Only professional corpse handlers were permitted to deal with the body, which would be exposed on some barren rocky ground where it could be fed upon by vultures and the bones bleached by the sun. Flat-roofed, open-air funerary towers[6] were developed as places where the corpse could be separated from the earth and exposed to scavenger birds. Later the bleached bones would be buried to await resurrection at the end of time.

In Zoroastrian thought, the tortures of the damned are not eternal. Hell was the creation of Ahriman whose aim is to doom all humankind to eternal suffering in the fires of hell. Although Ahriman is Ahura Mazda's primeval opponent, he is not equal to the Wise Lord. Ahriman has neither omniscience nor even the foresight to perceive his own future defeat and the triumph of Ahura Mazda, under whose rule humanity is destined to be reclaimed from evil. Salvation, in the end, is for all. Hell will last until the final resurrection when all people will be restored to their physical bodies.

The souls of both the righteous and the wicked will be re-united with their bodies – the bones being demanded back from the earth, the blood from water, the hair from plants, and the life from fire – so that they are reconstituted once again in their original materials. (Nigosian, 1993, p. 94)

For three days at the end of time, the re-embodied souls will experience even greater bodily bliss in paradise, or more intense physical suffering in hell. The last day is envisioned as a great fiery conflagration when the mountains of the earth will turn to molten metal. According to Zoroastrian scripture, the good will pass through the rivers of molten metal as through a bath of warm milk, while the wicked will experience it as supreme torture. However, after that final purification, the suffering of the damned will be over; all people will praise Ahura Mazda, all will live eternally in virtue and harmony. There will be no more procreation because creation would be finished, but human beings in their transformed state will experience all the pleasures of life forever on the earth, which itself would become an immortal realm. As for Ahriman and his retinue of demons, they would be defeated in a final great battle and thrown into the depths of hell to be sealed there for all eternity. For the Zoroastrians, then, good and evil are forces that continually battle one another on a cosmological level as well as in the heart of every human, but at the end of the story, life conquers death, good conquers evil, and salvation is the final chapter in the cosmic history of every human being. Only the demonic forces are eternally bound in hell; the earth and all its inhabitants are ultimately destined to be as they were in the beginning, perfect and pure.

The influence of Zoroastrianism on the development of Judaism, Christianity, and Islam is a hotly contested subject and one that is not easily resolved since the dates for Zoroaster and the early hymns of the *Avesta* are not conclusively established. Nevertheless, the similarities are undeniable; Nigosian lists the following concepts and beliefs shared by Zoroastrianism and the monotheistic religions:

> God and Satan (or the devil)
> Angels and demons
> Heaven and hell (and Purgatory in Christianity)
> Resurrection of the body and life everlasting
> Individual judgment at death and cosmic last judgment
> Arrival of the Messiah

Cosmic events during the end of the world
The Armageddon battle followed by a millennium period
(Nigosian, 1993, p. 97)

Although debatable, it is not implausible that the three major monotheistic religions of the world owe some of their characteristics to Zoroastrian influence.

Notes

1. In some tomb paintings, renewal of life is symbolized by a painting of the deceased being purified and cleansed with water poured by Horus and Thoth, the two gods who washed the newly born sun god at the beginning of the world (Taylor, 2001, pp. 52–53).
2. Cardboard-like material made of layers of linen or papyrus.
3. Dating of Egyptian dynasties and periods is approximate and debated among Egyptologists.
4. Anubis was associated with the embalmer's craft since he was the god who originally wrapped Osiris. Based on the existence of Anubis masks in ceramic and cartonnage, it is believed that during the mummification rituals, a priest wearing the mask was identified with Anubis.
5. The generally accepted view of Mesopotamian afterlife as entirely gloomy, pessimistic, and unrelated to judgment or moral behavior in life has been questioned by Gregory Shushan, who points to several texts that suggest a multiplicity of beliefs in the Mesopotamian world, some of which do offer possibilities for a beatific afterlife, and a range of fates for the dead based on the manner of their death or their status in life (Shushan, 2009).
6. The most famous in modern times are the "Towers of Silence" belonging to the Parsi community in Mumbai, India. However, the decline of the vulture population and other problems of modernity mean that many Zoroastrians now opt for cremation or burial.

References and Further Reading

Boyce, Mary. *Zoroastrians: Their Religious Beliefs and Practices*. London: Routledge, 2001.

Budge, Ernest Alfred Wallis, Sir. (Trans.) *The Book of the Dead*. New York: University Books, 1960.

Dalley, Stephanie. *Myths from Mesopotamia*. Oxford: Oxford University Press, 2000.

Davies, Jon. *Death, Burial and Rebirth in the Religions of Antiquity*. London: Routledge, 1999.

Faulkner, Raymond Oliver. (Trans.) *The Ancient Egyptian Pyramid Texts*, Vol. 1. Oxford: Clarendon Press, 1969.

Ikram, Salima. *Death and Burial in Ancient Egypt*. London: Longman Pearson Education, 2003.

Kellehear, Allan. *A Social History of Dying*. Cambridge: Cambridge University Press, 2007.

Lambert, W.G. "The Theology of Death." In Bendt Alster (ed.), *Death in Mesopotamia: Papers Read at the 26th International Assyriological Association*. Copenhagen Studies in Assyriology, Vol. 8: 53–66. Copenhagen: Akademisk Forlag, 1980.

Nigosian, S.A. *The Zoroastrian Faith: Tradition and Modern Research*. Montreal: McGill-Queen's University Press, 1993.

Shaw, Ian. *The Oxford History of Ancient Egypt*. Oxford: Oxford University Press, 2002.

Shushan, Gregory. *Conceptions of the Afterlife in Early Civilizations: Universalism, Constructivism, and Near-Death Experience*. New York and London: Continuum, 2009.

Sommer, Jeffrey. "The Shanidar IV 'Flower Burial': A Re-evaluation of Neanderthal Burial Ritual." *Cambridge Archeological Journal*, 9, 1 (1999): 127–129.

Taylor, John H. *Death and the Afterlife in Ancient Egypt*. Chicago: University of Chicago Press, 2001.

4

Jewish Perspectives on Death

The development of religious views on death and afterlife in Judaism is so interwoven with the early history of the Israelites that it is worth bearing in mind the following major foundational periods and events.[1]

c. 1900–1700 BCE   The age of the patriarchs. This covers the pre-history of the Hebrew tribes when they are led by their traditional forefathers, Abraham, Isaac, and Jacob, who is renamed Israel. With regard to dates for this period:

> ...it is difficult to speak of the so-called "patriarchal period" as a well-defined chronological entity ... It would seem rather that imbedded in this narrative cycle are

Understanding Death: An Introduction to Ideas of Self and the Afterlife in World Religions, First Edition. Angela Sumegi.
© 2014 Angela Sumegi. Published 2014 by Blackwell Publishing Ltd.

> reminiscences of centuries long historical processes... These extended time spans were telescoped in the biblical narrative into a mere trigenerational scheme – Abraham, Isaac and Jacob. (Malamat, 1976, p. 32)

c. 1550–1200 BCE	the Exodus of the Hebrews from Egypt and settlement in Canaan.
1025–928 BCE	The United Kingdom of Israel under Kings Saul, David, and Solomon.
928 BCE	Division of the kingdom into the northern Kingdom of Israel and the southern Kingdom of Judah.
722 BCE	Conquest of the northern kingdom by the Assyrians; the community displaced and assimilated. They become known as the 10 "lost tribes" of Israel.
586 BCE	Conquest of the southern kingdom by the Babylonians; the temple in Jerusalem destroyed, and the community leaders sent into exile in Babylon.
539–333 BCE	the Persian period.
333–63 BCE	The Hellenistic (Greek) period.
63 BCE	Beginning of the Roman period.

The Jewish people trace their ancestry to semi-nomadic tent-dwelling Hebrew tribes of the second millennium BCE. They belonged to a world of tribal migrations and trade caravans on the move that traveled between the region of the Euphrates, southern Syria, and northern Palestine. Unlike Egypt, whose culture, wealth, and relative political stability were protected by the seas, deserts, and mountains that surrounded it, this was an area besieged by invaders and bitterly contested by all who laid claim to power. According to the historian Abraham Malamat,

> The military history of Syria and Palestine represents, on the one hand, a continuous chain of conquests and oppression directed by the various powers against the local population. On the other hand, struggles were being waged simultaneously among the would-be conquerors, each aiming to enhance his own power status. (Malamat, 1976, p. 7)

The region was not only politically unstable but also extremely culturally and religiously diverse: "a patchwork of peoples and states, several entering upon the stage of history at one and the same time, others following upon each other in rapid succession" (Malamat, 1976, p. 7).

In the context of this atmosphere of insecurity, anxiety, and the numerous religious cults that worshipped a bewildering array of gods and goddesses, the narrative of the Hebrew patriarch Abraham tells of a tribal leader who puts his faith in one supreme protector. Abraham is called by God to "Go from your country and your kindred and your father's house to the land that I will show you. I will make of you a great nation, and I will bless you, and make your name great, so that you will be a blessing. I will bless those who bless you, and the one who curses you, I will curse; and in you all the families of the earth shall be blessed" (Gen. 12:1–3). Abraham enters into a binding covenant with God in which he promises to worship God alone and to obey all his commandments. God promises Abraham that he will have descendants as numerous as the stars and that he will give them a homeland. And so Abraham and his tribe began the long journey into Canaan, the land promised by God, where they settled down among the polytheistic Canaanites and kept to their belief in the one God.

According to the Biblical narrative, after Abraham's death, the tribe was led first by his son Isaac and then by his grandson, Jacob, who eventually became known as Israel, whose 12 sons founded the 12 tribes of Israel. In time, famine struck the area in which they lived and the tribes made their way into Egypt where they lived for many generations in peace under the rule of the Egyptian pharaohs. However, during the thirteenth century BCE, a pharaoh hostile to the Israelites came to power and their condition in Egypt changed to one of great oppression. Sometime around the mid-thirteenth century, the Israelites made their escape into the desert of the Sinai Peninsula. The Bible speaks of a great exodus out of Egypt led by the Prophet Moses and his brother Aaron that resulted in 40 years of wandering in the wilderness. Finally, the tribes of Israel came again to Canaan, the land of their forefathers.

Some argue that the advent of the Israelites into Canaan came about through peaceful migration with occasional conflict, but the traditional Biblical account tells a story of military conquest and negotiated peace (Malamat, 1976, pp. 47–48). The result was that the tribes of Israel settled in the mountains of Canaan but were continually under pressure on all sides from the indigenous Canaanites as well as from invaders who came out of the desert to the east and from sea-faring peoples, like the Philistines, who settled on the western coast. Throughout these battles, the Hebrew tribes were led by charismatic prophets who oversaw their adherence to God's laws and spearheaded their military campaigns. Eventually the tribes united to form the Kingdom of Israel under kings Saul, David, and Solomon. In Jewish history, the United Kingdom ushers in what is called the First Temple Period (1006–586 BCE) when the center of religious ritual was the great Temple in Jerusalem that housed the holy "Ark of the Covenant," a chest that represented the throne and the presence of the invisible God. In contrast to all the surrounding religious cults, the Israelites made no images of their God.

During the many long years that the Israelites wandered across the desert seeking a safe haven, they gained a renewed sense of themselves as a distinct people, a nation chosen by God, and a new understanding of their God. The God of the early patriarchs was a national or tribal god, worshipped exclusively by them, but still one among many. Through Moses, the Israelites came to know God as Yahweh (YHWH), the one universal God with no equal. This transformation is captured in the Biblical account from the Book of

Exodus of God's revelation to Moses on Mount Sinai when Moses received the core of the Hebraic Law, the 10 precepts that encompassed all the ethical guidelines for a nation. At that time also, the Israelites affirmed their covenant with God; it was no longer simply an agreement between God and the patriarch on behalf of the tribe but between God and the people, on behalf of all humanity. Through Moses, God tells the Israelites:

> Now therefore, if you obey my voice and keep my covenant, you shall be my treasured possession out of all the peoples. Indeed, the whole earth is mine, but you shall be for me a priestly kingdom and a holy nation. (Ex. 19:5–6)

The cornerstone of Jewish religious attitudes is the covenant relationship between God and the people of Israel, as a total entity. Therefore, in thinking of death and the self in Judaism, it is important to consider that the religious identity of the individual is very much linked to the collective identity of a people who are God's link with the world. In his comprehensive work on the history of the afterlife in western religion, Alan Segal comments:

> Jews understand themselves to be God's special people not in the sense that they are preferred above any other, but in the sense that they have been elected to a special responsibility: to serve as God's priests in the world. (Segal, 2007, p. 65)

Individual death, grievous as that is, does not affect the covenant with God because the contractual relationship is with the people as a whole. According to one writer, "classical Jewish thinking saw national catastrophe, not individual extinction, as the worst imaginable disaster" (Goldenberg, 1992, p. 99). Not surprising, then, the trauma to Jewish religious consciousness caused by the twentieth-century Holocaust. From a religious perspective, horrific as genocide is under any circumstances, for Judaism it went beyond the extinction of a particular group of people; it could be thought of as a cosmic threat because it endangered the relationship between God and humanity enshrined in the covenant.

The Beginning of Death

Although the collective identity of the Jews as a people is an integral part of Judaism, each person is responsible for upholding the covenant and death comes to each on an individual basis. Let us now examine Jewish views of how persons came to be, and how death came into the world.

> Then the LORD God formed man from the dust of the ground, and breathed into his nostrils the breath of life [*nishmat ḥayyim*]; and the man became a living being [or living soul – *nefesh ḥayyah*]. (Gen. 2:7)

There are a number of words in Hebrew that relate to the animating element that is the mark of a living being: *nefesh, neshamah, ruah*. They all have slightly different nuances but all relate to concepts of inhalation, breath, or wind. *Nefesh* is often translated "soul" in the sense of the personality, the quality of an individual that can become noble or debased, and *neshamah* or *ruah* are used to refer more explicitly to the life principle or life-breath (Segal, 1989, p. 144). Still, however we describe it – whether as animating principle, life-force, breath of life – that which makes living creatures alive is understood to come from God and upon death the life-breath departs the body. The main point here, however, is that in the Biblical creation story, human beings are not a duality of mortal body and immortal soul; God's breath animated the body made from the dust and the body became a living being. As Segal remarks: "In short the problem is that we use the term differently from the Hebrews: We think we have a soul; the Hebrews thought they were a soul" (Segal, 1989, p. 144). Upon death, the body returns to the dust from which it was formed and the life-breath returns to God from where it came. Personal identity, however, is not annihilated; the word *nefesh* is also used to refer to the shade or ghost of the person that remains after death, when the person is no longer a living soul but a dead soul. We will investigate this further below.

Having created the first man and woman at the beginning of time and the world, God places them in a beautiful garden and instructs them:

"You may eat freely of every tree of the garden; but of the tree of the knowledge of good and evil you shall not eat, for in the day that you eat of it you shall die." (Gen. 2:16–17)

The story of Adam and his mate Eve in the Garden of Eden is one of the great myths of world religions. It tells of beginnings: the beginning of the world and humankind as God's good creation; the beginning of human reasoning and moral responsibility; the beginning of self-consciousness and shame; the beginning of man's realization of death. In this narrative, Eve encounters another character in the Garden, the serpent, who directly contradicts God's statement: "You will not die; for God knows that when you eat of it your eyes will be opened, and you will be like God, knowing good and evil" (Gen. 3:4–5). And so doubt was born, and choice was born. The woman considered the serpent's words and judged that the fruit was both beautiful and good to eat, as well as desirable because it would make one wise, and so she chose to eat it, and offered it also to her husband who also ate of it. And as the serpent said, their eyes were opened and they felt shame in their nakedness. According to the Bible, God could no longer trust in their obedience, and lest they eat of the fruit of the Tree of Life and gain immortality, they are turned out of the Garden to fend for themselves and the Tree of Life is protected by angels with flaming swords.

This myth raises a number of questions related to death and afterlife. Adam and Eve are portrayed as having knowledge of death prior to the knowledge of good and evil since both God's commandment and the serpent's contradiction of it depend on that knowledge. Does that mean that they were created mortal and destined for death? Not necessarily; since the result of breaking God's commandment would be death, it could be thought that so long as they followed God's instructions, they would live forever in the Garden.

Or, it could mean that death would simply come to them sooner, at that moment, rather than later at the end of life.

Interestingly, Adam and Eve were not explicitly forbidden to eat of the Tree of Life, and one might note that the issue of immortality is of concern only *after* they had eaten of the Tree of the Knowledge of Good and Evil – would that imply that they would be immortal so long as they were ignorant or unselfconscious of their immortality? Does death come into the picture of life only when we are conscious of what it means to live and to make choices between life and death, good and evil? And how are we to understand the serpent – is this an evil presence in the primeval garden, coexistent and in conflict with God as Ahriman and Ahura Mazda in Zoroastrianism? Or is God the only one overseeing the future of humankind? In the Bible, there are a number of references that suggest God's intervention in human affairs in ways that may seem devious to us, but that are eventually shown to further a greater plan. For example, in the story of the wicked king Ahab (1 Kings 22:19–23), God sends a lying spirit into the mouth of his prophets so that Ahab may be deceived and drawn into the battle in which he is killed. This suggests the possibility that the snake in the Garden of Eden is doing nothing more than God's work by introducing Adam and Eve to that which makes them fully human and fully capable of worshipping God through their own free choice and the ability to discern good from evil.[2]

The Soul and Sheol

The breath of life is God's breath, but it is difficult to establish exact meanings for the terms used to describe that which makes the difference between life and death. Gillman explains that they can be used quite interchangeably in the Bible.

> Death is understood as the "going out" of the *ruah* [Psa. 146:4], or of the similar "going out" of the *nefesh* (as in Genesis 35:18), or of God's "taking away" the *nefesh* (as 1 Kings 19:4) or the *neshamah* (as in Job 34:14). (Gillman, 1997, p. 76)

Although the notion of something "going out" of the body might suggest ideas of a separate and immortal soul entity that survives and continues without the body, this is not the view expressed in the books of Genesis or Psalms or Job. In those texts that date prior to the Hellenistic period, a human being is regarded as a holistic combination of body and animating breath; the person does not possess a soul but is a soul, a being, living when the breath of life is present, dead when it is not. At that time also, it would seem that the beliefs of the Israelites regarding the afterlife, and Sheol as the place of the dead, were similar to those of the surrounding cultural environments of Mesopotamia and Canaan.

The idea that a dead person became a shade or ghost or spirit of some kind that dwelled in the land of the dead was common to Mesopotamian and Canaanite peoples. In Canaan, the Lord of Death was called Mot, who ruled over the underworld. Upon death, the vital element, equated with the "shade" or "soul" (npš – also related to breath, like the Hebrew *nefesh*) (Segal, 1989, p. 113), left the person and went to live in Mot's kingdom of death. It is important to note here that the shadowy figures that populated the Mesopotamian and Canaanite underworlds, those who, through necromantic rites, could be raised to communicate with the living, should not be understood to be disembodied souls, in the sense of an immortal immaterial essence that enjoys bliss or misery. They were ghosts, shadows of their former selves, cut off from life, devoid of the vitality of life. The Mesopotamian and Canaanite underworlds were places of neither punishment nor reward but simply the final destination of all the dead, regardless of their achievements or status in life. In all these ways, they resemble the Biblical concept of Sheol as the place of the dead – a place that the Book of Job calls "the land of gloom and deep darkness" (Job 10:21). Biblical references to Sheol are linked with the finality and the tragic nature of death.

> As the cloud fades and vanishes,
> So those who go down to Sheol do not come up . . . (Job 7:9)

It is a place from which one never returns, a place where one is cut off from God. In a traditional lament, the dying person finds no comfort in death.

> For my soul is full of troubles,
> and my life draws near to Sheol.
> I am counted among those who go down to the Pit;
> I am like those who have no help,
> like those forsaken among the dead,
> like the slain that lie in the grave,
> like those whom you remember no more,
> for they are cut off from your hand. (Psa. 88:3–5)

Again, the psalmist writes, "The heavens are the LORD's heavens, but the earth he has given to human beings. The dead do not praise the LORD, nor do any that go down into silence. But we [who are living] will bless the LORD from this time on and forevermore" (Psa. 115:16–18). In the tripartite cosmology of upper, middle, and lower worlds that the Israelites shared with the surrounding cultures, God is associated with the upper world of sky, and humans dwell in the middle world of earth, but the underworld of the dead is entirely disassociated from God and men.

There is a sense here, reminiscent of the Mesopotamian world-view, that only God is immortal, the inescapable fate of human beings is death, and death is a final end to life. The Book of Psalms also suggests that the dead are irrevocably separated from God and those who praise God – the living. So, for example, in the Book of Isaiah, we read that King Hezekiah who ruled the southern kingdom of Judah in the early seventh century BCE was sick unto death, but recovered and subsequently praises God, saying:

> . . . Sheol cannot thank you,
> death cannot praise you;
> those who go down into the Pit cannot hope
> for your faithfulness.
> The living, the living, they thank you,

as I do this day;
fathers make known to children
your faithfulness. (Isa. 38:18–19)

Such passages express a strong link between life, faith, and God.

In the death cults of the surrounding near eastern cultures, people made offerings to their ancestors, practiced necromancy, and worshipped not only celestial gods but also the gods of the underworld. The Israelite leaders rejected the entire polytheistic worldview with all its oracles, soothsayers, magic, and divination. The following passage from the Book of Deuteronomy traditionally represents the last exhortations of the Prophet Moses to the Hebrew tribes about to enter the promised land of Canaan:

> No one shall be found among you who makes a son or daughter pass through fire [child sacrifice], or who practices divination, or is a soothsayer or an augur, or a sorcerer, or one who casts spells, or who consults ghosts or spirits, or who seeks oracles from the dead. For whoever does these things is abhorrent to the Lord; it is because of such abhorrent practices that the Lord your God is driving them out before you. You must remain completely loyal to the Lord your God. Although these nations that you are about to dispossess do give heed to soothsayers and diviners, as for you, the Lord your God does not permit you to do so. (Deut. 18:9–14)[3]

Although all these practices were rejected by the Israelite leadership in their attempt to hold fast to the worship of the one and only God, and to separate their practices from those of the surrounding cultures, nevertheless, it would not be surprising if the beliefs and practices of the popular religion were influenced by the cultural environment. In Biblical denouncements of extravagant mourning and participation in Canaanite funeral rituals, Segal finds evidence of their infiltration into Israelite culture. He writes:

> ...there were a variety of funeral practices which offended the prophets, rites which resembled the funeral feasts of the Canaanites and Mesopotamians. Jeremiah 16:7 criticizes what appears to be banqueting: "No one shall break bread for the mourner, to comfort

him for the dead; nor shall anyone give him the cup of consolation for his father or his mother." Ezekiel 24 suggests the same, as well as questions other kinds of mourning customs: "Sigh, but not aloud; make no mourning for the dead. Bind on your turban, and put your shoes on your feet; do not cover your lips nor eat the bread of the mourners (v17). (Segal, 1989, p. 133)

The dead, however, are not easily ignored, especially when aid is needed. The most famous account of an Israelite engaging in forbidden rituals of necromancy is the story of the first king of Israel, Saul, and the woman from Endor whom he sought out to raise up the ghost of the dead priest Samuel, the one who had anointed him king. At this time, the Philistines were preparing for war against Israel. Saul finds himself in great distress, lacking God's assurance and blessing because he receives no answers to his prayers either through dreams or by casting lots, or by prophets. Desperate to know how he should proceed, even though he had expelled all the mediums and wizards from the land, Saul sends his servants to find a medium. In disguise, he visits the woman's house.

So Saul disguised himself and put on other clothes and went there, he and two men with him. They came to the woman by night. And he said, "Consult a spirit for me, and bring up for me the one whom I name to you." The woman said to him, "Surely you know what Saul has done, how he has cut off the mediums and the wizards from the land. Why then are you laying a snare for my life to bring about my death?" But Saul swore to her by the LORD, "As the LORD lives, no punishment shall come upon you for this thing." Then the woman said, "Whom shall I bring up for you?" He answered, "Bring up Samuel for me." When the woman saw Samuel, she cried out with a loud voice; and the woman said to Saul, "Why have you deceived me? You are Saul!" The king said to her, "Have no fear; what do you see?" The woman said to Saul, "I see a divine being coming up out of the ground." He said to her, "What is his appearance?" She said, "An old man is coming up; he is wrapped in a robe." So Saul knew that it was Samuel, and he bowed with his face to the ground, and did obeisance. (I Sam. 28:8–14)

Samuel speaks with Saul and confirms that God has indeed abandoned him for his disobedience and that there will be no success for him in the coming battle. Commenting on this story, Segal makes the point that the belief that the dead could be contacted and consulted was not questioned; the issue was one of obedience to God's laws and, in the eyes of the Israelite God, it was sinful to communicate with the dead as though they had divine powers equal to God or offered some refuge that could not be had from God (Segal, 1989, p. 126).

Besides the notion of Sheol, the Bible refers to another abode of the dead called in Greek Gehenna. This was originally a large ravine beside Jerusalem, which was apparently used as a city garbage dump and was also associated with a cult that practiced child sacrifice, those who "passed children through fire" (Segal, 1989, p. 135). During the Hellenistic period (333–63 BCE) and especially in the Christian New Testament, Gehenna becomes the metaphoric basis for ideas of hell as a place where the wicked dead are condemned to burn for all eternity, but in the Biblical records that date prior to the destruction of the First Temple in 586 BCE, there is no sense of the dead attaining either to the joys of heaven or the fires of hell. Sheol is described as a place of gloom and is associated with unwanted or untimely death (Segal, 1989, p. 139). The Bible, however, also speaks of death as a peaceful rest belonging to the natural order of things. At the end of a long and fruitful life, the dead one is "gathered to his people" (Gen. 25:8) or "sleeps with his ancestors" (1 Kings 1:21). Exactly what these phrases mean is not entirely clear, but what is clear is that in the First Temple Period of Israelite history, life was perceived as God's gift and all God's blessings and rewards were to be had in life, not after death. As the famous story of Job recounts, after he had suffered through all the trials laid upon him to test his faith, God rewards Job in life with great wealth, the love of friends and family, beautiful children, a long life, and a peaceful death: "After this Job lived one hundred and forty years, and saw his children, and his children's children, four generations. And Job died, old and full of days" (Job 42:16–17).

Resurrection and the World to Come

The textual evidence in the Hebrew Bible of an afterlife that is the object of hope and expectation is quite late and linked with particular historical circumstances. The first clear reference to the idea of resurrection in a literal sense comes from the Book of Daniel dated to *c.* 165 BCE. The author speaks of a time of great upheaval and trouble and a time when the dead will arise to face their destiny.

> At that time Michael, the great prince, the protector of your people, shall arise. There shall be a time of anguish, such has never occurred since nations first came into existence. But at that time your people shall be delivered, everyone who is found written in the book. Many of those who sleep in the dust of the earth shall awake, some to everlasting life, and some to shame and everlasting contempt. Those who are wise shall shine like the brightness of the sky, and those who lead many to righteousness, like the stars forever and ever. But you, Daniel, keep the words secret and the book sealed until the time of the end. Many shall be running back and forth, and evil shall increase. (Dan. 12:1–2)

The ideas expressed here of resurrection of the dead and everlasting life after death represent a complete reversal of those passages that portray death as a final state cut off from the God of the living. To understand this major shift in the Biblical approach to death, we need to ask, what is going on in Jewish history in the years leading up to 165 BCE? It is a time of great persecution, a time when pious Jews are being martyred for their faith. It is the reign of the Syrian Greek ruler Antiochus IV (175–164 BCE) who outlawed the Mosaic Law, the dietary laws, and defiled the temple in Jerusalem by setting up a statue of Zeus inside it and sacrificing a pig on the altar; the observance of the Sabbath and circumcision were banned on pain of death. There were many who were martyred for keeping the laws and refusing to eat pork. The persecution resulted in the Maccabean revolt, which began in 167 BCE, led by a priest called Mattathias and his five sons called the Maccabees. The movement eventually retook the temple in Jerusalem and their struggle and victory are commemorated in the Jewish holiday of Hannukah.

Although the Israelites were no strangers to national suffering and disaster such as the destruction of the northern Kingdom of Israel in 722 BCE and the destruction of Jerusalem and the temple in 586 BCE, these events had been interpreted by the Jewish prophets as God's punishment for Israel's sin; God's justice was previously never in question, but the reign of Antiochus IV ushered in a period of unprecedented persecution based only on adherence to their faith. Where was God's justice here? What would be the fate of those who died for their faith? To be denied their rightful length of days? To be cut off from God in death? It is in the context of these social and historical conditions that Jewish eschatology is established, and the doctrine of resurrection and a future beatific life after death comes to the fore in Jewish history.

Eschatology is religious study and thought relating to notions of the end of time, the end of human history, and what happens to the living and the dead beyond time and history. Although the cultures that surrounded the early Israelites did not assume an "end" towards which all human history is moving, they had much to say about what happens to the dead. Yet, on this issue, the early Biblical writings are silent or vague and inconclusive. Segal suggests that this silence about the fate of the dead has less to do with the belief that there is no afterlife and more to do with the struggle of the prophets against the infiltration into popular Israelite religion of the attractive but forbidden cults of fertility and ancestor worship that surrounded them (Segal, 1989, pp. 123–124). However, the question of what happens to the dead is not easily laid to rest, and in the Book of Daniel eschatological thinking finally bursts forth in the Bible accompanied by notions of a great apocalypse.

Prior to 165 BCE, there were prophets who used language that could imply resurrection and an apocalyptic eschatology, such as Ezekiel's famous vision of a valley full of dry bones:

> Then he [the Lord] said to me, "Prophesy to these bones, and say to them: O dry bones, hear the word of the LORD. Thus says the Lord

GOD to these bones: I will cause breath to enter you, and you shall live. I will lay sinews on you, and will cause flesh to come upon you, and cover you with skin, and put breath in you, and you shall live; and you shall know that I am the LORD." (Ezek. 37:4–6)

This passage is fairly easily recognized as a metaphor for the regeneration of the nation of Israel since the writer interprets the vision for us in the following words:

"Mortal, these bones are the whole house of Israel. They say, 'Our bones are dried up, and our hope is lost; we are cut off completely.' Therefore prophesy, and say to them, Thus says the Lord GOD: I am going to open your graves, and bring you up from your graves, O my people; and I will bring you back to the land of Israel." (Ezek. 37:11–12)

The following passage from Isaiah seems more literal but, due to issues of dating and authorship, there is still ambiguity regarding whether or not it refers to a literal interpretation of bodily resurrection or serves as a metaphor for the revival of a people (Segal, 1989, p. 258 ff.).

Your dead shall live, their corpses shall rise.
O dwellers in the dust, awake and sing for joy!
For your dew is a radiant dew,
And the earth will give birth to those long dead. (Isa. 26:19)

Segal points out that the theme of resurrection and a beatific afterlife gradually infiltrated Israelite thought. Referring to the passages above from Ezekiel and Isaiah, he concludes:

However, even if both these passages are taken as references to literal resurrection, they hardly affect the general tenor of Israelite religion, which emphasized life on this earth and behaviour in the world ... But these two passages are absolutely crucial for understanding whence the language of resurrection comes. Metaphorical here, resurrection becomes absolutely literal in Daniel 12. Therefore, these passages become the reservoir of images that illustrate what resurrection means. (Segal, 1989, p. 261)

In searching for the roots of this type of thinking, some scholars look to the much earlier Zoroastrian teachings on resurrection, heaven, and hell, but regardless of whether resurrection and belief in a beatific afterlife entered Judaism due to external cultural influence or was an internal development, it is at a particular moment of persecution in their history that the idea gains currency as a Jewish answer to the question of God's justice and an affirmation of God's power. In the Book of Daniel, there is still no idea of a universal resurrection of all people at the end of time to face God's judgment. At this point, it is a way to glorify God's justice and to give succor to those pious Jews who suffered and died for their faith. However, the belief in a renewed life in God's presence, once introduced, would never lose its appeal and by the time the Mishnah (collection of oral traditions) was compiled (*c.* 220 CE), resurrection was accepted as an article of faith in Rabbinic Judaism.

Not all Jews of the first century accepted these theological innovations. There was one group that rejected any idea of resurrection because it could not be found in scripture except for the very late Book of Daniel – these were the Sadducees, the aristocratic priestly class of the Hellenic Jewish world, the wealthy, who lived the good life here and now, whose pleasure gardens were a paradise on earth, and who had no need to look for rewards in another world. However, the Sadducees were a minority and the doctrine of the resurrection was carried forward by another more popular group, the Pharisees. They were a class of scribes and craftsmen known for their righteousness, simple lifestyle, and knowledge of the Mosaic laws. It is their emphasis on resurrection and the world to come that was inherited by the rabbis and irreversibly established in Jewish thought. Today, traditional worship services affirm this belief in the *Amidah* prayer:

You sustain the living with compassion; You revive the dead with abundant mercy. You support the falling, heal the ailing, free the captive; and maintain faith with those who sleep in the dust. Whose power can compare with Yours, who is comparable to you O King Who brings death and restores life and causes salvation to sprout! (Gillman, 1997, p. 123)

Although resurrection became an article of faith in Judaism, it is an awkward doctrine that elicits more questions than answers, theological questions like:

Will all the dead be resurrected to stand at the Last Judgment, or will the Judgment take place first to determine which of the dead are worthy of renewed life? Will the Messiah be the judge at this final tribunal, or appear only later to rule over those deemed worthy to witness his glory? Will the Messiah's kingdom last forever or be followed by something else? Is the so-called World to Come identical with the Messianic kingdom, or something that will come after? (Goldenberg, 1992, p. 98)

And not so theological questions like: "Will I be resurrected in the bodily form that I had at the time of my death? Will I be clothed or naked? Will I return with my arthritis or without it? Before my weight-loss or following it? With which one of my spouses will I be living?" (Gillman, 1997, p. 131). The Jewish tradition offers no definitive answers to such questions and although belief in the resurrection and the age to come is an integral part of Judaism, there is no systematized dogmatic scheme to which all Jews adhere regarding the specifics of just exactly what is the nature of the resurrection and the World to Come, or when, how, or where it will take place. This leaves a lot of room for speculation and personal belief regarding the afterlife. For many contemporary Jews, it is enough that the details are in God's hands, enough to know that God's justice will prevail. Although specific beliefs about the afterlife do not define Judaism, nevertheless a sense of personal immortality is enshrined in Jewish prayers that affirm God's power to return life to the dead.

The Journey of the Soul

In the fourth century BCE, the armies of Alexander the Great defeated the Persians and Palestine came under the rule of the Greeks. This was the beginning of the Hellenistic period in Jewish history and it marked another shift in the way Jewish thinkers approached the question of death and afterlife. Ideas of bodily resurrection, as we have seen, developed as a natural extension of faith in God's justice, to provide hope for those who gave up life rather than renounce their beliefs. The notion, however, that each material, mortal body houses an immaterial, immortal soul that continues after death and experiences a beatific afterlife can be traced to the influence of Greek thinkers and philosophers, most particularly Plato (*c.* fifth century BCE). For Plato, the soul was the essence of the human faculty of thought and reason, the essence of the individual self, and its departure signified death. Death was a welcome liberation of the soul from its bodily prison. To develop the soul was to develop one's intellect, reason, and appreciation of the Beautiful and the Good. Plato taught that the soul pre-existed the body and after many reincarnations was destined for its own divine life in a realm of perfect essences or Forms. In popular Greek mythology, the dwelling place of the immortal soul came to be identified with the Elysian Fields, the Isles of the Blessed located in the sky among the stars. As Segal explains:

> The soul's salvation for Plato was quintessentially an individual process. The soul is on an individual mission to purify itself. It travels through many bodies and cleanses itself from the impurities it gathers in human society . . . This contrasts quite strongly with the communal and sectarian nature of resurrection of the body in its Iranian and Jewish versions. (Segal, 1989, p. 237)

Such a view of soul is also alien to the ancient Hebrew concept of *nefesh* (the animating breath of God), which is used to refer to the individual immortal soul in the later Rabbinic tradition.

91

Greek philosophical ideas had a profound impact on Jewish thought, but while, in Greek thought, the body was ultimately dispensable, having served its purpose as a vehicle for the education of the soul, Judaism could not disparage the body that was created by God. Resurrection of the body as well as reconciliation between the teaching on resurrection and new ideas of spiritual immortality were difficult areas to navigate. The difficulties are brought out in the contradictory views of a variety of groups as well as in the writings of Jewish philosophers and theologians who held quite different views of the afterlife. The Jewish historian Josephus (39–100 CE) writes of various groups active in the late second century BCE: the Sadducees who denied the resurrection, the Essenes, and the Pharisees. The scriptures of the Essenes show that, like the Pharisees, they believed in resurrection (Segal, 1989, p. 298), but they were also a society of radical mystics who may have been more inclined towards notions of immortality of the soul than other Jewish communities. The Pharisees appear to have combined the idea of a personal soul and personal salvation with the doctrine of communal resurrection including the belief that the wicked and good souls are separated, each to experience its own destiny of reward or punishment. It is the general picture offered by the Pharisees that moves forward in Jewish history to be grappled with by philosophers and theologians.

Philo of Alexandria (first century CE) promoted a thoroughly Hellenized version of the afterlife that dispenses with resurrection: "But then we who are here joined to the body, creatures of composition . . . , shall be no more, but shall go forward to our rebirth, to be with the unbodied, without composition" (quoted in Goldenberg, 1992, p. 103). This view, however, was too alien to the Hebrew heritage, and Rabbinic scholars would later make the doctrine of resurrection a central feature of the Jewish faith; those who deny it would have no share in the beatific Age to Come. Resurrection and immortality of the soul were contradictory ideas that were more or less successfully reconciled in Jewish thought. Rabbinic stories made it clear that neither idea was to be left behind. In one Talmudic text, the question is put that if body and soul are separate entities, then how are they to be judged accurately when they come before God. "The body can plead: the soul has sinned, since from the day it left me, I lie like a dumb stone in the grave. The soul can plead: from the day I departed from it, I fly about in the air like a bird." In his answer, the Rabbi uses the example of two watchmen appointed to guard an orchard, one blind and the other lame. In order to steal the fruit, the lame climbs on the shoulders of the blind and they both eat. When the owner questions them, the lame one answers, "have I feet to walk with?" and the blind one answers, "have I eyes to see with?" but the owner placed them one on the other and judged them together: "So will the Holy One bring the soul, replace it in the body, and judge them together" (Gillman, 1997, p. 139).

The intellectual movement in Judaism, however, still tended away from a literal interpretation of the resurrection and belief in a bodily life of eating and drinking in the Age to Come and towards a more spiritualized version in which there would be no eating, drinking, or reproducing in the afterlife. The greatest attempt to reconcile the teachings of the Torah with the Greek emphasis on reason, the Good, and the immortal soul was made by the medieval philosopher Maimonides. He lists resurrection among the 13 Principles of Jewish belief, but in the writings of Maimonides, the Age to Come was completely spiritualized with no "bodily" component to it at all; the disembodied soul existed blissful in the presence of God. He was criticized for this and had to defend himself against the accusation that he essentially denied the resurrection. Maimonides' compromise was to separate the resurrection, which takes place during the Days of the Messiah on earth when Israel will be released from bondage to foreign kingdoms, from the Age to Come.

> [T]he individuals who will return to their bodies will eat, drink, marry, and procreate, and they will die after a long life, like those who live during the messianic age. The life, however, that is not followed by death, is life in the world to come, since it will be bodiless. (Quoted in Gillman, 1997, p. 159)

As Gillman explains, for Maimonides, "The eschatology of the individual is a drama in two acts: First, resurrection of bodies reunited with souls; and then, after our second death, spiritual immortality alone" (Gillman, 1997, p. 160). Although Maimonides' scheme still leaves many questions unanswered as to exactly when the Messianic Age will be ushered in, when or how exactly resurrection will take place, whether the Age to Come is to be understood as a communal or an individual reality, nevertheless, immortality of the soul and resurrection of the body were inextricably bound together in Jewish thought.

Just as theories of the resurrection raise questions about what kind of body is a resurrected body and what kind of activities one engages in with it, so theories of an immortal soul raised questions of what happens to the soul in the time between death and resurrection when the soul is rejoined with the body – where does it go, what is it doing? Such thoughts were the special provenance of Jewish mystics who elaborated the journey of the soul in great detail. Today, Jewish mysticism, like many other types of mysticism, has become a subject of popular interest. It is traditionally preserved among those who follow the way of Kabbalah, an ancient mystical tradition especially characteristic of the teachings of Hasidic sects. Hasidism was founded in the eighteenth century by a rabbi known as the Baal-Shem Tov – the Master of the Good Name. However, they are the inheritors of a much earlier kabbalistic literature based on texts such as the *Sefer haBahir* (*Book of Illumination*) and the Zohar (Radiance) dating to the twelfth and thirteenth centuries, as well as the teachings of Rabbi Isaac Luria in the sixteenth century, founder of Lurianic kabbalah.

Belief in the pre-existence of souls and their reincarnation or transmigration throughout many lives, called *gilgul* in Hebrew (lit. 're-volving'), is a key feature of the mystic tradition. In the kabbalistic version of creation, before the world is created God is All, God is infinite, God is eternal – there is no other. In order to make room for creation that is other than God, God contracts or limits himself and then emanates one aspect of himself as creation – the finite aspect. The perfection of creation, however, is marred by an accident that takes place during the process of God's emanation – the intensity of God's light shatters the vessels that were intended to carry the emanation and their fragments are scattered throughout the universe, thereby creating an element of disorder and disharmony. Due to this mishap, the infinity of God and finite creation became alienated from each other. In other words, the two aspects of God, the infinite and the finite, became divided from each other. The great mystic symbol for this alienation is exile – man's exile from God, which is equally God's exile from Himself. Exile means to be cast out of your home, to be a stranger wandering in a strange land, and this is an experience which has been of profound meaning to the Jewish people throughout their history from the time that it is said Abraham first left his home. It is not surprising, then, that kabbalistic teachings gained their strongest impetus at the end of the fifteenth century at a time when Jews were being expelled from Spain and Portugal.

According to kabbalistic thought, the goal of the mystic is universal and personal healing or "repairing" of the fragmentation and disunity that characterizes the world and the individual. Until the resurrection, every soul has numerous opportunities through reincarnation to participate in the process of cosmic healing by developing spiritually, following God's commandments and eventually reaching a state of perfect wholeness in union with God. Since a soul inhabits many bodies, however, during the course of its transmigration, it leaves its traces or "sparks" on each body and at the time of resurrection each person shares in the "soul sparks" of all those that have been associated with that body. "Thus, the resurrection of any one human affects the fate of the many other bodies which housed this particular soul" (Gillman, 1997, p. 179). Among the followers of Hasidism, the ideal of redemption is captured in the concept of *d'vekut* (clinging or cleaving to God – mystic communion with God). Through singing, dancing, and contemplation on God, when one experiences *d'vekut*, then one's soul becomes reunited with God, and all those souls who have shared in your countless bodily reincarnations as you journey to God also attain perfection in that moment. In that moment, both creator and created find their true home in each other; exile is over.

In the intellectual atmosphere of the eighteenth century when reason and science became the touchstone of civilization, kabbalistic beliefs and practices lost credibility and became relegated to folk tales and superstition, and it was so until today. The contemporary Jewish philosopher Neil Gillman likely expresses the thoughts of many mainstream Jewish leaders when he says, "Whenever I lecture on the afterlife to lay audiences, I am invariably asked about reincarnation. I am tempted to dismiss the doctrine as popular superstition, but that would seriously underestimate its importance both in Judaism and for many of our contemporaries" (Gillman, 1997, p. 177). Kabbalistic beliefs in the journey of the soul were never expunged from popular Jewish culture. They were indelibly imprinted in prayers and stories, and in the twenty-first century they offer a counterpoint to the dominance of the scientific model in understanding what it means to be human as well as an avenue for the exploration of the human spirit.

The idea of resurrection of the body and the idea of a disembodied soul enjoying eternal bliss were difficult to combine into a cohesive system, but just as the early Egyptians held many differing ideas about the fate of the soul, so belief in resurrection and belief in an immortal soul separate from the body were brought together and given space within the Jewish tradition. However, many devout Jews of today hold no strong beliefs regarding the nature or destiny of the soul or the details of resurrection; with regard to life and death, the Jewish emphasis remains firmly centered on life, well lived, according to God's laws. The importance of the different strands of belief regarding life after death that can be found in Judaism might well be thought of as different ways of contemplating the relationship between God and humanity. Resurrection of the body inspires us to consider the body as sacred, as God's creation, neither to be disparaged nor abandoned. It also speaks to us about the power of God who is able to return life to the dead. The notion of an immortal soul inspires us to consider the sacredness of the individual and the relationship of each person to God. The mystical journey of the soul speaks to us of personal continuity and the human striving to restore an imperfect self and world to perfect harmony and wholeness.

Rituals of Departure

Since the eighteenth century, a number of movements in Judaism – Reform, Conservative, Reconstructionist, Orthodox, Hasidic – have reflected the different ways that Jews have sought to engage with their religious faith. They represent a range of interpretations of religious doctrine and implementation of burial and mourning rituals. Here we will examine some differences and identify the main elements of Jewish death rituals. It is important to recognize at the outset, however, that what constitutes "traditional" burial practices is traditional from the perspective of European and North American modernity. Not only do burial customs differ among different Jewish communities around the world, but the long history of Judaism has seen many customs arise and fade. In his history of death rituals in rabbinic Judaism, David Kraemer comments that contemporary Jews would hardly recognize their own burial rituals and prayers in the ancient practices. He states:

> On the one hand, practices taken for granted by the classical rabbinic works, such as anointing the deceased, the standing and sitting ritual, overturning the beds, covering the upper lip, and reburial – to enumerate only a few examples – seem to find little or no memory in later Jewish practice. On the other hand, practices later generations view as central to death and mourning ritual, such as recitation of the kaddish, are totally unknown in this connection in the early rabbinic sources. (Kraemer, 2000, p. 133)

Even though belief in the afterlife and the conquest of death became entrenched in Jewish thought, nevertheless, Judaism maintained the ancient view of death as a reality that cannot be denied. Even today, mourners recite the psalm that says, "Mortals cannot abide in their pomp; they are like the animals that perish" (Psa. 49:12). The Greek view of death as a condition to be welcomed because it releases the immortal soul is not found in Judaism. Life, and the body, which came from God and returns to God, are of supreme value. Even in death, the body is to be respected and honored. This principle of respect underlies many Jewish burial practices. Out of respect, the body is treated with dignity and buried quickly; out of respect, if a coffin is used, it remains closed.

Although cremation is practiced by some liberal and reform Jews, it is a subject of theological debate even within those groups that allow for it. Burial, not cremation, is the traditional Jewish way of disposing of the dead for reasons that include honoring the body that was given by God, returning the body to the earth in as complete a form as it was given, and symbolizing the hope of resurrection, which has been interpreted both literally and symbolically throughout Jewish history. On the most literal side, in Jewish (and Islamic) folk religion, there is a tradition that the bone at the base of the spine called the "luz" bone does not decay and forms the kernel around which the body is resurrected on the Day of Judgment. In the modern scientific era, however, many take their cue from Maimonides, who emphasized the spiritual immortality of the soul over any kind of material or bodily delight in the afterlife. There is not space here to explore in any detail the past and present debates in Judaism over the nature of the resurrected body or the nature of the soul, but regardless of how it is understood, resurrection remains in Jewish thought as "ultimately an affirmation of the value of history and society, of the only life we know of, life as embodied individuals in space and time" (Gillman, 1997, p. 224).

The following are some of the main elements in Jewish death rituals that are followed more or less strictly according to the denomination (Lamm, 1969). Upon death, the eyes and mouth are closed and the face covered with a sheet by children, close family, or friends. The body is then attended to by members of the same sex as the deceased. The body is oriented ideally with the feet towards the door and a candle at the head; some place the body on the floor. From the time of death until the burial, which should take place within 24 hours if possible, the body is not left alone. The body is washed and ritually purified by members of a professional burial society called *Chevra Kadisha*. The body is not embalmed or beautified. It is dressed in plain white shrouds to signify the equality of all and to indicate that material wealth is of no consequence in the presence of God. Burial takes place in a plain wooden coffin so that there is the least interference with the return to the earth. Most traditional burials in Israel do not use a coffin of any kind; the body is simply placed on a wooden board, covered with a cloth, and lowered into the grave.

The funeral service is short. In general, it involves the reading of selections from the Psalms – especially the 23rd Psalm, which includes the well-known line "Though I walk through the valley of the shadow of death, I fear no harm, for You are with me" – the eulogy (delivered by the rabbi or by friends or family), and the Memorial Prayer in which the mourners pray for the soul of the dead and promise acts of charity in remembrance of the deceased. Another prayer always associated with death and mourning is the "Mourner's Kaddish." It is a communal prayer that has nothing mournful about it but is entirely an outpouring of praise and adoration of God, a declaration of faith and steadfastness in the face of human sorrow captured in the refrain "Let His great name be blessed forever and to all eternity!"

On the way to the cemetery, the procession stops a number of times (seven stops are customary among many communities) signifying, among other things, hesitation and grief of parting from the deceased. At the gravesite, friends, family, and community leaders assist in covering the casket with earth. To leave the cemetery, the principal mourners pass through two lines formed by those present who recite words of comfort. As Lamm says, after the interment, the theme of the ritual changes from honoring the dead to comforting the bereaved (Lamm, 1969, p. 67). After the funeral, the participants wash their hands in accordance with ancient rites of purification after contact with the dead. The family returns home to a meal prepared by the community and commences the first period of mourning. Jewish custom discourages extravagant displays of flowers at the funeral or on the grave, and encourages gifts to charity in the name of the deceased.

Two of the best known of Jewish mourning rites are *keri'ah* and *shivah* (Hauptman, 2002). *Keri'ah*, the rending of garments as a sign of grief, was once done upon hearing of the death, but now it is done either just prior to the funeral service or at the cemetery just prior to burial. In some communities, the mourners do not tear their own garments but tear a small black ribbon pinned to their clothes, which symbolizes the rending of the garment. The torn garment is worn for the duration of the seven-day mourning period called *shivah*. For seven days, beginning upon return from the cemetery, the mourners sit *shivah*, that is, they remain at home – do not work, bathe, shave, change clothing, wear leather, or engage in sexual relations. In the house of mourning, it is customary to cover all the mirrors (to indicate disinterest in vanity and personal appearance). Friends and relatives provide food and see to the needs of the immediate family who are the principal mourners. The mourners sit on lowered chairs while the community comes to offer condolences and comfort as well as to honor the dead by speaking of them and remembering them. Following the withdrawal from society and the intense mourning of *shivah*, there is a secondary period of mourning for 30 days. This is a time of reintegration into society when people can return to work but avoid all social festivities, celebrations, and such things as wearing new clothes. All mourning restrictions are lifted at the end of this 30-day period except if the deceased is a parent who is to be especially honored. For parents the mourning observances continue for 12 months and when garments are torn for a parent, they are torn on the left side, over the heart; all others are torn on the right side.

A Conversation on Understanding Death

With Josée Posen

Josée came to Canada from her native Holland as a young child. She was raised in the Roman Catholic faith, but as a convert married into a Jewish family she has been studying and practicing the beliefs, rituals, and observances of Judaism for nearly 25 years. Our conversation ranges from her experience of her Catholic mother's death some years ago to her anxiety over her husband's ongoing struggle with lung cancer. Josée comments that when she and her son arrived at her mother's death bed, "it seemed right to us" to recite the Jewish prayer for the dead, the Mourner's Kaddish. It also felt right to recite the prayer with her family after the cremation, but it "did not seem right" to carry on with any further Jewish rituals for her. The Catholic funeral mass provided as much completion as Josée needed, especially since she says, "I felt her spirit around me, I felt her standing in the choir saying goodbye." However, when she thinks of her own death or that of her husband, then she says, "I will find those [rituals like sitting *shivah*] quite comforting."

I ask Josée what she thinks about continuation after death – does she believe she will meet her husband again in the afterlife? Her answers lead me from death back to life and community. She says, "I do believe we continue," but, at the same time, "I don't know if I will see him again." She points out that her husband has a very secular scientific view – "when you're dead, you're dead" – and that the focus for both of them is not so much on believing the right thing as doing the right thing. Further, she notes, "there is not one Jewish system; when people think of Judaism, they are often thinking of the classical rabbinic system, but there are new kinds of Judaism being born as we speak."

What makes them Jewish? I ask, and her answer is, "a powerful sense of community and community connectedness – a very practical sense of other and duty to other." "Judaism," she says, "is geared to teaching you communal duty. Many religions focus on teaching you what and how to think or believe. Judaism teaches you how to behave appropriately towards God and towards each other – the beliefs that are taught, may or may not follow, but in either case, you'll be OK." That approach, in Josée's view, "allows for common expected behavior among a group of people, but divergence in beliefs regarding the nature of God, soul, resurrection, the afterlife, etc." "Not many of us," she comments, "believe in God the way the prayer book lays it out, and it's not that we're hypocrites because God is a vastness that cannot be filled – the prayer, though, is the glue that binds us together."

When our conversation touches on beliefs in the afterlife, Josée admits her attraction to Hasidic ideas of souls that travel through life together, encountering each other in various forms in various lives, but in general she says, "I don't think much about what happens after death." Further, "ideas of heaven and hell and resurrection are not real for many of us; what is real are the prayers, rituals, and observances – they link you to community and to something greater than you and the community, they remind us that we're all part of a bigger world that we are not aware of." For Josée, the Jewish way of preparing for death is all about "giving back to the community – strengthening the bonds of your connection to community." She notes that "withdrawal or isolation is a very unJewish way to approach death," because not only is the person disconnected from the community but the members of the community suffer also the disconnection from one of their own. Speaking for herself, Josée says that when her time comes, "I would connect with those people who are important to me, make a greater effort – have my last conversation with them while I could." For her, the rituals and observances surrounding death would also be very important because, as she says, "this is what gives the person a sense of belonging – so necessary at the time of death."

Notes

1. It is worth noting that almost every date relating to the origins and early history of the Israelites is subject to scholarly debate. The dates given here follow *The New Oxford Annotated Bible*, 3rd edition (2001).
2. Divine intervention for the sake of furthering the development of human beings is commonplace in many traditions. In traditional biographies of the Buddha, we are told that as a young prince he was protected by his father from all the ills of the world. On a pleasure outing through the city that his father had decreed to be cleansed of all its beggars and sick so that no ugly sight should disturb his mind, the gods, knowing that it was time for him to fulfill his destiny, arranged for the appearance of the old, the sick, and the dead so that Siddhartha would realize the human condition and pursue his destiny of becoming a Buddha.
3. Such exhortations were likely written sometime in the seventh century BCE when Canaanite cultural influences were threatening the purity of Israelite belief.

103

References and Further Reading

Gillman, Neil. *The Death of Death: Resurrection and Immortality in Jewish Thought*. Woodstock, VT: Jewish Lights Publishing, 1997.

Goldenberg, Robert. "Bound up in the Bond of Life: Death and Afterlife in the Jewish Tradition." In Hiroshi Obayashi (ed.), *Death and Afterlife: Perspectives of World Religions*. London: Praeger, 1992, pp. 97–108.

Hauptman, Judith. "Death and Mourning: A Time for Weeping, A Time for Healing." In John D. Morgan and Pittu Laungani (eds.), *Death and Bereavement Around the World*, Volume 1: *Major Religious Traditions*. Amityville, NY: Baywood Publishing Company, 2002, pp. 57–77.

Kraemer, David. *The Meanings of Death in Rabbinic Judaism*. London: Routledge, 2000.

Lamm, Maurice. *The Jewish Way in Death and Mourning*. New York: Jonathan David Publishers, 1969.

Malamat, Abraham. "Origins and the Formative Period." In H.H. Ben-Sasson (ed.), *A History of the Jewish People*. Cambridge, MA: Harvard University Press, 1976, pp. 3–87.

The New Oxford Annotated Bible, 3rd edition, New Revised Standard Version, ed. Michael D. Coogan. Oxford: Oxford University Press, 2001.

Segal, Alan F. *Life After Death: A History of the Afterlife in Western Religion*. New York: Doubleday, 1989.

Segal, Alan F. "The Jewish Tradition." In Willard G. Oxtoby and Alan F. Segal (eds.), *A Concise Introduction to World Religions*. Oxford: Oxford University Press, 2007, pp. 60–128.

5

Christian Perspectives on Death

Christianity began as a Jewish movement that eventually developed into an entirely separate religion. Christian perspectives on death and afterlife, then, developed out of a Jewish matrix that assumed the history of the Jews, their hopes and struggles as a people. When Jesus of Nazareth was born, nearly 300 years of Greek culture, language, and thought had deeply affected how some Jews engaged with their religion. The Hellenistic period in Jewish history probably accounts for the first major divisions or movements within Judaism, between those who regarded Greek thought and civilization as a modern, sophisticated, intellectually satisfying approach to the world, philosophers like Philo of Alexandria who attempted to reconcile Greek philosophy with their monotheistic faith, and those who retained a more traditional and conservative hold on their beliefs. By 63 BCE when Roman rule was established in Palestine, there were a number of Jewish movements that offered various interpretations of doctrine and practice. Among them were the Sadducees,

Understanding Death: An Introduction to Ideas of Self and the Afterlife in World Religions,
First Edition. Angela Sumegi.
© 2014 Angela Sumegi. Published 2014 by Blackwell Publishing Ltd.

who represented the priestly class that presided over the sacrificial rituals and offerings made at the temple in Jerusalem; they adhered strictly and narrowly to the written Torah and, therefore, rejected the doctrine of resurrection, the belief in a coming Messiah, and the idea that history was moving towards a cataclysmic end, none of which appears explicitly in the scriptures. They were also the wealthy aristocrats of the time and the most Hellenized of the Jewish community. Oddly enough, despite their integration into Greek culture, in their literal interpretation of the Bible and rejection of resurrection, they could be thought more "traditional" than any of the other groups.

Millennialism and apocalyptic eschatology, however, prevailed among the less Hellenized Jewish population at large, although it should be remembered that apocalyptic expectations were expressed in both moderate and extreme ways involving differing combinations of religious belief and political activism. The Pharisees represented a relatively moderate approach. They believed that Moses received from God both a written Torah and an oral Torah (transmitted orally until it was written down as the Mishnah in the second century CE). The Pharisees emphasized study of the Torah and believed that it was necessary for God's Laws to be explained and interpreted by teachers (rabbis) with the skill and wisdom to do so. According to the Jewish-Roman historian Josephus (39–100 CE), they believed in resurrection, individual rewards and punishments after death, and that souls have "deathless vigour" (Gillman, 1997, p. 116).

A more extreme movement was the Essenes, a mystical and ascetic community of celibates who separated themselves from society and lived a communal life of purity in the desert. Although the Essenes believed in resurrection, they are also characterized as believing in a very Platonic version of the immortality of the soul (Segal, 1989, p. 298 ff.). Finally, on the far end of the spectrum were the Zealots, who were political activists driven by social discontent and dedicated to the overthrow of the Romans and the freedom of the Jews from foreign rule. None of these movements should be thought of as a homogeneous group but as encompassing many variants, rising up usually under the leadership of charismatic figures who would impress their own vision on their followers. Besides organized groups, there were also individuals whose religious fervor gained them disciples, inspired the common people, and placed them in the tradition of the ancient prophets. Jesus of Nazareth can be counted among such individuals.

Jesus was a reformer and his preaching reflected the popular apocalyptic orientation towards belief in the resurrection of the dead and divine retribution for the oppressors of Israel. His teaching, however, which emphasized the spirit of the law over the letter of law and the meaning of purity over the rituals of purity, offended many traditional Jews among all groups. The Pharisees were known for their virtue and piety but Jesus' relationship with God as Father is portrayed by his disciples as more than mere pious devotion. In the famous scene of his baptism by John the Baptist, "just as he came up from the water, suddenly the heavens were opened to him and he saw the Spirit of God descending like a dove and alighting on him. And a voice from heaven said, 'This is my Son, the Beloved, with whom I am well-pleased'" (Matt. 3:16–17). Even though in the Gospels Jesus does not call himself "Son of God," others do (Matt. 14:33), and there is a sense in which Jesus' relationship to God is not only special but peculiar to him. In the volatile political atmosphere of his time, Jesus' teaching was disturbing not only to the state but also to the high priests of the temple and other Jewish groups who found his preaching threatening and heretical.

The Death of Jesus

When it was noon, darkness came over the whole land until three in the afternoon. At three o'clock Jesus cried out with a loud voice, "Eloi, Eloi, lema sabachthani?" which means, "My God, my God, why have you forsaken me?" When some of the bystanders heard it, they said, "Listen, he is calling for Elijah." And someone ran, filled a sponge with sour wine, put it on a stick, and gave it to him to drink, saying, "Wait, let us see whether Elijah will come to take him down." Then Jesus gave a loud cry and breathed his last. And the curtain of the temple was torn in two, from top to bottom. Now when the centurion, who stood facing him, saw that in this way he breathed his last, he said, "Truly this man was God's Son!" (Mark 15:33–39)

The death of Jesus resounds through the ages wherever Christian communities have established themselves. It was a defining moment in the Jewish movement that eventually became Christianity, and forever symbolized the conquest of death in death itself. The story, as it appears in the Gospels of the New Testament, is one of high drama. Jesus is betrayed by one of his own closest disciples for a purse of silver, accosted by an armed mob, and taken away to be tried by a court of high priests who find him guilty of blasphemy and turn him over to the Roman governor of Palestine, Pontius Pilate.

Jesus belonged to the apocalyptic movement in Judaism, a movement that had been growing stronger since the time of the Maccabean revolt, and which taught that a time was soon to come when a Messiah would lead them through a great cataclysmic upheaval in which the old corrupt age and government would be overthrown, the martyred dead resurrected, and the wicked face God's Judgment; a time when a new world order would be established in which the righteous would take their proper place. There are indications that Jesus preached this message of urgent salvation in such passages as:

> For the Son of Man is to come with his angels in the glory of his Father, and then he will repay everyone for what has been done. Truly I tell you, there are some standing here who will not taste death before they see the Son of Man coming in his kingdom. (Matt. 16:27–28)

As an apocalypticist who believed in the resurrection, his teaching would have been regarded as rebellious by both the Roman government and the established priestly class of the Jews. At his trial, Jesus is questioned, scourged, and mocked; he is accused of setting himself up as the son of God and the king of the Jews. The Biblical account, which we must remember was written by those who believed in him and his message, emphasizes that he was innocent of all the charges; the Roman governor is portrayed as finding no good reason to execute him except for the pressure of the priests who claim that he has blasphemed against the Jewish religion, and so Jesus is condemned to suffer the agonizing death of crucifixion. His execution, however, is carried out by Roman soldiers under Roman law. His death becomes a flash point for the movement and its interpretation the foundation of Christian doctrine ever after. As Alan Segal summarizes,

> Jesus lived as a Jew and died for his Judaism. His politics were seen as subversive to the Romans. He must have been an apocalypticist himself, otherwise there would have been no adequate reason for his movement to have expected his return immediately. He was the leading figure in a small movement of apocalyptic Jews who saw his death as a martyrdom, like many previous Jewish martyrdoms. . . . Whatever Jesus' Jewish and Roman politics were, they were not considered primary to his church, once the church understood his message as the salvation of the world. (Segal, 1989, pp. 388–389)

Jesus' death, like his life, is portrayed as the fulfillment of prophecy. At the moment of his arrest, he claimed that he could call on God to send legions of angels to his defense, "But how then would the scriptures be fulfilled, which say it must happen in this way?" (Matt. 26:54). Jesus was destined to die as all humans are, but his was not the death that comes to those at the end of their days, having lived a full and fruitful life; his was a horrifying, untimely death in the prime of life and it came to represent in Christianity the deepest suffering that a human being can undergo. The New Testament gives an intimate portrayal of Jesus praying fervently to be spared this death and in the end his heart-wrenching cry of abandonment can be heard wherever human despair reaches its breaking point. There is no sense here that death is an illusion; Jesus' suffering and death are understood to be as real as the suffering and death of any person. But in Christianity, Jesus is not just any person, and his tortuous death is understood as an historical event that had implications not only for all people who were to come after him, but

109

also for all those who had lived before him. These implications are revealed in the story of Jesus' resurrection.

We are told that when his disciples went to visit his body in the crypt, the tomb was empty. The fact that his body went missing, never to be found, is, in itself, no proof of resurrection. However, in the Biblical accounts, the women who discover the empty tomb also encounter angels who tell them that Jesus is risen. They hurry to tell the others but their reports are met with disbelief and skepticism. Later, Jesus appears to groups of his disciples. What was the resurrected body of Jesus like? In some accounts, he appears as a stranger, walking and talking with them for a long way, unrecognized by his disciples. Sometimes he appears inexplicably amongst them, for example, in a room that was bolted and barred, but despite his strange or miraculous appearances, he identifies himself as Jesus by showing them, and allowing them to touch, the physical wounds that he received on the cross; he proves that he is not merely a ghost or a spirit by eating and drinking with them, and convinces even the most doubtful that he indeed lives again. The nature of the resurrected body, however, contains an inherent tension between ordinary (flesh and blood) and sublime (transformed/resurrected) that becomes a subject of debate from the earliest establishment of the church.

Eventually, the Bible accounts say Jesus was taken up bodily into the sky to be with God, and the disciples were filled with faith in the truth of his resurrection. Regardless of the ways in which Jesus' death and resurrection have been interpreted throughout the history of Christianity, it was that leap of faith among his first disciples that established the profound significance of his death. In the apocalyptic view, the resurrection of the dead was associated with the upheaval that would mark the end of the current world order, so for those who lived in the time of Jesus and shortly after, Jesus' resurrection was the sign that the end times were upon them. The fulfillment of all their hopes was not a distant event; it was now, maybe this evening, maybe tomorrow, certainly in this lifetime. Jesus' disciples and the early Christian mission were imbued with a sense of urgency and expectation driven by the belief in Jesus' resurrection.

Developments in Christian Thought on the Soul

Despite the fervent hope and belief of first-century Jews and Christians, the expected cataclysm and the overthrow of the old world order did not materialize; the resurrection of the dead became an expectation that was pushed further and further into the future. This meant, however, that God's justice would also be delayed to some indefinite and unknown time, an unsatisfactory situation for both communities. For both Jews and Christians, the answer lay in the destiny of the soul at death. Where and under what conditions would the soul exist after leaving the body upon death? Jewish and Christian apocalyptic writings describe two locations – heaven and hell. While the soul waited to be rejoined to the body in the resurrection it experienced the bliss of heaven or the torments of hell. But if the soul is immortal and goes directly to heaven or hell, then where is the need for resurrection? The question represents the fundamental problem that Greek soul theories presented for Judaism and Christianity. In both traditions, the question is answered by a reinterpretation of "soul." In the Platonic view, death is the separation of soul and body; the soul is the pre-existing, immortal aspect of a person – it is the intellect, the faculty of reason and thought, that which strives after and realizes wisdom, virtue, truth, beauty, and the ultimate good. In life, the soul is bound to the body, distracted and thrown off course by the body and its demands. In Plato's *Phaedo*, Socrates argues that although suicide is not morally justified, death is to be welcomed as the release from the impediment of the body that all true philosophers seek.

> The body presents us with innumerable distractions, because of the necessity of looking after it . . . The body fills us with emotions of love, desire, and fear, with all kinds of phantasy and nonsense . . . we are slaves in its service . . . even if we do get some time off from looking after it, and turn to some investigation, it keeps on turning up everywhere in our search, and causes disturbance and confusion, and thoroughly dumbfounds us, so that because of it we cannot catch a glimpse of truth; it really is proved to us that if we are ever going to

111

have pure knowledge of anything, we must get rid of the body and survey things alone in themselves by means of the soul herself alone; *then*, it seems, we shall have our heart's desire, that of which we claim to be lovers, even wisdom – when we die, as the argument indicates, but not so long as we live. (Bluck, 1955, pp. 50–51)

The Greek notion of an immortal soul that survives death and the emphasis on the value of the intellect were very attractive to Jewish thinkers and philosophers in the Hellenistic period; eventually the immortal soul and its destiny became doctrine in both Judaism and Christianity, but not without some major changes. Denigration of the body and belief in a pre-existent immortal soul proved untenable for Judaism and Christianity, even though some, like the first-century Jewish philosopher Philo and the third-century Christian theologian Origen, leaned towards such an understanding of soul.

For Biblical traditions, God's role in human life and death would be compromised if the soul were naturally immortal. Both Jewish and Christian understandings of "soul" retained the emphasis on the whole person that comes into being due to God's life-giving action. Whatever immortality is attributed to the person is equally a result of God's action and not an intrinsic quality. Nevertheless, the notion of the soul continuing after death as a separate if immaterial entity does become entrenched in both Judaism and Christianity. It is difficult to say when this idea began to take hold, but over time as immediate eschatological expectations fell away, the importance of the soul as distinct from the body became increasingly prominent: "In other words, when the apocalyptic end receded, the intermediate state in heaven [or hell] became more and more important" (Segal, 1989, p. 490). For Judaism, the conflicting ideas of resurrection and immortal soul were reconciled in the overriding belief in God's power – the power to bring body and soul together at the time of Judgment. However, the details of exactly when the resurrection is to take place, exactly what kind of body a person will have, exactly what heaven and hell are like, or where the soul is after death are not given any great prominence. In Judaism, preoccupation with life and the details of living it in accordance with God's Laws takes precedence over preoccupation with the fate of the dead. It is enough to believe generally as the Talmudic prayer says:

> My God, the soul that you have given me is pure. You created it, You fashioned it, You breathed it into me, You safeguard it within me, and You will eventually take it from me and return it to me in time to come. As long as the soul is within me, I thank You O Lord, my God and God of my ancestors, Master of all things, Lord of all souls. Praised are you Lord who restores souls to dead bodies. (Gillman, 1997, p. 135)

The situation was somewhat different for Christianity. As in Judaism, the resurrection and immortality of the soul are contradictory after-death scenarios, but increased emphasis on the details of resurrection and the expectation of the Second Coming of Christ in victory (however far in the future that might be) was accompanied by an increase in concern with the fate of the person from the time of death until the final judgment day. Would all the dead simply rest peacefully until that time? Justice seemed to require a more immediate consequence for wicked as opposed to pious individuals. The notion of the immortal soul served this need for immediate rewards and punishments very well and became the way in which Christianity negotiated the afterlife. The tension between the notions of resurrection and immortal soul, however, was the subject of theological debate, reconciliation, and clarification from the time that the Christian mission expanded beyond its Jewish roots and became established among Hellenized gentiles.

The apostle Paul who took the Christian message to Greece and Macedonia spoke vigorously against some in those churches who were denying the resurrection in favor of belief in the immortal soul and its salvation. Paul made it clear that to deny resurrection was to deny salvation itself. For Paul, Jesus' resurrection was the foundation of the salvation hope: "For since death came through a human being, the resurrection of the dead has also come through a human being; for as all die in Adam, so all will be made alive in Christ" (1 Cor. 15:21–22).

In Paul's view, death is inextricably linked with sin. Mortality and death came into the world due to mankind's sin of disobedience. It is an enemy as sin is an enemy. Jesus' death and resurrection establish a new world order for humanity, one in which salvation from sin and the conquest of death become an option for all those who believe in him. For Paul, to abandon belief in resurrection would be to give death/sin victory over the body. This would be a way out for those who believe that the body is a prison which the soul must escape, but would pose a problem for the monotheistic traditions that uphold a holistic view of the person as created by an all-powerful God. Paul explained to the Corinthians that the resurrected body was not one of ordinary flesh and blood, but neither was immortality merely a "soul" feature: it was characteristic of the entire person who would be bodily transformed into an immortal being. Paul does not deny that this is a mysterious and extraordinary claim. He says:

> What I am saying, brothers and sisters, is this: flesh and blood cannot inherit the kingdom of God, nor does the perishable inherit the imperishable. Listen, I will tell you a mystery! We will not all die, but we will all be changed, in a moment, in the twinkling of an eye, at the last trumpet. For the trumpet will sound, and the dead will be raised imperishable, and we will be changed. For this perishable body must put on imperishability, and this mortal body must put on immortality. (1 Cor. 15:52–53)

Resurrection and Eternal Life

In the centuries following the death of Paul in 64 CE, the fortunes of the Christians changed dramatically. From a small religious minority rejected by the Jewish community as having strayed too far beyond the bounds of Judaism to be considered a Jewish sect, therefore, not regarded as a legal religion by the Romans and persecuted as enemies of the state for not worshipping the Roman emperor as a divinity, Christianity eventually became the official religion of the Roman Empire thanks to the conversion of Emperor Constantine (ruled 306–337 CE). During these early centuries, Christian theologians continued to struggle to formulate the doctrines that would direct religious belief for the future. Much of the debate amongst themselves and against their pagan critics focused on arguments relating to the immortality of the soul and the nature of the resurrected body.

As Paul had done, the Church Fathers rejected any notion of the soul as possessing natural or intrinsic immortality – salvation was not a matter of the immortal soul freeing itself from the body and finding its way to God, salvation was entirely dependent on the belief that Jesus was the means by which God entered into the world to become the sacrifice that released mankind from the heritage of Adam's sin into which each person is born. Jesus was called the second Adam and his resurrection was the proof of his victory over death and a new beginning for all those who believed in him. Christianity does not place any value on immortality itself, which was associated with the pagan gods and Greek notions of the nature of the soul. In Christianity, eternal life is associated with the idea of a person dwelling constantly in the presence of God, an opportunity that is only available because of the death and resurrection of Jesus. Creed or belief, therefore, becomes much more important in Christianity than in Judaism, and the church, as it set about formulating what was "orthodox" belief, put great effort into fighting heretical or incorrect beliefs regarding not only the nature of the soul but also, more problematically, the nature of the body, which is related to the nature of resurrection, to the nature of Jesus as a human being, and ultimately to the understanding of one's own identity as an individual facing death.

As we have seen, Paul suggested that the body that is raised is a spiritual body, not a body of flesh and blood, but the Gospel narratives present us with a much stronger sense that Jesus is resurrected in the flesh. Arguments among Christian theologians and philosophers in the first three centuries after the death of Jesus follow both these lines of thought, some emphasizing a spiritual interpretation and others leaning towards a more literal interpretation of the "body" that is resurrected. On one end of the spectrum were

115

those for whom Christianity was most influenced by an intellectual Platonic worldview. For example, the Docetists believed that Jesus was a divine being who only "seemed" to live and die, untouched in reality by the suffering and problems related to fleshly existence. Another movement that held similar ideas was Gnosticism. Gnostics believed that the body and worldly life were worthless, that the soul is a prisoner of the flesh; they emphasized a mystical relationship to Jesus and that salvation comes about not merely through faith but through a special kind of esoteric knowledge (gnosis). However, by denying the value of the body or by spiritualizing it out of fleshly existence, these movements reduced the crucifixion to a display of divine magic, took Jesus out of the realm of the human, and made his suffering essentially unreal and, therefore, meaningless. Remembering that the first to the third centuries were a time of persecution and martyrdom when Christians underwent tortures for their faith, it is not surprising that many Church Fathers regarded such teachings as intolerable heresy; martyrs died believing in the resurrection of their bodies to eternal life. On the other end of the spectrum, then, were arguments for belief in bodily resurrection. These included appealing to the power of God. The second-century bishop Iranaeus claimed that it should be more difficult to believe that God had the power to make the first living person out of non-existent bones, veins, etc. than to believe that he has the power to reconstitute what was already made, "For, if God does not give life to what is mortal and does not recall the corruptible to incorruptibility, then he is not powerful" (Dewart, 1986, p. 93). Another early Church Father, Ignatius of Antioch, proposed that resurrection must be the resurrection of the entire fleshly body, not merely some spiritualized version of it. He linked his belief to the reality of the crucifixion and the suffering of Jesus:

> Now, He suffered all these things for our sakes, that we might be saved. And He suffered truly, even as also he truly raised up himself, not, as certain unbelievers maintain, that He only seemed to suffer . . . For I know that after His resurrection also he was still possessed of flesh, and I believe that He is so now. (Segal, 1989, p. 545)

At the beginning of the third century CE, Tertullian continued the emphasis on fleshly resurrection:

> If God raises not men entire, He raises not the dead. For what dead man is entire ... What body is uninjured, when it is dead? ... Thus our flesh shall remain even after the resurrection – so far indeed susceptible of suffering, as it is the flesh, and the same flesh too; but at the same time impassible, inasmuch as it has been liberated by the Lord. (Segal, 1989, p. 568)

In these writings of the early Church Fathers, bodily resurrection is affirmed in the strongest terms, including the idea that somehow the transformed resurrected body is a physical body of flesh.

There were others, such as Clement of Alexandria and Origen, who, rather than rejecting Gnosticism outright as heresy, attempted to reconcile its emphasis on the immortal soul with the resurrection beliefs of Jewish apocalyptic thinking. Origen agreed with the Gnostics and Platonists that the immortal soul was pre-existent and that in life it is entangled with the passions driven by the nature of the body. By appealing to the Apostle Paul's statements that the resurrected body is a spiritual body and that flesh and blood cannot inherit the kingdom of God, Origen was able to preserve the idea of resurrection as the resurrection of a "spiritual" being, not a person of flesh and blood. His approach was a way of making sense of the discord between belief in resurrection and belief in the immortal soul, both of which were entrenched in Christian thought. These debates raged throughout the newly Christianized Roman Empire but eventually the Gnostic-leaning views of the Greek Fathers like Clement and Origen were declared heretical, and "orthodox" church doctrine came down firmly on the side that stressed the resurrection of the body. It was left to the North African theologian Augustine (354–430) to formulate a reconciliation between Biblical ideas and Greek philosophy that set the tone for centuries of Christian theology after him. Augustine emphasized the connection between human mortality and the state of original sin that every human inherits at birth:

> The law of death is that by which it was said to the first man, "You are dust and unto dust you shall return," for we are all born of him in that state because we are dust and we shall return to dust as a punishment for the sin of the first man. (Dewart, 1986, p. 164)

This is the case for the body, but at death the soul separates from the body and enters into an intermediary state where it experiences peace or misery:

> Now in the time intervening between a man's death and the final resurrection, the soul is held in a hidden retreat, enjoying rest or suffering hardship in accordance with what it merited during its life in the body. (Segal, 1989, p. 592)

For Augustine, "body" has two meanings – the body of corruptible flesh that dies because of original sin and the resurrected "spiritual body," which is immortal not because it is purely immaterial spirit but because of God's power to transform the corruptible into the incorruptible:

> We shall see the corporeal bodies of the new heaven and the new earth in such a way that, wherever we turn our eyes, we shall, through our bodies that we are wearing and plainly seeing, enjoy with perfect clarity the vision of the sight of God everywhere present and ruling all things, even material things. (Dewart, 1986)

Finally, on the Day of Judgment, all will be resurrected to receive their eternal reward or punishment. In both cases the body is necessary in order that the identity of the person be fully restored to bear the punishment of hellfire or the beatitude of heaven.

Despite the best efforts of Christian theologians, however, reconciliation between a vision of the future as the fulfillment of history centered on communal resurrection at the end of time and a vision of the future as fulfillment of the individual centered on the fate of the soul after death was never entirely successfully achieved. It remained a difficult topic, becoming even more difficult with the rise of science and the dawn of the Age of Enlightenment and Reason, and culminating in the fierce eschatological debates of the eighteenth and nineteenth centuries that questioned the nature of hell, one's fate beyond death, and sometimes even the notion of future immortality altogether (Rowell, 1974).

Heaven and Hell

In the established eschatology of Christianity, the theme of resurrection consists of a number of stages. First is the resurrection of Jesus, which is understood to have taken place three days after his death and in which the faithful see the promise of eternal life for all who believe in him. Second is the resurrection of the saints, the martyred dead, and third is the resurrection of all people to face God's judgment; each individual, at that time, receives and enters into his or her final and eternal destiny of heaven or hell. Christian imagery of heaven and hell, which was greatly expanded upon during medieval times, finds its most prominent Biblical reference in the last book of the New Testament commonly called Revelation or the Apocalypse of John. It was written towards the end of the first century CE and is a profoundly symbolic, visionary, apocalyptic text inspired by the martyrdom of Christians. Of it the modern novelist D.H. Lawrence wrote: "when we read Revelation, we feel at once there are meanings behind meanings" (Lawrence, 1980, p. 47). Over the years, this text has been subjected to various interpretations, both literal and metaphorical, but in general it speaks of the comfort and hope offered to the faithful by Jesus who states: "I was dead, and see, I am alive forever and ever; and I have the keys of Death and of Hades" (Rev. 1:18). In Revelation, the martyred dead are portrayed as risen in glory, dressed in white robes before God's throne:

> They will hunger no more, and thirst no more; the sun will not strike them, nor any scorching heat; for the Lamb at the center of the throne will be their shepherd, and he will guide them to springs of the water of life, and God will wipe away every tear from their eyes. (Rev. 7:16–17)

In the New Testament, Jesus has very little to say about the details of the afterlife, but Revelation provides strong imagery and certain details that have had a great influence on Christian doctrine, among them the idea that resurrection takes place in two stages beginning with the resurrection of the Christian martyrs, avenged by God's wrath poured out on the wicked of the world. The visions of John provide dramatic images:

> ... the sun became black as sackcloth, the full moon became like blood, and the stars of the sky fell to the earth as the fig tree drops its winter fruit when shaken by a gale. The sky vanished like a scroll rolling itself up, and every mountain and island was removed from its place. Then the kings of the earth and the magnates and the generals and the rich and the powerful, and everyone, slave and free, hid in the caves and among the rocks of the mountains, calling to the mountains and rocks, "Fall on us and hide us from the face of the one seated on the throne and from the wrath of the Lamb; for the great day of their wrath has come, and who is able to stand?" (Rev. 6:12–17)

The resurrection of the martyrs also marks the beginning of a thousand years of Christ's rule, a messianic kingdom, during which time Satan is bound and powerless. At the end of this period of righteousness, Satan is again released and a final battle takes place, at the end of which Satan and all those deceived by him are thrown into a lake of fire and sulfur. Following this, in the second stage, all the dead are resurrected to stand before God's throne and receive His judgment according to their deeds, either gaining eternal life or condemned to be thrown into a lake of fire.

In Revelation, the community of the saints will dwell in the heavenly city of Jerusalem, deathless and sorrowless, in light, beauty, and purity.

> Then I saw a new heaven and a new earth; for the first heaven and the first earth had passed away, and the sea was no more. And I saw the holy city, the new Jerusalem, coming down out of heaven from God, prepared as a bride adorned for her husband. And I heard a loud voice

from the throne saying, "See, the home of God is among mortals. He will dwell with them; they will be his peoples, and God himself will be with them; and he will wipe every tear from their eyes. Death will be no more; mourning and crying and pain will be no more, for the first things have passed away." And the one who was seated on the throne said, "See, I am making all things new." (Rev. 21:1–5)

According to Revelation, the city of God on earth is made of gold, jasper, and every precious gem; within it grows the tree of life, and through it flows the river of the waters of life – reminders of the primeval Garden of Eden; its gates are always open and there will be no more night, no need for sun or moon because God's light will shine everywhere and always. Early theologians like Tertullian interpreted this to be the way in which the martyred saints lived out the millennium, the thousand years of Christ's rule, after which all others are resurrected and those destined for heaven are changed in a moment into angel-like beings, by the putting on of incorruption (McGrath, 2008, p. 53). Although the symbolism and visionary nature of Revelation allow it to be interpreted in many different ways, one gets the sense that in this text, resurrection implies not only the return to life and transformation of human beings but also the transformation and revitalization of their entire material environment, regardless of whether or not that is understood literally.

The notion of the perfect city with its saintly inhabitants ruled by Christ further implies the redemption of history itself. Like Judaism, Christianity carries the weight of history. God's relationship with humanity is played out in events that are set apart and bounded by time. Unlike the religions of the East which carry a different burden, the burden of never-ending time, the religious events of Christianity are fixed moments in human history. Once, and for all time, Jesus was born, crucified, and rose again and because of those events, once and for all time, there will be a resurrection, a last judgment, and a final destiny for each person whose opportunity for salvation is determined by the choices made in the course of one life. Salvation, however, in monotheistic traditions, refers not only to salvation of the soul; in the doctrine of resurrection the body is also redeemed from death and made incorruptible, free from all imperfection. God's final relationship with the faithful, therefore, is one of perfection in all its parts, but human history is a story of failing and imperfection, and if it were to end simply with the destruction of the world, then God's relationship to human history would be left imperfect, lacking wholeness. The new heaven and new earth of Revelation, the city where God dwells among the people, and the thousand years of Christ's rule all relate to the idea that included in God's redemption of humanity is the opportunity for humans to experience history and society as a perfected state. The essence of religious identity and personhood in Christianity is not to be found in ideas of soul or resurrected body but in the person's relationship to God. However, individuals are embedded in place and time – in their earthly environment and in their history – so for the whole person to experience fulfillment, time and place cannot be ignored, they also must be transformed in relation to God.

In an excellent book that pulls together many facets of Christian eschatology, the contemporary theologian Ramon Martinez de Pison emphasizes the essential nature of the personal relationship to God *as person* in Christian identity. He suggests that this crucial aspect is in danger of being eroded by popular attraction to new age theories of reincarnation that conceive of God as "the manifestation of the divine contained in all humanity, as the Energy of the whole universe, and not as a person," and which provide an easy way to confront death by seeing it as "only one step among many in the cycle of life" (Martinez de Pison, 2007). For Martinez de Pison, "If life beyond death is no longer linked with a personal God, and if life is not seen as our accomplishment of our communion with the Holy One, our bodily condition is no longer integrated with and an essential expression of what we are as relational beings" (Martinez de Pison, 2007).

Heaven as a place or state of eternal joy in the presence of God is the focus of Christian hope; similarly, the idea of hell as a place or state of eternal torment for the unrepentant has had a long tradition in Christian thought. However, whether literally or metaphorically interpreted, for all Christians, the idea of heaven affirms God's love and redemption from the consequence of original sin, but the notion of hell as everlasting torment for the unrepentant has been the subject of intense debate. The problem of hell in Christianity reflects the relationship between the infinite and the finite, between God and humankind. It reflects the primeval problem of choice in all its subtlety and depth. Do we truly have the freedom to choose between good and evil? If I, in my finite knowledge, choose to reject God, does God, in his infinite wisdom, mercy, and power, have the choice to save me? As Geoffrey Rowell comments in his work *Hell and the Victorians*:

> In a sense it can be rightly said that hell is the fundamental problem of ethics, for it is concerned with the ultimate nature and consequences of a man's actions and decisions, and the relation of those actions and decisions to the character and purposes of God. (Rowell, 1974, p. 217)

If God's purpose is the fulfillment and salvation of humankind, then eternal hell is a sign of God's ultimate failure, but if all are to be eventually saved, then of what ultimate significance is our individual moral choice? There have been many attempts to answer this question, which essentially is one of relationship. The importance of a person's relationship to God in this life was underscored by the third-century theologian Augustine, for whom there could be no hope of improving one's lot after death – beyond death there is only judgment: "let no one hope to obtain, when he is dead, merit with God which he earlier neglected to acquire" (Segal, 1989, p. 593). This view implies that once death has come, one's fate is sealed; heaven and hell are the results of one's relationship with God in this life. Following on Augustine's thought, the pattern of Roman Catholic eschatology was eventually established as summarized here by Rowell:

> ... the departed soul immediately underwent the particular judgment [i.e. judgment for one's individual life up until death], and was assigned to heaven, hell, or purgatory, there to remain, experiencing joy or pain as the case might be, until the Day of Judgment. At the

123

Day of Judgment the resurrection took place and souls were once more united with their bodies to be assigned either to heaven, to enjoy the perfection of bliss, or to hell, to suffer just punishment. The punishment suffered in hell consisted both of the deprivation of God (*poena damni*) and the positive torment (*poena sensus*), and the punishment would be apt – "the pattern of a man's sins will be the pattern of his punishment"... (Rowell, 1974, p. 23)

The notion of purgatory (purification) in Roman Catholicism was first officially presented in a papal letter of 1253 (Turner, 1993, p. 127). It was defined and finally confirmed as church doctrine in a series of Church Councils, the last of which was the Council of Trent (1563). Purgatory, as an intermediate place or state of suffering and purification, does not have direct Biblical support but was developed in response to a number of issues. One relates to contemplation on the nature of sin and the nature of individual judgment that takes place upon death. Individuals are not equal in their virtue or their sin; the saints in whom virtue is paramount are thought to be in heaven and the unrepentant wicked may be destined for hell, but the majority of people, though not wicked through and through, fall short of saintly virtue, so how are they to be judged at death? This question disturbed many, and the church during the Middle Ages engaged in a constant battle to maintain orthodoxy against the numerous heretical groups that formed around charismatic preachers with their own ideas of Christianity.

In her book on *The History of Hell*, Alice Turner suggests that the doctrine of purgatory helped to keep the faithful within the orthodox fold as it offered a chance for purification after death and hope for the innocent or unbaptized dead (Turner, 1993, p. 128). Another factor in the development of purgatory was the yearning for the salvation of loved ones who had died; Christian hope called for a space in which the soul could be purified of sin and made ready for heaven. Purgatory may seem illogical given the Christian belief that judgment of the soul takes place at death and that the only opportunity for salvation takes place during one's earthly life; however, that belief is to be tempered with the belief in God's infinite power and grace on which all hope for salvation is based.

From the third century on, it had been accepted that the prayers of the faithful could benefit the dead. By the Middle Ages, it was popularly thought that the saints, and especially Mary, could intercede on behalf of the souls in purgatory to relieve the amount of penance required of them and shorten their stay. Eventually, pardons called "indulgences" were widely promulgated and sold by church authorities who played on the popular belief that loved ones suffering in purgatory could be released sooner from their pains by means of such divine pardons.[1] By the time of the Protestant Reformation marked by Martin Luther's complaint in 1517 against the corruption of the church, the sale of indulgences had created an atmosphere in which financial offerings to the church translated into the remission of sins. This was rejected by the Protestant movement, as was the idea of purgatory as a method of "paying" for sins after death. Although the church subsequently addressed the issue of corruption raised by the Protestants, and banned the sale of indulgences and the association of prayers for the dead with any kind of fees or financial transaction, these doctrines remained an integral part of the faith. However, Protestants who abandoned the idea of purgatory were left, upon death, with the stark alternatives of heaven or hell. Luther proposed that the dead "sleep" until the Last Judgment, but others like Calvin maintained that the soul spent the intermediate time in a state of heaven-like joy or hellish misery.

Around the time of the Reformation as well, the heretical writings of Origen, the second-century Greek Church Father, began to be circulated. Origen had proposed a universal theory of salvation and leaned towards ideas of reincarnation as a way in which the soul could continue its journey towards purification and communion with God. By the seventeenth century, criticism of the doctrine of an eternal hell appeared in earnest and the controversy gained in strength over the eighteenth and nineteenth centuries. Nevertheless, alongside those who questioned the doctrine, there were those in the late nineteenth century like the Reverend Joseph Furniss who were happy to make the horrors of hell the primary focus of their sermons. Furniss wrote in sadistic detail of the shrieking souls in hell, including the tortures of little children agonizingly twisting and turning in the fire (Rowell, 1974, p. 172). Such language and beliefs became more and more unpopular until finally in the 1980s it became apparent to sociologists and church historians that hell had disappeared from religious sermons and the personal belief systems of many Christians – even strong evangelical Christians seemed to have trouble with it. The University of Virginia sociologist James Hunter commented to *Newsweek* that "many evangelicals have a difficult time conceiving of people, especially virtuous non-believers, going to hell," and that "People say now, 'I think there is a hell, but I hope it will be a soul-sleep'" (Kvanvig, 1993, p. 13). The novelist David Lodge humorously assigned the disappearance of hell to the rise of the permissive society sometime in the 1960s. In his satire *How Far Can You Go?* he writes:

> At some point in the 1960s, Hell disappeared. No one could say for certain when this happened. First it was there, then it wasn't. Different people became aware of the disappearance of hell at different times...By Hell we mean, of course, the traditional Hell of Roman Catholics, a place where you would burn for all eternity if you were unlucky enough to die in a state of mortal sin. (Lodge, 1980, p. 113)

For many modern theologians, both Catholic and Protestant, heaven, hell, and purgatory are no longer described or understood in literal terms but as states of the soul in relationship to God. The Protestant theologian Rudolf Bultmann argued that in today's world, we can no longer hold to the supernatural beliefs of a past age:

> What meaning, for instance, can we attach to such phrases in the creed as "descended into hell" or "ascended into heaven"? We no longer believe in the three-storied universe which the creeds take for granted. The only honest way of reciting the creeds is to strip the mythological framework from the truth they enshrine...No one who is old enough to think for himself supposes that God lives in a local heaven. There is no longer any heaven in the traditional sense of the word. The same applies to hell in the sense of a mythical underworld beneath our feet. And if this is so, the story of Christ's descent into hell and of his Ascension into heaven is done with. (Bultmann, 1961, p. 4)

Bultmann claims that the mythological view of the world is obsolete but does not discount the purpose of myth, which he says:

> is not to present an objective picture of the world as it is, but to express man's understanding of himself in the world in which he lives. Myth should be interpreted not cosmologically, but anthropologically, or better still, existentially. (Bultmann, 1961, p. 10)

It is this existential approach that is evident when the suffering associated with purgatory and hell is interpreted not as punishment inflicted by God but as the sad result of the soul's inability to love God. According to Pope Paul II,[2] hell is "the ultimate consequence of sin itself." And although the pope's words do not preclude hell as a place of confinement, he emphasizes that "hell indicates the state of those who freely and definitively separate themselves from God, the source of all life and joy."

There are other voices, however, that resist the demythologizing tendency promoted by Bultmann. For the evangelical theologian Reverend R.C. Sproul, the supernaturalism of the New Testament goes hand in hand with belief in God and the Bible. In the preface to his book that asserts a literal interpretation of heaven, hell, and the angels and demons of the Bible, he states:

> I believe that if we are to be consistent Christians, believing all of the Bible rather than portions of it, we must recognize that the supernatural places and beings described on its pages are real. There is an uncompromised supernaturalism at the heart of the Christian worldview, and we must not let the world's skepticism with regard to these things affect our belief systems. We must trust and affirm that there is much more to reality than meets the eye. (Sproul, 2011)

Although, for many in contemporary Christianity, eternal hell may have lost its literal fire and brimstone, it has not lost its reality and theologians continue to struggle with the problem of reconciling God's love and mercy with that reality. Rowell highlights the efforts of Nicolai Berdyaev, Ian Ramsey, and Paul Tillich. Berdyaev emphasizes the subjective nature of hell. Rather than any objective action of God on the soul, he states, hell is: "the state of the soul powerless to come out of itself, absolute self-centeredness, dark and evil isolation, i.e. final inability to love" (Rowell, 1974, p. 218). However, the belief that Christ descended into hell to minister to those cut off from God underpins the hope that God's salvation has the power to reach even to the depths of hell. Anglican Bishop Ian Ramsey notes that a theory of universal salvation (which threatens to undermine the moral significance of actions) could only be acceptable to Christianity if the belief in God's ultimate love, power, and justice is maintained alongside the belief in "the cosmic significance of moral decision, the cosmic loneliness and separation it involves and so on" (Rowell, 1974, p. 219). And Tillich reminds us that "absolute judgments over finite beings or happenings are impossible, because they make the finite infinite" (Rowell, 1974, p. 219). In whatsoever ways the problem is approached, however, overall, Christian hope reflects the words of the wise woman of Tekoa from Second Samuel:

> We must all die; we are like water spilled on the ground, which cannot be gathered up. But God will not take away a life; he will devise plans so as not to keep an outcast banished forever from his presence. (2 Sam. 14:14)

Rituals of Departure

Among the world's religions, Christianity today claims the majority of adherents worldwide; under its vast umbrella, the 2001 *World Christian Encyclopedia* counts over 33,000 sects, communities, or groups that identify themselves as Christian, each with its own funeral rituals. Further, the diversity in funeral rituals among Christians extends not only to the differences among sects, but also to cultural differences among communities adhering to the same church. For example, the death rituals of Roman Catholics in North America would be substantially different from those of Catholics in Africa or Mexico.

In the Catholic Church, when a person is near death, it is customary to call a priest to hear the person's last confession and administer the Sacrament of Anointing the Sick (previously known as the Last Rites or Extreme Unction). Following death, the main features of a North American Roman Catholic funeral include: the transfer of the body from the home or hospital to the funeral home where the body would be prepared for disposal (embalmed or not, according to the wishes of the family); a period of one or two days of visitation and viewing the body by friends and relatives, eulogies, and condolences – this is called the wake or vigil and includes the Vigil service; the wake is carried out differently by different communities and can range from very modest to an extended and elaborate time of eating, drinking, and celebrating the life of the deceased; the coffin is then taken to the church for the funeral mass (service), in which the participants take part in the ritual of Holy Communion commemorating the last meal that Jesus shared with his disciples; prayers for the dead are said in the hopes that the deceased will quickly be purified and be found worthy to pass from purgatory to heaven. The coffin is then transported to the gravesite or the crematorium (cremation is accepted among mainstream Christian churches) where more prayers are said commending the soul to God; there is no strictly defined mourning period, but masses for the dead can be requested for many years after. As previously said, there is great flexibility and diversity in the form of Christian burial rites. The following is a brief example of Catholic death rituals in the popular culture of Mexico taken from Kristin Norget's ethnographic research in the 1990s (Norget, 2006).

In the folk culture among the poor of Oaxaca, death rites follow the basic outlines of an orthodox Roman Catholic funeral, but much is different, reflecting a layer of folk belief that permeates the way people engage with their religion. As elsewhere, a priest is called to hear confession and provide the dying person with absolution. Upon death, a cross is drawn on the floor in ash or white lime and the body laid out on the cross. The cross is thought to absorb the person's soul or spirit so that when it is removed only the corpse is placed in the coffin; the spirit remains embedded in the cross. Norget comments:

> The rituals of death thus carefully mark the separation of those two dimensions or aspects understood to make up personhood: body and soul. At first, the physical, corporeal form of the person, represented by the body in the coffin, and the spirit (*espíritu*) or soul, embodied in the cross of lime (*cruz de cal*), lie side by side but separate. From this point on, their journeys will increasingly diverge: the body will be committed to the earth, and the soul will be cast on the atmosphere, to wander and seek rest. (Norget, 2006, p. 122)

Once the body is in the coffin, the wake or visitation begins. The door of the house is left open to indicate that all are welcome to attend the wake, including passing strangers. The family provides an abundance of food and drink but guests also bring offerings of flowers, food, or money as contribution to the wake. Prayers are recited throughout the night for the salvation of the soul and the body watched over until morning. The day after the wake, the body is taken to the church for the funeral mass, at the end of which the priest draws a cross with earth on the head of the coffin. The procession to the gravesite is led by a person bearing a wooden cross and may include live musicians who play popular hymns and other religious melodies. When the coffin is lowered into the grave each person tosses in a handful of dirt; the grave is filled in by the men in the group and the wooden cross placed at its head; flowers and lighted candles are arranged all along the grave. For the nine nights following the funeral (called *novenario*) prayers are said over the lime cross in the house; the cross is often adorned with elaborate artistic paintings made around it in colored sand or sawdust. The idea that prayers can relieve or shorten the suffering of the dead in purgatory is the driving force behind the practice of the *novenario*, at which the length of time spent in prayer, the sincerity of the petitioners, and the number of people praying are all considered to be factors in mitigating God's punishment on the soul (Norget, 2006, p. 160).

On the final night, the ceremony of Raising the Cross (*Levantada de la Cruz*) is held. Accompanied by prayers, the cross, painting, and flower decorations are scraped up in a set order and placed into boxes, which are the next day taken and interred into a cross-shaped depression made at the head of the grave. During the nine nights of the *novenario*, the soul is believed to be present in the lime cross and the *Levantada* symbolizes the final departure of the soul from its earthly realm. Forty days after the end of the *novenario*, the soul is thought to arrive at its final destination – heaven for the saintly and the *angelitos* (sexually innocent children), hell for the unrepentant wicked, or purgatory for most. The period of active penitence in purgatory is thought to last for a year, the end of which is marked by the ceremony of *cabo de año*. In popular belief, this time coincides with the end of penitence, and is also related to the minimum time that it takes for the flesh to entirely decompose; "the dissolution of the deceased's body is taken to be a metaphor for the soul's social and moral transformation" (Norget, 2006, p. 141). The soul is then thought to have completed its penitence and is worthy to be called upon for assistance in earthly affairs. From this point on, the deceased joins all those who are commemorated with ritual offerings on November 1, the annual Day of the Dead, celebrated in Mexico as a national holiday.

A Conversation on Understanding Death

With Trevor and Marjorie Myers

Trevor and Marjorie were born and raised in Jamaica. They were married there and raised their own two boys to adulthood on the island. Social unrest and the deteriorating political situation, however, changed their lives. They were in their late forties when they immigrated to Canada in 1977. They carried with them $55 (the limit of the funds that could be taken out of Jamaica at the time) and a wealth of Christian faith. "We knew there was a place for us here." Hard work, family support, a positive attitude, and their constant faith resulted in a new life from which they have never looked back. They became strong supporters and community members of the Presbyterian Church where they lived, so it is from this perspective that our conversation takes place.

During our conversation on understanding death, it is obvious that on these subjects they are of one mind and speak with the harmony and consonance of 61 years of marriage. What comforts you, I ask, when you must face the death of a loved one? The answer is not as straightforward as I expect. "I am comforted in that person's faith in Jesus and that death is not a final annihilation of the person, because then I know that they are in a better place; that they will be at peace. But if that person does not believe, then I am not sure of their fate and it is more difficult to find comfort." "In that case, I pray for the person to rest in peace." Trevor points out, however, that "it is not for us to judge what may be the last thoughts of a person on their deathbed, or what may transpire between that person and God at the end." He reminds us of Jesus' words in the Gospel of Luke to the criminal who was to be crucified with him: "Truly I tell you, today you will be with me in paradise." In the end, there is comfort in the magnitude of God's love. As far as preparing for one's own death, "We are preparing every day. One has to live life as though any day could be your last. This is not the way we normally think but it is important to live life so that one is ready to die at any time."

Marjorie notes that this way of thinking also comes with taking Jesus as one's personal savior and making Him an integral part of one's ordinary everyday life: "I talk to Him daily, not just during prayers in church, but while cooking, walking, lying in bed, as a friend who is always there to support me and give me the strength to face whatever life brings, including death." "As much as we may think that life is good and beautiful and to be preferred over death, I look forward to even more beauty and goodness beyond death, I look forward to a joyful reunion when I will again see all my loved ones that have gone before me." "You should not think that I do not feel afraid when I think about the death of myself or those I love dearly, we are only human and I do, but then I remember, this is not the way to think; Satan's influence is present in life, so in fact life is guaranteed to be full of hardship and injustice, but faith in Jesus sustains us through every hardship and when being with Jesus is a reality in every moment, then no problem, no loss is too great to face." "Death is a great hardship, but when we see it as the doorway to a greater life, then it is turned around."

We discuss other more theological questions of the soul, of resurrection, of heaven and hell, but the tensions and conflicts inherent in these issues are not something that disturbs them. Marjorie quotes her mother who taught her that "we are not meant to understand everything." "Simple faith," she emphasizes, "in the truth of the Bible, in God's omnipotence and love, and in the saving grace of Jesus – this is enough for us."

Notes

1. It should be noted that the actual teaching of the Roman Catholic Church on indulgences is much more subtle and complex, but this did not prevent the abuses that accompanied the sale of indulgences.
2. Quoted in 1999 in *L'Osservatore Romano*, the newspaper of the Holy See; see http://www.ewtn.com/library/papaldoc/jp2heavn.htm#Hell.

References and Further Reading

Bluck, R.S. (Trans.) *Plato's Phaedo*. London: Routledge and Kegan Paul, 1955.
Bultmann, Rudolf, et al. *Kerygma and Myth: A Theological Debate*. New York: Harper and Row, 1961.

Dewart, Joanne E. McWilliam. *Death and Resurrection (Message of the Fathers of the Church Vol. 22)*. Wilmington, DE: Michael Glazier, 1986.

Gillman, Neil. *The Death of Death: Resurrection and Immortality in Jewish Thought*. Woodstock, VT: Jewish Lights Publishing, 1997.

Kvanvig, Jonathan L. *The Problem of Hell*. New York: Oxford University Press, 1993.

Lawrence, D.H. *Apocalypse and the Writings on Revelation*. Cambridge: Cambridge University Press, 1980.

Lodge, David. *How Far Can You Go?* London: Secker and Warburg, 1980.

Martinez de Pison, Ramon. *Life Beyond Death: The Eschatological Dimension of Christian Faith*. Ottawa, Canada: Novalis, 2007.

McGrath, Alister E. *A Brief History of Heaven*. Oxford: Blackwell, 2008.

Norget, Kristin. *Days of Death, Days of Life: Ritual in the Popular Culture of Oaxaca*. New York: Columbia University Press, 2006.

Rowell, Geoffrey. *Hell and the Victorians: A Study of the Nineteenth-Century Theological Controversies Concerning Eternal Punishment and the Future Life*. Oxford: Clarendon Press, 1974.

Segal, Alan F. *Life After Death: A History of the Afterlife in Western Religion*. New York: Doubleday, 1989.

Sproul, R.C. *Unseen Realities: Heaven, Hell, Angels and Demons*. Christian Focus, 2011.

Turner, Alice K. *The History of Hell*. New York: Harcourt Brace, 1993.

6

Muslim Perspectives on Death

La ilaha illa Allah
Muhammad rasul Allah
(There is) no god but The God
Muhammad is the messenger of God

Historically, Islam is the youngest of the three major monotheistic religions of the world. The words quoted above constitute the *shahadah*, the primary proclamation of faith for all Muslims. To recite it is to bear witness to the utter uniqueness of Allah and to the belief that the Prophet Muhammad (to whose name devout Muslims will always add the phrase "peace be upon him") imparted God's final and definitive revelation to the world. According to Islam, existence itself, every tiny part and piece of it, is a sign and proof of God and the oneness of God. Just as a magnificent palace cannot appear without a master architect and builder, so the well-ordered cosmos is

Understanding Death: An Introduction to Ideas of Self and the Afterlife in World Religions,
First Edition. Angela Sumegi.
© 2014 Angela Sumegi. Published 2014 by Blackwell Publishing Ltd.

evidence of its creator. In the poetic words of the twentieth-century Turkish intellectual Said Nursi, to deny God and the unity of God is like denying the existence of the sun,

> on a cloudless day at noon, when its traces are to be observed and its reflection is to be seen in every bubble on the surface of the ocean, in every shining object on dry land, and in every particle of snow ... For if one denied and refused to accept the existence of the single unique sun, he would be compelled to accept the existence of a whole series of minor suns, each real and existent in its own right, as numerous as the drops and bubbles of the ocean, as countless as the particles of snow. (Nursi Studies, n.d.)

The word Islam is usually translated as submission or surrender; the follower of Islam is a Muslim, one who submits or surrenders (to God's will). From the outset, the opportunity for cultural mis-understanding is present because submit and surrender are words that, in English, tend to have connotations of intimidation, coercion, and compulsion, whereas in Arabic, the root of the words Islam and Muslim, *s-l-m*, resonates with notions of peace, acceptance, com-mitment, wholeness, soundness, and safety. The intent of the word Islam, then, is to bring to mind the inner peace, wholeness, and safety that result from the free acceptance of and surrender to God's way or will. From a Muslim perspective, not only humans are Mus-lim, the whole natural world submits to God's way in the cycle of the seasons, the ebb and flow of ocean tides, the instinctual behavior of animals. Humans, however, are different in that their surrender to God is one of choice – not the irrelevant choice of picking and choosing clothes to wear or food that one likes, but an existential choice for which one will be held accountable by God on the Day of Judgment, a choice that leads to a future life beyond death of eternal happiness or unimaginable fear and pain. According to Islam, every child comes into the world not only pure and sinless but also with a natural tendency towards submission to the way of God. If that ten-dency is not fulfilled, however, and the person chooses to turn away from God, then the time will come when he or she must account for that choice and receive God's judgment.

Islam situates itself within the Biblical tradition that it honors as its heritage, but at the same time Islam offers a unique expression of monotheism. Judaism, Christianity, and Islam all trace their roots to a common religious ancestor, Abraham, whose devotion to one God set him and his tribe apart from the surrounding polytheistic peoples of Mesopotamia. According to the Biblical story, Abraham and his wife Sarah were childless into old age, and Sarah gave him her handmaid Hagar that he might have a son, and she bore him Ishmael. When the boy was 13, God told Abraham that Sarah would also bear him a son to be called Isaac, with whom God would establish his covenant; and Abraham was worried for the fate of Ishmael and said, "O that Ishmael might live in your sight!" And God said, "As for Ishmael, I have heard you; I will bless him and make him fruitful and exceedingly numerous; he shall be the father of twelve princes, and I will make him a great nation" (Gen. 17:18; 20). In her ninetieth year, when Abraham was a hundred years old, Sarah bore Isaac. Soon Sarah told Abraham that Hagar and Ishmael must be sent away from the household, which greatly distressed Abraham because of the love he had for his son, but God told him that Ishmael was blessed and that he should do as Sarah asked. So Abraham sent Hagar and Ishmael away. The Bible, which follows the events of the offspring of Isaac, tells us very little of what happened after that or of how Hagar and Ishmael reached the valley of Mecca, except to say that at the end of their journey, the waterskin was empty and Hagar lay the child, who she thought was dying, under a bush, and wept.

> And God heard the voice of the boy; and the angel of God called to Hagar from heaven, and said to her, "What troubles you Hagar? Do not be afraid; for God has heard the voice of the boy where he is. Come, lift up the boy and hold him fast with your hand, for I will make a great nation of him." Then God opened her eyes and she saw a well of water. She went and filled the skin with water, and gave the boy a drink. (Gen. 21:17–19)

In Islamic tradition, when the water was finished, Hagar (Arabic: Hajar) ran between two hills seven times in all looking for someone to help but there was no one, and when she stopped to rest, the angel spoke to her.[1] The water was a spring that is said to have appeared under Ishmael's (Arabic: Isma'il) heel as he lay on the ground. It became known as the well of Zamzam, and because of the presence of water, the area became a thriving oasis in the desert and a halting place for caravans and travelers. According to the Qur'an, Abraham later visited his son in the valley of Mecca and God told him where and how to build the holy sanctuary called the Ka'ba (meaning cube, according to its shape). Embedded in its eastern corner is its holiest object, a celestial stone that was said to have been brought to Abraham from a nearby hill by an angel (Lings, 1983, p. 3). The Qur'an also places the establishment of the pilgrimage to Mecca known as the Hajj in the time of Abraham and his son Ishmael.

> Proclaim the Pilgrimage to all people. They will come to you on foot and on every kind of swift mount, emerging from every deep mountain pass . . . (Sura 22:27)

As the centuries passed, Islamic tradition says that the well of Zamzam was buried and forgotten,[2] and the purity of the worship of the one God became contaminated with idol worship. Following the work of the eighth-century historian Muhammad ibn Ishaq, Martin Lings writes:

> The descendants of Ishmael became too numerous to live all in the valley of Mecca; and those who went to settle elsewhere took with them stones from the holy precinct and performed rites in honour of them. Later, through the influence of neighbouring pagan tribes, idols came to be added to the stones; and finally pilgrims began to bring idols to Mecca. These were set up in the vicinity of the Ka'bah, and it was then that the Jews ceased to visit the temple of Abraham. (Lings, 1983, p. 4)

By the time of the birth of Muhammad in the sixth century CE, the shrine called the Ka'ba had come to be chief among the sacred places of Arabia. Mecca, therefore, was a rich city, not only because it was a trading center, but because it was also a religious center that hosted thousands of pilgrims in an annual religious festival that attracted the desert tribes people from all quarters. The powerful Quraysh tribe into which Muhammad was born ruled over the valley and were the guardians of the sanctuary.

Among the various kinds of people in Meccan society were those known as *hanifs* (pious ones). They were attracted to the monotheism of Judaism and Christianity but did not belong to either community – they were impressed with the desert hermits who secluded themselves in caves and other lonely places to prey, contemplate, and come to know God. Scholars think that Muhammad may have been one of these "pious ones" since we know that he had a reputation for fairness, justice, honesty, and compassion, and that he abhorred the idol worship that was then a prominent aspect of the Ka'ba. Every year during the month of Ramadan he would spend days in seclusion in a cave in the mountains close to Mecca. And it is during one of these retreats that he experienced the first of the overwhelming visitations said to be by the angel Gabriel, the content of which eventually formed the sacred scripture of Islam, the Qur'an. The message that Muhammad preached was not convoluted or complicated – worship and submission to the will of the one God, generosity to the poor of society, and a day of punishment and reward, the Day of Judgment when the faithful will be rewarded with eternal paradise and those who reject God punished in a fiery hell.

As a distinct religious path, Islam is founded on the revelations recorded in the Qur'an (derived from the root of the word *iqra* meaning "read" or "recite"). The Prophet Muhammad was born *c.* 570 CE and in 610, when he was 40 years old, he is said to have received the first revelatory vision of the angel Gabriel who commanded him:

Read![3] In the name of your Lord who created: He created man from a clinging form.[4] Read! Your Lord is the Most Bountiful One who taught by [means of] the pen, who taught man what he did not know. (Sura 96:1–5)[5]

139

Although the Qur'an is the Holy Book of Muslims just as the Bible with the New Testament is the Holy Book of Christians, and the Hebrew Bible that of the Jews, it would be a mistake to think that they are regarded in the same way by their proponents. For Muslims, the Qur'an was not written or composed by any human being, no matter how holy or inspired; the Qur'an is the direct and living word of God transmitted in Arabic by God through the angel Gabriel, heard and revealed to others by the Prophet Muhammad. The Qur'an is only available in Arabic; any translation, however well done, cannot claim the status of Qur'an. This means that as a text, the Qur'an has been preserved essentially unchanged from the time that it was compiled from scattered collections soon after the death of Muhammad in 632 CE. However, there has always been and continues to be a lively tradition of exegetical commentary dedicated to elucidating and understanding the meanings of the text. Along with the Qur'an and its commentaries, Muslims also look for guidance to the sayings attributed to the Prophet that have been passed down through the generations by oral transmission; these are called *hadith*.

The Names of God

Based on the primary article of faith – the oneness (*tawhid*) of God – the gravest sin in Islam is the association (*shirk*) of anything or anyone with God. God is utterly transcendent and utterly supreme over all things, which are his creation, and the relationship of humankind to God is one of service, worship, and submission to the will of a supreme creator and master. If one were to ask, "what kind of master is God?," the answer would be found in the Islamic tradition of the 99 beautiful names or attributes of God. Foremost among the names of God is Ar-Rahman "The All Merciful" and Ar-Rahim "The All Beneficent"; others include: The Knower of All, The Absolute Ruler, The Pure One, The Preventer of Harm, The Satisfier of All Needs, The All Powerful, The Compeller, The Originator, The Shaper of Beauty, The Maker of Order, The Forgiver, The Loving One, The Generous, The Perfectly Wise, The Abaser, The Exalter, The Bestower of

Honors, The Watchful One, The Responder to Prayer, The Truth, The Giver of life, The Taker of Life, The Avenger, The Patient One, The Just (Sheykh Tosun Bayrak, 2000). God's attributes indicate his transcendence and power over all creation; the proper relationship of humans to God is that of a servant to a supreme ruler, one who worships and submits to the will of the master, one whose life is completely circumscribed by God's will. In the relationship of God to humans, God provides the total meaning for human life, which is his creation. In their book *The Islamic Understanding of Death and Resurrection*, Smith and Haddad emphasize that:

> As part of God's creation man can be assured of two things: first, that the difference between himself as the created and God as the creator is virtually without limit, and thus his best effort is crowned with success only insofar as that is within the scope of God's will and choice; second, that behind the flow of events, birth in the natural and human orders, is a divine plan, and that all of man's life from birth to death is a microcosmic part of that overall macrocosmic scheme. (Smith and Haddad, 1981, p. 11)

In Islam, time, history, and human life have a direction and a purpose. All is created, directed, and maintained by God who will eventually bring all of creation to an end. At that time, human beings, who have been endowed with reason and choice, who have been honored by God as his vicegerents on earth, having dominion over all other creatures, will be held accountable for their choices and the way in which they lived their lives. Along with the belief in the oneness of God and the role of prophecy, belief in a Day of Judgment is essential to the Islamic faith.

Like other monotheistic religions, Islam has a history of debate and controversy over the relationship between the human freedom of will and the absolute will and authority of God. It would seem only reasonable that if one is to be responsible and accountable for one's choices, then this is an area over which God does not have absolute power, yet that flies in the face of God's will, which directs all things. Among the classical theological schools of the ninth and tenth centuries, the Mu'tazila argued against predestination and held to the idea that human free will is necessary for justice to have any meaning and to guard against any association of God with sin. However, the dominant view was that God's authority is total and that all events and acts take place according to his will. A rather convoluted compromise was put forward by the al-Ash'ari school, which claimed that although all acts are created according to God's will, they are placed in the human heart and become owned or appropriated by the person, who is then individually responsible for them. What is apparent is that regardless of the theological difficulties presented by free choice, human responsibility and culpability are upheld. On this, Smith and Haddad state:

> The battle over human free will was waged *not* on the grounds of whether or not we will be called to account at the final rendering – an issue never debated – but rather of whether or not the implication of free choice in any way impugns the understanding of God as absolutely free in his own actions and knowledge. (Smith and Haddad, 1981, pp. 13–14)

Modern Islamic thought emphasizes that human beings have freedom of choice to follow God's commands or not, and, therefore, will be judged by God according to their actions. However, human beings along with their thoughts and actions are not independent of God, whose will and authority are all-encompassing, and who knows from the beginning what the end will be. For most ordinary Muslims, as for those who belong to other monotheistic traditions that struggle with freedom of human will versus divine will, such theological difficulties are resolved in the love of, and surrender to, God. Once the entire self – body, speech, and mind – is given up to God, the problem is no longer a problem. But for many the question remains – how can God call me to account for my thoughts and actions if all is God's will? One way of understanding how humans can be free to make their own choices and yet not be independent of God is to think of the limitations of human choice. Every choice is circumscribed by the conditions under which it is made – conditions of knowledge, of capacity, of time and place. One cannot choose from a banquet table an item that is not on the table, but that does not mean that one cannot make healthy or unhealthy choices from what is available. According to Islam, God is the creator and owner of the entire banquet of existence and it is by his will that human beings are created responsible and account-able, free to choose what to accept and what to reject; what is not on the table, however, what cannot be refused, is God's freedom and God's will. So, for example, Smith and Haddad point to a modern writer like Mustafa Mahmud, "who says that we might do what is not acceptable to God, but we cannot do what God does not will. All events and actions occur within the divine will, even if some are out-side the divine *rida* [satisfaction, contentment]" (Smith and Haddad, 1981, p. 204 n. 68)

Ruh and *Nafs*

Like Christianity and Judaism, Islam accepts the idea of the conti-nuity of some form of the person after death, the essence or indi-viduality of the individual, so to speak, that will be reunited with the body at the time of resurrection to receive God's judgment and recompense for the life that has been lived. Two words are used to speak of the non-physical aspects of a person – *ruh* (spirit) and *nafs* (soul). In general, *ruh* refers to the life breath, the divine spirit that enlivens the material body, and *nafs* refers to the self or soul, the ethi-cal character of a person, the aspect which pertains to rationality and intelligence that can develop in noble or base ways, that can change and grow towards God or away from God. What exactly continues after death, however, has been debated by Islamic theologians over the centuries and the debate is compounded by the fact that in many cases *nafs* and *ruh* are used interchangeably. The distinction between them is sometimes drawn on the basis of the difference between death and sleep. The Qur'an states:

> God takes the souls of the dead and the souls of the living while they sleep – He keeps hold of those whose death He has ordained and sends the others back until their appointed time – there truly are signs in this for those who reflect. (Sura 39:42)

In the interpretation of this verse some have understood that God takes the rational soul (*nafs*) during sleep, while the life breath (*ruh*) remains with the body. At death, then, it is the rational soul that dies with the body and the divine spirit or breath of life that continues. Smith and Haddad explain that:

> while the terminology sometimes differentiates between *nafs* and *rūḥ* and sometimes suggests two varieties of *nafs*, there is a general understanding in both the classical and modern writings that the rational soul, which directs the activities of the body, perishes at physical death, while the life-infusing soul or spirit continues and awaits the coming of the Hour. (Smith and Haddad, 1981, pp. 19–20)

This view, however, is still not entirely satisfactory because it does not answer the question of how the person maintains individuality after death if that aspect which is associated with the individual personality dies. This is a question for which Ibn Qayyim al-Jawziya, the fourteenth-century author of *Kitab al-ruh* (The Book of the Spirit), one of the most famous classical works on the traditional Islamic concept of soul, says there is no definitive or authoritative answer. Some say that the soul is distinct only when associated with the body, but Ibn Qayyim argues that the soul is taken from the body in a form that is recognizable to others, "influenced and proceeding from its body as the body is influenced and proceeds from it" (Smith and Haddad, 1981, p. 56). The notion of the quasi-materiality of the soul has a long history in Islamic literature. In Ibn Qayyim's work, *ruh* is applied both to the spirit that comes from God and the human soul. Ibn Qayyim rejects the notion of a totally immaterial soul. For him, the soul is like a subtle body (*jism latif*) possessing a different nature from the body of flesh and blood in that it is "luminous, elevated, light, alive and in motion. It penetrates the substance of the body organs, flowing therein in the way water flows in roses, oil in olives, and fire in charcoal" (Marmura, 1987, p. 225). At death, when the soul is separated from the body, it maintains its distinctiveness and individuality because in life body and soul interact and mold each other's characteristics.

Contemporary Muslim writers are divided in their understanding of the relationship between *nafs* and *ruh*. Some hold to a strict distinction between these two concepts but others point out that, historically, these concepts have been used interchangeably and suggest that it may be more profitable to think of them simply as referring to different expressions of that which makes a human being human – *nafs* being used to speak of the personal or human essence associated with the body and *ruh* being used to refer to the same essence when it is separated from the body at death (Smith and Haddad, 1981, p. 20).

A more nuanced line of thinking is expressed by the contemporary Qur'anic exegete al-Khatib, who "concludes that (1) *ruh* gives life; man and animals have spirits and the difference between them, as between the spirits of men, is in rank not in kind; (2) the *nafs* distinguishes man from animal, the human essence [*al-dhāt al-insānīya*] being created by the meeting of the *ruh* and the body" (Smith and Haddad, 1981, p. 202 n. 40). In this vein, the western scholar William Chittick explains the relationship between soul (*nafs*) and spirit (*ruh*) in relation to the cosmos and the human being who is a microcosm of the universe.

In his article "'Your Sight Today is Piercing': The Muslim Understanding of Death and Afterlife" (1992), Chittick relates the cosmos (macrocosm) to the human being (microcosm). The cosmos appears like a series of layers, the outer layer or shell being the visible world which we inhabit, the physical world devoid of the divine characteristics of life, knowledge, speech, generosity. At the core is the world of pure spirit, the invisible realm of the angels, which the Qur'an says God created out of light. Compared with the pure light of the invisible realm, the visible world is a world of darkness. The space in between the world of angels and the world of materiality is the realm of beings that are neither purely spiritual nor purely physical. This is the place of spirit beings like the jinn[6] who are said to be made out of fire and, like fire, which is halfway between material flames and immaterial light, the jinn occupy an intermediate space in the cosmos, invisible but not always. In Islam, the human being is seen as a mirror image of the cosmos – a microcosm. If we think of the creation of the first man, Adam, the Qur'an concurs with the Bible that God created Adam's body out of clay or earth and breathed into him the divine animating spirit (*ruh*). Similar to the cosmos, then, human beings have a visible outer shell of clay as the body and an invisible inner core of spirit. What, then, corresponds to the intermediate worlds of the cosmos? According to Chittick, this is where the Islamic idea of the soul comes in. As al-Khatib suggests, the soul (*nafs*) comes into being due to the joining of body and spirit, and is characterized neither by the pure light of spirit nor by the pure darkness of the physical. The soul reflects the degree to which the person has developed the divine qualities that are present in all humans as potential. The soul represents the essential character of the person and each soul is a unique combination of divine spirit and clay, each soul will possess the divine qualities of knowledge, justice, love, generosity, forgiveness, power, and strength in differing degrees. The soul is the meeting place of spirit and body – therefore, partaking of the materiality of the body but not entirely (Chittick, 1992, p. 132).

The questions and debates regarding the concepts of *nafs* and *ruh*, and how they relate to the resurrection of the body in Islamic thought, are manifold and complex. Both classical and modern authors have held many differing opinions, but there is general agreement that resurrection and life after death pertain to individual identity, and that there is some aspect of one's identity that will experience the events that take place between death and resurrection, whether pleasurable or painful.

The Trial of the Grave

> Does man think We shall not put his bones back together? In fact, We can reshape his very fingertips.[7] Yet man wants to deny what is ahead of him: he says, "So, when will this Day of Resurrection be?" (Sura 75:3–6)

Along with belief in the unassailable oneness of God and the role of prophecy in human existence, eschatology – the study of the endtimes and the hereafter – forms the third great theme or principle in Islamic thought (Chittick, 1992, p. 125). Death is the end of this life, which is the arena for action; at the same time, it is the beginning of an eternal life, in which one experiences the results of this life of action. The Qur'an describes in great detail the events of the Day of Judgment and what is to be expected if one attains the reward of paradise or the punishment of hell but it does not reveal much about the period between individual death and collective resurrection, a conjunction of time and place that came to be known as *barzakh*, a word that literally means barrier or separation – the separation between the world of the living and the world of the dead. According to the Qur'anic verse:

> When death comes to one of them [evildoers], he cries, "My Lord, let me return so as to make amends for the things I neglected." Never! This will not go beyond his words: a barrier [*barzakh*] stands behind such people until the very Day they are resurrected. (Sura 23:99–100)

The implication here is that upon death, there is no possibility of return to this life, no possibility to alter or atone for what has been done in this life; after death, one can only wait for the day of reckoning. Islam generally rejects the idea of reincarnation or rebirth in future lives; nevertheless, as do all religions, it contains many voices and we should be aware that in the history of Islam there have been schools of theology like the Mu'tazila that argued that God's justice required a second chance for certain people whose good and bad deeds were exactly even, and there are certain sects among the Shi'a that hold to the doctrine of the transmigration of the soul, not in the Hindu sense of endless cycles of existence but in the sense of opportunities for growth and purification of the soul before the time of Resurrection.

Descriptions of exactly what happens after death, how the soul leaves the body, and the stages of the afterlife are based on a few Qur'anic verses along with a multitude of traditions (*hadith*) drawn together in various eschatological manuals. As Smith and Haddad point out, however, the concern of Muslim theologians has not been to establish a fixed sequence of events but to use scripture and the traditions to emphasize the overarching concern of Islam that the choice one makes to follow God's way or not has serious ramifications beyond this life (Smith and Haddad, 1981). Here we will examine the events that take place after death up until the final allocation to paradise or to hell based on the writings of one of the greatest thinkers of classical Islam – the Persian theologian al-Ghazali (1058–1111). The text that we will follow in this section and the next is called *The Remembrance of Death and the Afterlife* (Al-Ghazali, 1989). It is the final book in his 40-book theological exposition on Islamic faith, *The Revival of the Religious Sciences*. In it, al-Ghazali contextualizes what is to come by beginning with an exposition on the excellence of the remembrance of death as an antidote to the pursuit of, and indulgence in, worldly desires. Knowledge of the afterlife and its relation to this life is regarded as the necessary impetus to overcome moral frailty and the baser inclinations of human beings. According to the Qur'an,

> On that Day you will be brought to judgement and none of your secrets will remain hidden. (Sura 69:18)

We might think of it as the divine counterpart to transparency in business and government that keeps people honest. After death and before resurrection, however, the soul exists in an intermediate place and state called *barzakh*. Although there are many variations regarding the events that take place upon death and during the *barzakh*, modern and traditional accounts agree that the soul after death is aware of its environment, able to see and hear the laments of the living; that angels visit the grave and question the soul, that the soul is visited by representatives of its good and bad deeds; and that while awaiting resurrection, the soul already receives punishment or reward according to its former deeds. *Barzakh*, then, is not a period of peaceful oblivion; upon death, the soul faces an immediate trial, the results of which foreshadow the misery or bliss that is the soul's ultimate destiny. The experiences begin from the very moment of death when the person is visited by 'Izra'il, the angel of death, who comes to take the soul away from the body. Sometimes two or four angels are said to arrive at the dying one's side. Al-Ghazali describes them as "the angel who pulls the soul from his right foot, the angel who pulls it from the left foot, the angel who pulls it from his right hand, and the angel who pulls it from his left hand" (cited in Smith and Haddad, 1981, p. 36). The separation of soul and body is further understood to be easy for the good person and difficult for sinners. "The good soul slips out like the jetting of water from a waterskin, but the profligate's spirit squeaks out like a skewer from wet wool" (cited in Smith and Haddad, 1981, p. 37).

On the first night in the grave the person is questioned by two angels called Munkar and Nakir. Here you should not think of lovely young ladies floating in white dresses or cherubic infants – the angel of death and those who carry out the questioning in the grave are beings so fearsome that even the staunchest believer might be terrified. A popular Shi'a account from the nineteenth century describes them as:

Two men [who] were strong and hefty like giants. Smoke and fire bellowed from their mouths and nostrils. In their hands were iron rods, so red hot that it seemed as if flames were leaping up from them. Suddenly they thundered in voices so sharp that the heavens and earth trembled, "Who is your Lord?" (Quchani, 1994, p. 3)

The questions asked relate to the foundation of Islam – Who is your Lord? What is your religion? Who is your Prophet? There are other questions as well that probe the person's knowledge:

"What say you of the Prophet?" they demand of him. Now if he is a believer he will reply, "He is God's bondsman and Emissary." "We had known that you would speak thus," they say, and his grave is widened for him by seventy cubits by seventy, and he is given light therein, and is told to sleep . . . and he sleeps like a bridegroom, who is awakened only by the most beloved of his family, until he is raised up from his bed.

149

And if he is a hypocrite he will say, "I know not; I used to hear the people saying something, so I said it also." And [the Angels] say to him, "We had known that you would speak thus!" Then the earth is commanded to draw tightly around him, and it is so until his very ribs protrude. In torment he thus remains until God resurrects him from his bed. (Al-Ghazali, 1989, pp. 144–145)

According to your answers, then, the grave becomes a pleasant or unpleasant place to wait for the day of judgment. If you have many good deeds to your credit, then the grave becomes a spacious and beautiful place and you will be visited by a man with a beautiful face, sweet-smelling, and wearing beautiful garments. He represents your own good deeds and tells you that things will be well for you. If you are unable to answer the angels' questions properly, then the grave becomes a place of suffering.

The Garden (*Janna*) and the Fire (*Jahannam*)

The Qur'an presents the results of God's Judgment in stark contrast. It describes in sensuous detail the afterlife enjoyed by the faithful in paradise, which is portrayed as a divine garden or series of gardens. Those fortunate ones, clothed in silk and brocade, adorned with silver bracelets, recline on couches under shady trees with hanging clusters of fruit, eating and drinking pure food and drink from silver plates and silver goblets in a garden that knows neither extreme heat nor cold (Sura 76:12–21). Similarly, the experiences of hell are clearly pictured: "We have prepared chains, iron collars, and blazing Fire for the disbelievers" (Sura 76:4). However, before the final allocation to the Garden or the Fire, Islamic eschatology provides a wealth of detail regarding the events of the Day of Resurrection and Judgment.

The Day of Judgment, its time and hour known only to God, begins in a cataclysmic destruction of the entire universe above and below, a day when the only emotions are fear and the desire to save oneself.

On that Day the mountains shall be shaken to dust . . . On that Day the heavens shall be split apart . . . On that Day tongues shall be struck dumb, and limbs shall speak out loud. [It is] the Day on which the secret things are rendered public, the Day on which no soul shall aid another . . . the Day on which one shall have no refuge from God . . . On that Day . . . Hellfire is brought near and its simmering water brought to a boil; the Inferno moans, the unbelievers despair . . . (Al-Ghazali, 1989, pp. 184–187)

As with accounts of the *barzakh* period, there is no consensus re-garding the exact sequence of events of the Resurrection and Judg-ment since the traditions are manifold and varied. According to al-Ghazali, the first stage of this final end is heralded by the sound of the trumpet blown by the angel Seraphiel. This cosmic blast marks the destruction not only of the physical world, but also of every liv-ing being including all the angels, and, in a surprising turn of events, in order to fulfill God's words that "every soul shall taste death," the angel who heralds death himself must die – only God remains in the totality of his oneness. Al-Ghazali writes: "Three times He asks, 'To whom belongs the Kingdom this day?' No one answers Him so He answers Himself, saying, 'To God, who is one alone, victorious!'" (cited in Smith and Haddad, 1981, p. 72).

Such utter annihilation, however, is not the ultimate fate of mankind; the divine plan is one of return to God. Therefore, God causes the earth to be rejuvenated and Seraphiel, restored to life, sounds the fearsome trumpet once more to call the dead from their graves. On that day, the Qur'an says:

When the sun is shrouded in darkness, when the stars are dimmed, when the mountains are set in motion, when pregnant camels are abandoned, when wild beasts are herded together, when the seas boil over, when souls are sorted into classes, when the baby girl buried alive is asked for what sin she was killed,[8] when the records of deeds are spread open, when the sky is stripped away, when Hell is made to blaze and Paradise brought near: then every soul will know what it has brought about. (Sura 81:1–14)

All are gathered in front of God's throne "barefoot, naked, and uncir-cumcised" to stand, waiting in agonizing anticipation for judgment to be handed down. In some traditions, the period of waiting is said to be 50,000 years. When the Judgment finally begins, each one is brought before God to be interrogated:

> "Did I not bless you with youth? How did you employ it? Did I not grant you long life? How did you spend it? Did I not bestow wealth upon you? Whence did you come by it, and how did you expend it? Did I not ennoble you with knowledge? How did you act by what you knew?" (Al-Ghazali, 1989, p. 191)

Not only ordinary people are questioned. Everyone, including the angels and all the prophets and messengers of God, are questioned as to their actions and the responses that they received – all are as abjectly humble and terrified in the face of God's wrath as any sinner.

After the questioning comes the weighing of the good and evil deeds. Al-Ghazali speaks of three groups among the resurrected – those who have not a single good deed to their credit would be immediately assigned to hell; those who have not a single bad deed to confess would be immediately taken to paradise. The majority will constitute the third group, those with a mixture of good and bad deeds. The books and scrolls that record a lifetime of deeds that each person carries around his neck are weighed in the cosmic balance and then returned to each one:

> Anyone who is given his Record in his right hand will say, "Here is my Record, read it. I knew I would meet my Reckoning," and so he will have a pleasant life in a lofty Garden, with clustered fruit within his reach. It will be said, "Eat and drink to your heart's content as a reward for what you have done in days gone by." But anyone who is given his Record in his left hand will say, "If only I had never been given any Record and knew nothing of my Reckoning. How I wish death had been the end of me. My wealth has been no use to me, and my power has vanished." "Take him, put a collar on him, lead him to burn in the blazing Fire, and [bind him] in a chain seventy metres long ... " (Sura 69:19–32)

Al-Ghazali records a tradition of the Prophet which states that there are three places where a person will think only of himself:

> when the scales are erected and actions are weighed, so that the son of Adam shall watch to see if his balance shall be heavy or light; and at [the Assessment of] the Scrolls, so that he watches to see if he is to receive his book in his right hand or in his left; and at the Traverse. (Al-Ghazali, 1989, p. 196)

Another element in the eschatological drama of classical Islam is the Traverse, the bridge over hell – sharper than a sword and thinner than a hair.

> Mankind after the terrors . . . shall be driven to the Traverse, which is a bridge stretched over the gulf of Hell, sharper than a sword and thinner than a hair. Whosoever has in the world kept upright on the Straight Path . . . shall bear lightly upon the Traverse . . . and will be saved. But whosoever deviates from uprightness in this world, and weighs down his back with burdens and disobeys his Lord, shall slip upon taking the first step on the Traverse and shall go to perdition. (Al-Ghazali, 1989, p. 207)

Although the traditions regarding the elements and sequence of events of the Day of Judgment are diverse in their descriptions, there is a sense that all of what transpires is perceived and encountered according to the character and qualities of the person. So, for example, there is a tradition that recounts the Prophet's answer to his wife, Aisha, when she expresses dismay at the fact that even true believers must go through all the terrors of the grave. He answers her:

> O 'Ā'isha, the voice of Munkar and Nakīr in the hearing of the believer are like antimony [khol, the cosmetic used to darken and beautify the eyes] in the eye and the pressure of the tomb to the believer is like the compassionate mother whose son complains to her of a headache and she strokes his head gently. But O 'Ā'isha, woe to those who doubt God – how they will be squeezed in their graves like the pressure of a boulder on an egg. (cited in Smith and Haddad, 1981, p. 46)

153

Similarly, with regard to the Traverse, each person crosses it in his own way according to the strength of the good deeds that he has accumulated in his lifetime.

> Mankind shall pass over the Inferno's Traverse, upon which are thorns, hooks and grapples, which snatch at them from left and right. On either side are the Angels, who say, "O Lord God, deliver!..." There are some among mankind who shall cross like a shaft of lightning; others shall pass over like the wind, others like horses at a gallop, others shall run, still others walk, while others crawl on their hands and knees or creep along on their bellies.... (Al-Ghazali, 1989, p. 208)

It should never be thought, however, that success is dependent entirely on one's own efforts; one attains to paradise only in the context of God's mercy. There is an interesting tradition which says that on the Day of Judgment God will provide light to each person according to their works; the one who has the least good works will receive a light only on his big toe that is sometimes shining and sometimes dark. That one will crawl across the Traverse with hellfire licking at his legs and upon crossing over will say: "Praised be to God! He has granted me something never given to anyone else, for He has delivered me from Hell after I had beheld it!" (Al-Ghazali, 1989, p. 208).

Modern Islamic Views on Heaven and Hell

Although there is a strong emphasis in Islam on the awesomeness of God's Judgment that assigns people to eternal bliss or to terrible suffering, whether the gardens of paradise and the fires of hell are to be understood literally is a subject of debate among modern Muslim thinkers. Some writers take an entirely spiritualized position. In the words of Muhammad Iqbal:

> Heaven and Hell are states, not localities. The descriptions in the Qur'ān are visual representations of an inner fact, *i.e.*, character. Hell,

154

in the words of the Qur'ān, is "God's kindled fire which mounts above the hearts" – the painful realization of one's failure as a man. Heaven is the joy of triumph over the forces of disintegration. (Quoted in Smith and Haddad, 1981, p. 138)

Others take a more popular middle position that says pleasure and suffering in the afterlife can be both physical and spiritual, with each person experiencing the afterlife at a level in accordance with what they deserve. Still others, like Muhammad al-Mubarak, reject literal, symbolic, or analogic interpretations and point out that the truth of the afterlife cannot be related to the realities of this life, that it is beyond our comprehension because there is no way for the human mind to conceive of what it has not experienced. In their summary, Smith and Haddad state:

> More important for these writers than the nature of the joys and tor-
> ments of the hereafter as described in the Qur'ān and traditions, then,
> is the purpose of these detailed and seemingly sensuous characteri-
> zations. Whether inciting fear of what is to be avoided or extending
> hope for what is to be attained, in the minds of many contemporary
> Muslims they are intended for the primary purpose of encouraging
> man to live in this world with the concrete and immediate awareness
> that he will be called to accountability for his actions in the next. "Thus
> the hereafter is a reality [the Muslim] lives," says Aḥmad Fā'iz, "and
> not a distant promise. He is in certitude and has no doubt that each
> soul will be recompensed for what it has earned. . . . And this is the
> secret of his piety and awe." (Smith and Haddad, 1981, pp. 140–141)

The eternity of a blissful afterlife for the saved in the Garden is never doubted as it is the manifestation of God's justice for the faithful, but Islamic theologians have struggled with the question of whether or not the torments of the damned are never-ending, a question that is related to the idea of intercession. With regard to the Muslim community, it has long been believed that based on God's mercy and Muhammad's intercession (as the purveyor of God's mercy) for his community, the wrong-doers among them will be punished but eventually released from the Fire and brought to the Garden. Hellfire in this case would function more like the Christian idea of purgatory – a period of painful purification. More problematic is the issue of non-Muslims and whether God's mercy might extend to them as well. Those who argue for eternal hellfire point to Qur'anic passages which state that the inhabitants of hell will not pass away. However, others point out that while the bliss of paradise in the presence of God is for all eternity, there is no indication in the Qur'an that hellfire is eternal, so those passages can be interpreted as saying that sinners will suffer as long as the Fire lasts. In general, the modern view is that for both Muslim and non-Muslim, hell is not intended as a place of torture designed by a vengeful God but as "a remedy, to heal the spiritual diseases which a man has incurred of himself and by his own negligence, and to enable him to start again on the road to the higher life" (quoted in Smith and Haddad, 1981, p. 144). God's mercy, therefore, is regarded as supreme and God's will prevails over all conditions. In that vein, we will close this section with the report from Smith and Haddad that:

> This understanding of God as merciful bears on several issues related to the nature of punishment, of which eternity is only one. In recent interviews with some Egyptian thinkers the authors posed the question of whether or not those who do not know about Islam will be punished (for whatever length of time) for their ignorance. The answer in each instance was a denial of such a possibility according to the mercy of God. Muḥammad Nuwayhī of the American University of Cairo, for example, indicated that in his opinion in 90% of the cases where people have heard the message of Islam it has been in such distorted forms that they could not be blamed for not accepting it. Urging again the significance of divine mercy, he reflected on how much better it is for God to promise wrath and then show mercy than the opposite. (Smith and Haddad, 1981, p. 47)

Rituals of Departure

The practice of cremation is prohibited in Islam, as is the practice of embalming or autopsy (except if legally required). Burial should take place as quickly as possible, preferably within 24 hours, and the family should pay any debts owed by the deceased as quickly as possible. When a person is close to death, verses from the Qur'an are read at the bedside and if possible the dying one is encouraged to recite the *shahadah*, the declaration of faith that is the basis of the call to prayer five times daily, or it is whispered into the person's ear. A religious authority such as the imam may be called to help comfort the dying and remind them of God's love and mercy. The Qur'anic passage most often recited when a person hears of a death is Sura 2:156, "We belong to God and to Him we shall return." Upon death, the eyes and mouth are closed, the body covered. It is also customary in some places to lay the body on its right side facing the *qibla* (direction of prayer). The body is to be washed, preferably by relatives of the same sex, and shrouded in plain white cloths. Weeping and grieving for the deceased are natural, but excessive displays of grief such as ritual wailing or beating one's breast, or lengthy periods of mourning, are discouraged since death takes place according to God's will, which is always for the good, regardless of human beings' ability to understand God's actions.

The body is taken to the mosque for the Funeral Prayer, which is usually said outside the mosque in a courtyard or special area. The Funeral Prayer is a communal obligation and includes prayers of supplication (*dua*) on behalf of the deceased and the total community: "O God, forgive our living ones and our deceased ones, and those of us who are present and those who are absent, and our young ones and our old ones, and our males and our females. O God, those of us whom Thou grantest life, keep them firm on Islam, and those of us whom Thou causest to die, cause them to die in the faith" (quoted in Davies, 2002, p. 122). Only men are permitted to accompany the coffin to the gravesite, where the body is lowered into the grave, preferably without the coffin. Flowers, candles, or other grave decorations are generally discouraged. These are some main features of Muslim death rituals but, as in all religions, actual cases are influenced by the cultures among which Islam has spread. The following description of funeral rituals among the Safaliba Muslims of northern Ghana is from the preliminary ethnographic research of Jennifer Schaefer (Schaefer, 2008).

Among Safaliba Muslims, funeral activities carry on until the fortieth day of death. On the first day, the washing, shrouding, and burial take place. The coffin is brought into the room where the body was washed and dressed, and the Qur'an is read over the body inside the coffin. It is then brought out of the room and set down by the door, where more prayers are said over the body. The coffin is then taken by the men to the cemetery where the grave has been dug by the young men of the community.

On the second day, everyone in the community goes to greet and comfort the bereaved family. On the third day, the family prepares fried millet cakes to offer to the imam, important elders, and family heads among the Muslim community. Since all are welcome at the funeral, friends and strangers alike, on this day also the rest of the village prepares food to help the bereaved family feed the strangers who attended the funeral. On the fourth day, the bereaved family makes the rounds of the village thanking those who helped to prepare the food for the strangers. The funeral is also the occasion for a celebration feast that allows for all the scattered family to gather and remember the deceased. This begins on the seventh day when a sheep is killed and the family shares out the meat and other food with the Muslim elders and leaders, with one hind leg going to the grandchildren.

On the eighth day, the family again go out to thank those who contributed to the food for the gathering the day before. If the deceased is an old or important member of the community, then the rituals continue and on the twelfth day, there is a special reading of the Qur'an for three hours, after which a cow is killed, again one hind leg going to the grandchildren, who cook it along with other food that they take into the deceased's room and leave there as an offering to the soul until evening when they can eat it. Throughout the afternoon, the imam and elders gather with the family and friends to read from the Qur'an. Finally, on the fortieth day, the funeral rites come to an end as the family again fries the traditional millet cakes to distribute to the elders and community leaders. Although the main features of washing, shrouding, and burial would be recognized by all Muslims, the cultural values underlying the rituals show an emphasis on social solidarity and relationship that is evident in the numerous occasions for greeting and sharing food with the community. Also, the practice of leaving food for the dead reflects the pan-African concern for the ancestors and the continued welfare of the soul.

A Conversation on Understanding Death

With Mine Khan

Mine was born in a small town close to Ankara, Turkey. She met Zakaria from Pakistan, her husband to be, when both were university students in Germany. They came to Canada as a newly married couple in 1975 and settled here to raise a family. We meet at her home to have this conversation and I feel as though I have been transported to Istanbul with traditionally designed carpets under my feet, flowing Arabic calligraphy on the walls, linden flower tea, and a plate of artfully presented delicacies in front of me. But Mine defies any stereotyping; she is solidly grounded in her Turkish culture and Islamic religion, yet reaches out to contemporary Canadian culture and the modern world of information technology in which she has worked for 35 years.

Mine begins our conversation with a quote from the Qur'an: "Every living soul will taste death." "So," she says, "from newborn to 120 years, death can come at any age, at any time, but I find comfort in knowing that everything has been given to us temporarily, in trust – all that I have, including my children, belong to God, who is their owner and who can take them back." "Of course, I can still pray for my loved ones to live long, but being patient with ourselves and with our grief is part of faith. I know that when loved ones die, they go back to where they belong, to where they will be treated right." "We need to replace grief for those we have lost with prayer for their sins to be forgiven." "I am thankful to Allah for all that I have, but I know that all belongs to Him." "Another way of finding comfort is to do a good deed on behalf of one who has died – give to charity, or feed the poor, make supplications, read Qur'an, or make a Hajj (pilgrimage) or an *umra* (minor pilgrimage) to Holy Kaba in Makkah on behalf of the deceased, as I did for my father who did not have the chance when he was alive." "When we first hear of a death, there is a moment of disbelief, but then we must accept the will of Allah – this acceptance diverts attention away from oneself and prevents us from asking things like 'why did this or that happen?'; we do not oppose Allah's will but simply plan how to benefit the one who died by making supplications, giving to charity, or doing a sacrifice in their name."

When Mine mentions her father, she adds the phrase "May God be pleased with him," and continues to say, "when he died, I tried to think what would be pleasing to him if he were alive, what would make him happy, because I know Allah will let him know of my actions – and I knew that he would be pleased for me to look after my young brother and see him safely on his way through life." Mine notes that although she was raised in a culturally Muslim family, they were not extremely religious or very strict practitioners and her personal engagement with Islam really came about in the context of being Muslim in Canada. "I wanted to know more about my own religion, to make it part of my life and be able to explain it to others, and the more I read the Qur'an, the more interested I became in the afterlife." A final turning point came in 1984 when the whole family took part in the Hajj. She explains how "the Hajj separates you so completely from the things of this worldly life," and "after the Hajj, I remembered death much more and the thought of death became part of my life." "What this means is that the afterlife took more of my thoughts, I started practicing my religion more, for example, having never worn the hijab, I am now moved to begin wearing it." "I call myself to account, ask myself, 'Am I ready to die today? What have I missed and how can I make it up?" "I try to remember that nothing is mine, not even my life." "Strangely, these thoughts actually make me happy, make life easier, and help me to face whatever problems will come because my perception of daily problems has changed – I look for the good in it, or take it as a lesson or a test of patience." "So whatever happens, I thank God for the good in it, for the opportunity for spiritual growth, and for the power and value that is to be found in hardship."

When I ask Mine how she would prepare for her own death, she answers, "be diligent in worship, share what I have, whether wealth or knowledge or time, and repent for my shortcomings." "This world," she tells me, "is the preparation for the next." Again she comments on the life-changing nature of the Hajj. "It changed my whole view of my life, changed my understanding of my responsibility to the wider community, it showed me that helping others is my personal responsibility." And finally she sums it all up for me: "Work hard, do your best to benefit self, family, religion, society – work as if you are never going to die, and worship as if you will die tomorrow."

Notes

1. In commemoration of Hagar's distress and God's salvation of her and her child, the rites of the Hajj pilgrimage include the pilgrims passing

back and forth between the two hills of Safa and Marwah seven times. Although the Bible implies that Ismael was 13 years old when he and his mother were turned out of the household, Islamic tradition portrays him as a suckling infant when the miracle of Zamzam took place.

2. The well was said to have been rediscovered by Abd al-Muttalib, the grandfather of the Prophet Muhammad (Lings, 1983, pp. 10–11).
3. The word also means recite and the sense is to read aloud or recite.
4. Often translated as a clot of blood referring to the undeveloped embryo that clings to the womb.
5. All Qur'anic quotations are taken from *The Qur'an: A New Translation* by Abdel Haleem (Oxford: Oxford University Press, 2004).
6. These are spirits who can be helpful or harmful, like the fearsome spirits of the desert who feature in the stories of the Arabian Nights.
7. Emphasizing God's ability to restore the individuality of each person marked by their unique fingerprints.
8. Refers to the pagan Arab practice of female infanticide.

References and Further Reading

Al-Ghazali. *The Remembrance of Death and the Afterlife*. Cambridge: Islamic Texts Society, 1989.

Chittick, William C. "'Your Sight Today is Piercing': The Muslim Understanding of Death and Afterlife." In Obayashi Hiroshi (ed.), *Death and Afterlife: Perspectives of World Religions*. London: Praeger, 1992, pp. 125–139.

Davies, Douglas J. *Death, Ritual and Belief: The Rhetoric of Funerary Rites*. London: Continuum, 2002.

Lings, Martin. *Muhammad: His Life Based on the Earliest Sources*. Rochester, VT: Inner Traditions International, 1983.

Marmura, Michael E. "Islamic Concepts of the Soul." In Lawrence E. Sullivan (ed.), *Death, Afterlife, and the Soul*. New York: Macmillan, 1987, pp. 223–231.

Nursi Studies. WORDS.pdf, http://nursistudies.com/downloads/pdf/THE, n.d.

Quchani, Hujjatul Islam Najafi. *Journey to the Unseen World*. Karachi: Peermahomed Ebrahim Trust, 1994.

Schaefer, Jennifer. "Funeral Rites of the Safaliba People." *G.I.L.L.B.T. Working Papers Vol. 2: Proceedings of the 2005 and 2006 Seminars*. Tamale,

Ghana: Ghana Institute of Linguistics, Literacy and Bible Translation, 2008, pp. 98–106.

Sheykh Tosun Bayrak. *The Name and the Named*. Introduction by William Chittick. Louisville, KY: Fons Vitae, 2000.

Smith, Jane Idleman and Haddad, Yvonne Yazbeck. *The Islamic Understanding of Death and Resurrection*. Albany: State University of New York Press, 1981.

7

Hindu Perspectives on Death

Historical beginnings are difficult enough to establish for religions like Christianity or Buddhism that are linked to a founding figure, but the origins of those without a founder merge into the amorphous beginnings of a people or peoples and their long-past religious beliefs and practices. This is the case for the religious systems of the Hindus, which have been fed by numerous streams of influence; among them, the beliefs and practices of the Indo-Aryan-speaking peoples who began migrating into the subcontinent during the second millennium BCE, the people of the Indus Valley whom they encountered, indigenous tribal peoples, and the Dravidians of southern India. With regard to the religions that developed in India, the most ancient texts that we know of are the Vedas (meaning "knowledge"), the sacred scriptures of the semi-nomadic Indo-Aryan-speaking tribes.

The Vedas consist of four major collections: the *Rig*, *Sama*, *Yajur*, and *Atharva*, composed over a period of centuries from

Understanding Death: An Introduction to Ideas of Self and the Afterlife in World Religions, First Edition. Angela Sumegi.
© 2014 Angela Sumegi. Published 2014 by Blackwell Publishing Ltd.

approximately 1750 to 600 BCE. In these collections we find hymns in praise of various gods, instructions for ritual sacrifices, as well as more contemplative, philosophic writing. Although it is commonly held that the earliest Vedic texts do not reflect the major religious beliefs and concerns of classical Hindu thought, such as belief in rebirth, the immortal soul (*atman*), and liberation (*moksha*) from *samsara* (the continuing round of birth and death), we should regard the changes as a shift in emphasis rather than a radical break in the religious response to death. As we will see, the continuity of Vedic thought is preserved in contemporary Hindu rituals and in the fact that the four major branches of Hindu religion focused on Vishnu, Shiva, the Mother Goddess, and the tradition of Advaita (non-dualism) all regard the Vedas as revealed scripture. We will begin this chapter, then, with a look at the ancient Vedic approach to death and life after death.

Feeding the Ancestors

In the Vedic age (1500–800 BCE), religion centered around the sacred nature of fire, either as household rituals around the domestic fire or the elaborate fire sacrifices offered to the divine powers or gods (*devas*) who were closely associated with the powers of nature. The primary purpose of religious activity was to ensure, through worship, praise, and offerings, the blessings of the gods; blessings that were understood very concretely and practically – health, wealth, many children, cattle, and a long life. The Vedic emphasis was firmly fixed on this-worldly concerns; the aim of religion was to achieve a long, prosperous, and joyful life. Concerns regarding what happens after death were situated within this general world-affirming, life-affirming picture, not the other way around, as would be promoted in later Vedic texts called the Upanishads (800–600 BCE), which represented a tradition of renunciation focused on attaining liberation from existence in this unreliable and impermanent world.

The Vedic universe was divided into four realms: the celestial realm of the sky gods like the sun and the moon; the atmospheric realm, where the gods of the atmosphere like Vayu (god of wind) and Indra (god of storms) held sway; the earth, where humans lived, and which was the realm of terrestrial gods of rivers, lakes, and earth; and the world of the fathers, the dwelling place of the ancestors. The most elaborate religious ritual was the fire sacrifice. It required the expertise of many types of priests who were trained in the chants and procedures of the ritual. The offerings were made to Agni the god of fire who fulfilled the functions of consuming, transforming, and transporting the offerings, thereby reaffirming the interconnections between gods, men, and cosmos.

The cosmic significance of the Vedic fire sacrifice was illustrated in its form. Three fire altars symbolized the universe and its inhabitants. In the west a round altar represented the earth and humanity: it signified the home or domestic fire in which the offering was cooked. In the east, a square altar represented the sky: it held the fire into which the offering was put to be sent to the celestial gods. In the south, a semi-circle represented the atmospheric region between sky and earth: it held the offerings intended for the ancestors and was called the Southern fire (Olivelle, 1996, pp. xlii–xliv). When the offering was taken from the home fire and placed in the sky fire, it symbolized the interrelatedness of earthly beings and *devas*, the shining ones above.

Although animal sacrifice was a feature of other ancient religious systems such as those arising out of Mesopotamia in the same period, the Vedic fire sacrifice was not carried out as a ritual of atonement for sins, neither did the animal offering represent a form of ransom. Among the Indo-Aryans, the sacrifice was a ritual affirmation of the bond between gods and men, between the universe as macrocosm and the individual as microcosm. The Vedic fire ritual is the earliest expression of one of the most characteristic of Hindu religious ideas – that the universe is the physical manifestation of the Divine, that gods, humans, and cosmos originate from a single source and are held together in a grand homology, a web of hidden correspondences and correlations that, if known, brings all power to the knower. The fire that consumes the sacrifice was regarded as the prime symbol of transformation and of the interrelatedness of all things. Agni, the god of fire, manifests in the sky as the sun, in the atmospheric region as lightning, and on earth as the cooking fire and the fire of earthly rituals. By means of the fire ritual, humans reaffirmed their place in the universe and played their part in nourishing and upholding the cosmos.

In the development of Vedic thought, the notion of a metaphysical soul (*atman*) as the undying essence of a person does not become prominent until the period of the Upanishads. Prior to that, the existence and continuity of personhood, whether of immortal gods, mortal humans, or dead ancestors, depended on some form of food or nourishment. The sacrifices and offerings made to the gods and the ancestors provided the nourishment needed to sustain their "bodies" (Reat, 1990, pp. 63, 90–91). In return, humans received the blessings of the gods and the good will of their ancestors in the form of health, long life, and prosperity. Individual and universal harmony and balance, therefore, depended on the efficacy and continuity of the offerings made to gods and ancestors by means of daily household rituals and the fire sacrifices performed by the priests.

Embedded in their scriptural heritage, the Aryan tribes also bequeathed to future generations a society organized into hereditary classes or castes based on occupation. According to an ideal fourfold division, the priestly (*brahmin*) class memorized the Veda and conducted the fire ritual; the warrior nobility (*kshatriya*) ruled the people and fought to protect them; the merchant class (*vaishya*) represented the commercial sector of society; and landless laborers (*shudra*) served others and worked the land. As the Aryan tribes integrated themselves into the subcontinent, there were some, like the indigenous tribal peoples or those whose occupations were ritually polluting, who were considered entirely outside of the caste system, therefore termed "outcaste."

The First Sacrifice

The most famous Vedic expression of the relationship between life and death is the *Purusha Sukta*, in which the universe emerges from

the primordial sacrifice of the primordial Person, the Cosmic Man
(*Purusha*).

1. The Man has a thousand heads, a thousand eyes, a thousand
    feet. He pervaded the earth on all sides and extended beyond
    it as far as ten fingers.
2. It is the Man who is all this, whatever has been and whatever
    is to be. He is the ruler of immortality, when he grows beyond
    everything through food.
    . . .
8. From that sacrifice in which everything was offered, the melted
    fat was collected, and he made it into those beasts who live in
    the air, in forests, and in villages.
9. From that sacrifice in which everything was offered, the verses
    and chants were born, the metres were born from it, and from
    it the formulas were born.
10. Horses were born from it, and those other animals that have
    two rows of teeth; cows were born from it, and from it goats
    and sheep were born.
11. When they divided the Man, into how many parts did they
    apportion him? What do they call his mouth, his two arms and
    thighs and feet?
12. His mouth became the Brahmin; his arms were made into the
    Warrior, his thighs the People, and from his feet the Servants
    were born.
13. The moon was born from his mind; from his eye the sun was
    born. Indra and Agni came from his mouth, and from his vital
    breath the Wind was born.
14. From his navel the middle realm of space arose; from his head
    the sky evolved. From his two feet came the earth, and the
    quarters of the sky from his ear. Thus they set the worlds in
    order. (RV 10.90)

In this well-known text, the ritual of the sacrifice is presented as
a symbol of the cosmos and the primordial dynamic of creation in
which all things are consumed, all transformed, all nourished. The

169

sacrificial offering is the Cosmic Man, the *Purusha*, "who is all this, whatever has been and whatever is to be." And who is yet more than all this, who pervades everything, spreading out "into that which eats and that which does not eat." The Man, who is everything, is sacrificed by the gods, and from the parts and pieces of his body, everything is born – the Vedas themselves, the sun, the moon, the sky, all types of animals, and all types of people, everything set in its proper social and cosmic order. It was understood that the principle of harmony and order (*rta*) in the universe, both earthly and divine, was upheld and maintained by the sacrificial rituals performed by gods and men.

It may appear that the *Purusha Sukta* presents us with creation as the result of a ritual death and dismemberment. However, the act of creation here is not situated in a temporal moment from which history streams forth; creation is embedded in a series of correspondences and correlations that constitute the whole. On this, Walter Kaelber states:

> Through yajña [sacrifice] a series of homologies is established wherein components of (1) the Cosmic Person, (2) the primordial sacrifice, and (3) the cosmos itself are equated or linked in a network of identities. (Kaelber, 1989, p. 8)

In other words, the hymn speaks to a beginningless cycle of interconnectivity affirmed through the ritual of the sacrifice in which death is homologized with the living totality, the allness of existence. Therefore, the *Purusha* is not only the sacrificial offering but also the one to whom the sacrifice is offered, not only the creator but also the created. Cremation is called the "last sacrifice" (*antyeshti*), and the primordial ritual of creation is echoed in a hymn that tells the deceased:

> May your eye go to the sun, your life's breath to the wind. Go to the sky or to the earth, as is your nature; or go to the waters, if that is your fate. Take root in the plants with your limbs. (RV 10.16.3)

Death as sacrifice defeats death as destruction.

The destructive aspects of death associated with the sacrifice, however, create concern over the path by which the deceased may reach the world of the gods. In the *Rig Veda*, death is told:

> Go away, death, by another path that is your own, different from the road of the gods. I say to you who have eyes, who have ears: do not injure our children or our men. (RV 10.18)[1]

Eventually, two paths are identified as available to the person after death: the way leading to the world of the fathers and the way leading to the world of the gods. In the Upanishads, these pathways are worked out in more detail; the world of the fathers becomes associated with reincarnation, while the world of the gods represented the attainment of immortality. Both paths lead to heavenly worlds, but the outcome is different according to the knowledge and practice of the person. Therefore, in the *Brihadaraṇyaka Upanishad* we are told that those who live in solitude in the forest, who know the esoteric truth of the homology between sacrifice and creation, death and life, go to the highest heaven of Brahma and do not return to earthly life (BU 6.2.9–14). The hidden correspondences are explained in terms of the sacrificial fire:

> A fire – that's what the world up there is, Gautama. Its firewood is the sun; its smoke is the sunbeams; its flame is the day; its embers are the quarters; and its sparks are the intermediate quarters. In that very fire gods offer faith, and from that offering springs King Soma [the Moon]. (BU 6.2.9)

The passage continues to equate the sacrificial fire with: the rain cloud; this world down here; man; and woman. The gods offer faith[2] as the sacrifice into the fire that is "the world up there," i.e., the celestial realm, and from that sacrifice Soma[3] is born; Soma is consumed by the fire that is the rain cloud and from that sacrifice comes rain; rain is consumed by the fire that is "the world down here," and from that sacrifice comes food; food is consumed in the fire that is a man and that sacrifice produces semen; semen is offered into the fire that is a woman and from that sacrifice is born a child. The child lives and grows and finally dies and is offered to the cremation fire, and from that sacrifice one "of brilliant color" emerges. According to the text, those wise ones who know these interconnections are guided on the path of the gods to the highest heaven and do not return. In his analysis of this passage Arindam Chakrabarti notes the relationship between destruction and creation, "behind every birth there is a sacrifice" (Chakrabarti, 2006, p. 14).

Those, however, who do not have such esoteric knowledge, those who strive for heaven by means of ordinary sacrificial rituals, ordinary offerings, and the performance of austerities, go forward after death to the world of the fathers, and from there to the moon, the lunar celestial realm of the ancestors, where they dwell for some time, being food for the gods, but after that they pass into the sky, and from the sky into the wind, and from the wind into the rain, and from the rain to the earth, where they become again food consumed by man and take birth again from the semen sacrificed in the fire of woman.

These two paths, then, are differentiated by knowledge: those who understand the hidden interconnections between all things, who know how they have come to be and who they truly are, and those who think that immortality is the result of ritual. The *Kausitaki Upanishad* makes this difference even clearer.

> When people depart from this world, it is to the moon that they all go. By means of their lifebreaths the moon swells up in the fortnight of waxing, and through the fortnight of waning it propels them to a new birth. Now the moon is the door to the heavenly world. It allows those who answer its question to pass. As to those who do not answer its question, after they have become rain, it rains them down here on earth, where they are born again in these various conditions . . . each in accordance with his actions and knowledge. (KsU 1.2)

Here, the moon is the gateway to the path of the gods and when the dead arrive, the moon god asks, "Who are you?" If the dead one has the knowledge to answer correctly, to show the correspondences that result in the answer "I am you!," then the moon lets him pass onto the path of the gods. Eventually he reaches the highest abode of Brahman, and Brahman also asks, "Who are you?" Again, the answer is "I am who you are." Then Brahman asks, "Who am I?" and the one who knows the answer to that question – that Brahman is this whole world, the real, the truth (*satyam*), the inner self (*atman*) of every being, then that is one who knows the true nature of self and world, and that one wins the immortal world of Brahman (KsU 1.2–7).

Death, the Immortal

In the context of Vedic thought, creation and destruction, mortality and immortality are not irresolvable polarities but necessary and constitutive elements of each other. These paradoxical ideas are further explored in the Vedic myths of Yama, the Lord of Death. Yama is an ambiguous and complex figure. He appears in later mythology as a fearsome noose-wielding god who binds and carries away the souls of men, women, and children or as a stern judge presiding over the dispatching of souls to heaven or hell, but in the Vedic period, he is portrayed as the progenitor of the human race, the first mortal to die, the first to reach the celestial world of the gods. Yama is a forefather, a forerunner of men; he shows the path beyond death, he is the link between this world and the other world.

In the lead-up to the following passage from the Brahmanas (ritualistic sections of the Vedas), the gods have won immortality based on their knowledge of how to build the fire altar so that it properly corresponds to the divine cosmos, but Death objects that this merely technical route to immortality will leave no role for him, since anyone can learn it.

> Death then spoke to the Gods: "If this is so, then surely all men will become immortal. What will then be my fate [*share*]?" The Gods said: "From now on no one will become immortal with the body. After you have taken the body as your portion, then only shall whoever is going to become immortal, either by wisdom or works, become immortal, that is, after having laid down the body." (SB 10.4.3.9)[4]

Immortality, then, is not a matter of escaping death, nor does dying necessarily bring immortality, but immortality cannot be gained except through death that is the link between humanity and divinity. One of the most prominent divinities in Vedic literature is the sun, symbol of eternal life and the light of wisdom. In a striking association, the Vedic seers identify Yama (Death) as the son of the sun god, and portray him enveloped by the light of the sun:

> 3. He verily is Death, that person in the yonder orb [the sun]. That orb's blazing ray is the immortal; thus Death cannot die either, for he is enclosed within the immortal; thus Death cannot be seen, for he is enclosed within the immortal.

> 4. On this point there is a verse: "Within Death there is immortality" [*antaraṁ mṛtyor amṛtam*] . . . "Death clothes itself in Light," for Light, to be sure, is yonder Sun, because this light changes day and night, and so Death clothes itself in Light and is surrounded on all sides by Light, "The self of Death is in the Light" . . . (SB 10.5.3–4)[5]

Death is presented as a paradox, then, encompassing both the vulnerability of life and the indestructibility of life. Human beings, however, strive to negotiate the paradox, and so the speaker in the following verse from the *Rig Veda* prays to be released from death, which is naturally bonded with life, but not from immortality that is equally bound to death.

> Just as a cucumber is removed from its stalk
> So from Death's bonds may I be removed
> But not from Immortality! (RV 7.59.12)[6]

The Inner Controller

As we have seen, religious activity in the Vedic world was focused on the procurement of a long and prosperous life through the correct performance of rituals that ensured a harmonious relationship between all the spheres of the cosmos. Alongside the emphasis on the mechanics of ritual, however, we also find the seeds of more philosophical thinking. The *Atharva Veda* pronounces:

> Desireless, wise, immortal, self-existent,
> full of bliss, lacking in nothing,
> is the one who knows the wise, unaging,
> youthful *atman*: he fears not death! (AV 10.8.44)[7]

The death that was to be feared was untimely death (*akala mrtyu*); for the wise one of knowledge who had lived out his lifespan, death belonged to the order of the cosmos and was the gateway to immortality. *Veda* means knowledge and throughout the Vedas, it is the "one who knows" that is assured of bliss and immortality. The question is: what is it that the knowers know? This is the driving question behind the philosophic discussions and disputations of the Upanishads, the latest Vedic texts composed 800–600 BCE. In these texts, we find not so much a rejection of the earlier Vedic sacrificial worldview as a continuation of certain strands of thought, an attempt to work out the philosophical implications of earlier ideas, a rethinking of the meaning of death, of the relationship between life and death, of what it means to be a person, what it means to attain immortality and how that is achieved. Through their questioning, the Upanishadic sages explored certain concepts that became the hallmark of later Hindu thought and philosophy, concepts that bear directly on the understanding of death and what happens after. Among them: the concepts of *karma* (moral action); *samsara* (the cycle of birth, death, and rebirth); *moksha* (liberation); *atman* (individual soul); and *brahman* (universal ground of existence).

Karma is a word meaning "action." In the Vedic period, it referred to the ritual action of the sacrifice that brought about effects such as good crops and wealth. By the time of the Upanishads, karma becomes associated with intention and will, positive or negative, and according to one's positively or negatively intentioned deeds, one proceeds after death to positive or negative states. In the following passage, the great sage Yajñavalkya is questioned about the status of a person after death:

> "Yājñavalkya," Ārtabhāga said again, "tell me – when a man has died and his speech disappears into fire, his breath into the wind, his sight into the sun, his mind into the moon, his hearing into the quarters, his physical body into the earth, his self (*atman*) into space, the hair of his body into plants, the hair of his head into trees, and his blood and semen into water – what then happens to that person?" Yājñavalkya replied: "My friend, we cannot talk about this in public. Take my hand, Ārtabhāga; let's go and discuss this in private."
>
> So they left and talked about it. And what did they talk about? – they talked about nothing but action. And what did they praise? – they praised nothing but action. Yājñavalkya told him: "A man turns into something good by good action and something bad by bad action."
> (BU 3.2.13)

The implication here is that the understanding of karma and its significance to the person after death was secret esoteric knowledge to be passed privately from teacher to student. Compared to the material view of the person as distributed into the elements of the universe, this was an entirely different way of conceiving of the continuity of self; otherwise, as Arindam Chakrabarti asks, "why should talking about the results of one's actions answer a question about the status of the soul after death?" (Chakrabarti, 2006, p. 12).

The concept of karma (action) as having consequences for the person beyond death relates to another concept developed in the Upanishads, rebirth. We have seen that the Upanishads contained the notion of a cyclical return to life as a mechanistic process by which the constitutive elements of the dead person dissolve into the natural elements, thereby contributing to the conditions that bring about a new human birth. Alongside that idea is the concept of karma as intentional action that results in a future rebirth related to one's past actions. *Samsara*, then, is the unending cycle of death and rebirth fueled by karma; it is the arena for the working out of the consequences of action. It is from this karma-driven, birth-leading-inevitably-to-death process that liberation (*moksha*) is sought. Such liberation is further related to the Upanishadic concepts of *atman* and *brahman*. Both words have multiple meanings and are used differently in different contexts. *Atman* can function simply as a reflexive pronoun (myself) or refer to the person holistically as a living entity, or it can have a more spiritual connotation referring to the innermost immaterial essence of a human being. Similarly, *brahman* in the earliest Vedic texts refers to the powerful force generated by the correct performance of sacrificial rites; it also means "a formulation of truth," or it can refer to the Supreme Being, or an impersonal absolute – the ultimate ground and essence of the universe. The meanings that we will explore are of *atman* as innermost essence and *brahman* as universal ground of existence.

With regard to liberation from *samsara*, the Upanishads uphold the idea of what they call the "Imperishable," the ultimate foundation of all existence. It is described as:

> Neither coarse nor fine; it is neither short nor long; it has neither blood nor fat; it is without shadow or darkness; it is without air or space; it is without contact; it has no taste or smell; it is without sight or hearing; it is without speech or mind; it is without energy, breath, or mouth; it is beyond measure; it has nothing within it or outside of it; it does not eat anything; and no one eats it. (BU 3.8.8)

> This is the imperishable . . ., which sees but can't be seen; which hears but can't be heard; which thinks but can't be thought of; which perceives but can't be perceived. Besides this imperishable, there is no one that sees, no one that hears, no one that thinks, and no one that perceives. (BU 3.8.11)

This imperishable is identified with the inner self in a multidimensional way. So with regard to nature it is said,

> This self (*atman*) of yours who is present within but is different from the earth, whom the earth does not know, whose body is the earth,

and who controls the earth from within – he is the inner controller, the immortal. [The same for water, fire, air, wind, sky, sun, moon, stars, space, darkness, light.] (BU 3.7.3–14)

And with regard to the human body,

> This self of yours who is present within but is different from the breath, whom the breath does not know, whose body is the breath, and who controls the breath from within – he is the inner controller, the immortal. [The same for speech, sight, hearing, mind, skin, perception, and semen.]

> He sees, but he can't be seen; he hears, but he can't be heard; he thinks, but he can't be thought of; he perceives, but he can't be perceived. Besides him, there is no one who sees, no one who hears, no one who thinks, and no one who perceives. It is this self of yours who is the inner controller, the immortal. (BU 3.7.16–23)

These passages, then, give us an understanding of *atman*, "this self of yours," as the imperishable, ineffable innermost essence not only of a human being but also of the entire universe. A corresponding concept is found in the idea of *brahman*. *Brahman* is the imperishable foundation of existence that pervades all and at the same time transcends all phenomena. On the one hand, *brahman* cannot be defined or described by any language whatsoever because language operates only in the realm of duality and limits, whereas *brahman* is one, without another by which it can be characterized; therefore, all that can be said of it is "*neti, neti*," "not this, not that." On the other hand, *brahman* pervades all existence, so the Upanishads say:

> You are woman; you are man; you are a boy or also a girl. As an old man you totter along with a walking stick. As you are born, you turn your face in every direction.
> You are the dark blue bird, the green one with red eyes, the raincloud, the seasons, and the oceans. You live as one without a beginning because of your pervasiveness, you from whom all beings have been born. (BU 4.3–4)

The nature of *atman* and *brahman* and the relationship of these concepts to each other and to the concepts of karma and rebirth take up many discussions in the Upanishads and continued to be debated among Hindu philosophers centuries later. In general, *brahman* refers to the imperishable spiritual core, the sustaining essence of the universe, understood either as an impersonal indescribable absolute or as a personal God that is transcendent yet enters into all things. *Atman* refers to the immutable, imperishable sustaining essence or soul of an individual living being, any individual being, human or animal. The soul itself is not differentiated, so the innermost essence of a human is no different from the innermost essence of an ant, but due to karma, the unchanging *atman* becomes associated with a new body in each birth – the nature of that body depending on past karma. So long as a person has not recognized or realized the true nature of the innermost self, so long does the individual carry out ego-oriented intentional action (karma) and reap the results of such action, life after life in *samsara*. To be liberated from the cycle of rebirth and redeath is to realize that *atman*, the foundation and essence of the individual, is identical with *brahman*, the foundation and essence of the universe. In the *Chandogya Upanishad*, a father teaches his son that the innermost essence of a living creature is the very self or innermost essence of this whole world. Just as the finest unseen essence of a seed is the foundation of the immense banyan tree, so:

"The finest essence here – that constitutes the self of this whole world; that is the truth; that is the self (*atman*). And that's how you are [*tat tvam asi*], Śvetaketu." (CU 6.8.7)

There are differing interpretations of the unity between the individual soul and *brahman*. Those philosophers who view *brahman* from the perspective of impersonal absolute regard *atman* and *brahman* as identical and, therefore, liberation is the realization of this nondifference. For those who interpret *brahman* as personal God, liberation is the inseparable union of the individual soul and the Supreme

Being. As we will see below, this latter interpretation supports the popular path of devotion.

In the House of Death

The story of the Brahmin boy, Naciketas, who questions the Lord of Death and learns from him the truth of what happens after death ties together the ritual world of the Vedas and the philosophical inquiry of the Upanishads. According to the dialogue found in the *Katha Upanishad*, Naciketas is watching as his father presents a procession of cattle as offerings for a sacrifice; he notices that the cows are all barren and milked dry. To make up for these inferior gifts he suggests three times to his father that he (the son) should be offered as a gift: "Father, to whom will you give me?" The father, angered by the implication that he has not offered his best possessions, finally shouts at him, "I'll give you to Death!" (KaU 1.4). Naciketas, as an obedient son, follows his father's wishes and goes to the house of Yama, but finds him absent. After three days, Yama returns, and in order to make up for this breach in protocol in receiving an honored guest, he offers Naciketas three favors.

For his first wish, Naciketas requests that his father's anger be appeased and that he would greet him joyfully when he returns. Yama agrees to release the boy and tells him that his father will be happy to see him released from the jaws of death. For his second wish, Naciketas asks to be taught how to build the fire altar that leads to heaven. Yama teaches him all that he needs to know and is pleased with his student's aptitude. Finally, for his third wish Naciketas asks to be taught the truth about the existence of a person after death. "There is this doubt about a man who is dead. 'He exists,' say some; others, 'He exists not.' I want to know this, so please teach me" (KaU 1.20). Yama is not eager to give this teaching and begs to be released from this wish. He presses Naciketas to ask any other favor of him: he could choose to live as long as he wished, or he could choose untold wealth; or both together. Yama is ready to grant any wish but the one that has been asked. Naciketas, however, is not to be deterred:

> Since the passing days of a mortal, O Death,
> Sap here the energy of all the senses;
> And even a full life is but a trifle
> So keep your horses, your songs and dances!
>
> With wealth you cannot make a man content;
> Will we get to keep wealth, when we have seen you?
> And we get to live only as long as you will allow!
> So, this alone is the wish that I'd like to choose. (KaU 1.26–27)

Yama realizes that Naciketas is wise enough to choose the good over the immediately gratifying and agrees to grant his wish. Yama first teaches him how to use the sacred syllable OM as a meditative support for the deepest realization. Then he tells him:

> The wise one –
> He is not born, he does not die;
> He has not come from anywhere;
> He has not become anyone.
> He is unborn and eternal, primeval and everlasting.
> And he is not killed, when the body is killed. (KaU 2.18)

The implication here is that Naciketas' question does not apply to the reality of things. The essential self of a person cannot be said to exist or not exist after death because questions of existence and non-existence apply only to that which is born and which dies. The *atman*, however, is unborn and undying. It cannot be grasped by speech or mind or sight, and can only be realized by those whose desires have all been cut:

> When they are all banished,
> Those desires lurking in one's heart
> Then a mortal becomes immortal,
> And attains *brahman* in this world

When the knots are all cut,
that bind one's heart on earth;
Then a mortal becomes immortal –
For such is the teaching. (KU 6.14–15)

In the Upanishads, then, we find the notion that after death a person either attains the world of the fathers, from which he or she returns, or the heaven of *Brahman*, from which there is no return, but there is also the suggestion that liberation from *samsara* is not a matter of going anywhere after death, but a matter of realizing *atman*. The theme of the nature of the soul and the pathways that a person can take to achieve liberation is taken up in the *Bhagavad Gita*, one of the most popular and revered of Hindu texts.

The Three Paths to Liberation

The *Bhagavad Gita* (Song of the Lord) was composed sometime between 200 BCE and 200 CE and forms part of the great epic called the *Mahabharata*, which tells the story of a war between two sets of cousins together with their allies: the five Pandava brothers and the one hundred Kaurava brothers. The *Gita* portrays a conversation between Arjuna, the greatest warrior of the Pandavas, and Krishna, his charioteer. When this conversation takes place, Arjuna is about to enter into battle. He and his army represent Dharma (truth and righteousness); on the opposing side are his Kaurava cousins and uncles, and the teachers they have shared growing up together. Although Arjuna knows that he is fighting to uphold righteousness against evil, he is smitten by doubt and the feeling that to kill family members and revered teachers is a great moral evil that will bring him to hell. In this state of mind, he listens to the counsel that Krishna, the charioteer, offers him.

Krishna reveals himself to Arjuna as no ordinary charioteer but the divine lord of all, Vishnu, who has incarnated on earth in the form of Krishna to protect and guide his devotees. In the *Gita*, God is not an impersonal absolute about which nothing can be said. Vishnu/Krishna describes himself as the essence of all things, the ultimate source, as well as the sustainer, and destroyer, of the universe.

> Learn that this is the womb
> of all creatures:
> I am the source of all the universe,
> just as I am its dissolution.
>
> Nothing is higher than I am;
> Arjuna, all that exists
> is woven on me,
> like a web of pearls on thread.
>
> I am the taste in water, Arjuna,
> the light in the moon and the sun,
> OM resonant in all sacred lore,
> the sound in space, valor in men.
>
> I am the pure fragrance
> in earth, the brilliance in fire,
> the life in all living creatures,
> the penance in ascetics. (*Gita* 7.6–9)

In his counsel to Arjuna, Krishna tells him that he must find the courage to do his duty, to uphold righteousness against evil. He tells him that his actions are not what they seem because the soul transcends time and the body:

> You grieve for those beyond grief,
> And you speak words of insight;
> But learned men do not grieve
> For the dead or the living.
>
> Never have I not existed,
> Nor you, nor these kings;
> And never in the future
> Shall we cease to exist.

Indestructible is the presence
That pervades all this;
No one can destroy
This unchanging reality.

Our bodies are known to end,
But the embodied self is enduring,
Indestructible and immeasurable;
Therefore, Arjuna, fight the battle!

It is not born,
It does not die;
Having been,
It will never not be;
Unborn, enduring,
Constant and primordial,
It is not killed
When the body is killed. (*Gita* 2.11)

As mentioned above, Hindu thought, from the time of the Upanishads, proposed that until the nature of the innermost self (*atman*) was realized and liberation obtained, the person was reborn life after life, appearing in various forms according to karma. This is *samsara*, the constant round of birth and death in which all individual lives are subject to suffering and destruction. In order to escape this cycle that is bound to death, the *Gita* describes three paths (*marga*) to liberation: the path of action, the path of knowledge, and the path of devotion. Each of these paths or ways involves its own type of discipline or *yoga*.

The path and discipline of action (*karma yoga*) has its roots in the Vedic ritual world where karma meant the ritual action of the sacrifice that brought about effects such as good crops and wealth, and that resulted after death in the person being able to find his way to the world of the fathers. In the *Gita*, however, the path of action is related to the Upanishadic notion of karma as intentional action driven by one's desires, positive or negative. Karma yoga, then, means the discipline of acting according to Dharma without fear of punishment or hope of reward; simply dedicating all actions to God and letting go of desire for, and attachment to, the results of one's efforts:

> A man who relinquishes attachment
> and dedicates actions to the infinite spirit
> is not stained by evil,
> like a lotus leaf unstained by water.
>
> Relinquishing the fruit of action,
> the disciplined man attains perfect peace;
> the undisciplined man is in bondage,
> attached to the fruit of his desire. (*Gita* 5.10, 12)

Ordinary worldly action, even religious rites and rituals, if they are self-oriented, serve only to bind the person to death and rebirth, but through the karma yoga described in the *Gita*, one can participate in the world, carrying out one's worldly duties in such a way that action leads to liberation.

The path and discipline of knowledge (*jnana yoga*) refers to the study of the scriptures and philosophic analysis through which one comes to understand the nature of ignorance and the ways in which human beings are bound or released. Beyond mere book knowledge, however, is the knowledge or realization of the innermost essence (*atman*) arising from the yogic discipline of restraining the senses in meditation:

> Disciplining himself,
> his mind controlled;
> a man of discipline finds peace,
> the pure calm that exists in me.
>
> Absolute joy beyond the senses
> can only be grasped by understanding;
> when one knows it, he abides there
> and never wanders from this reality. (*Gita* 6.15, 21)

This is the path of scholars, philosophers, and strong meditators.

Finally, the path and discipline of devotion (*bhakti yoga*) is the one most strongly advocated in the *Gita*. Krishna says, "Arjuna, know that no one devoted to me is lost" (*Gita* 9.31). It is the surest path and the simplest, open to everyone, saints and sinners, rich or poor, those with many duties or those with few, regardless of gender or social standing; one need only turn to God with true loving devotion and it will be returned.

> Relinquishing all sacred duties to me,
> Make me your only refuge;
> Do not grieve,
> For I shall free you from all evils. (*Gita* 18.66)

Arjuna asks Krishna which type of discipline is better, the path of devoted action or the path of knowledge. Krishna responds that both ways lead to liberation, but the path of knowledge is more difficult, whereas liberation through devotion requires only that a person love Krishna, and make him the object of all their faith, dedicating all actions to him, seeing him in all things and all things in him.

> Whatever you do – what you take,
> What you offer, what you give,
> What penances you perform –
> Do as an offering to me, Arjuna! (*Gita* 9.27)
>
> He who sees me everywhere
> And sees everything in me
> Will not be lost to me,
> And I will not be lost to him.
>
> I exist in all creatures,
> So the disciplined man devoted to me
> Grasps the oneness of life;
> Wherever he is, he is in me. (*Gita* 6.30–31)

Rituals of Departure

Although burial is not unknown among Hindus,[8] from Vedic times until the present, the most common form of disposal has been cremation, called the "last sacrifice" (*antyeshti*) because it is regarded as an offering to the fire god. The death rituals and annual post-cremation rituals called *shraddha* (ancestral rites) are traditionally performed by the eldest son and relatives of the deceased. These rituals consist of offerings intended to establish a new body for the deceased in the world of the fathers, thereby transforming the deceased from a ghost (*preta*) into an ancestor, and subsequently are intended to sustain the deceased and all the past ancestors. As we will see, contemporary Hindu funeral practices reflect an amalgam of beliefs that embrace: the world of the fathers as the ancient Vedic dwelling place of the ancestors; the Upanishadic vision of ultimate liberation from an endless cycle of rebirth; and the hope of attaining to the heaven of a beloved deity enshrined in devotional Hinduism.

In her comparison of Hindu death rituals in India and Britain, Shirley Firth (1997) outlines nine stages: (1) preparation for death; (2) the moment of death; (3) preparation of the body; (4) procession to the cremation ground; (5) cremation; (6) disposal of the ashes; (7) *shraddha* rituals; (8) *sapindikarana*;[9] (9) annual *shraddha* ritual. Firth's work shows how difficult it is for traditional rituals to be maintained in a culturally alien environment, especially because death, which is a home and communal affair in traditional societies, has become, in western culture, the domain of medical and funeral establishments and professionals who do not always assign importance to, or opportunity for, traditional customs. State laws and bureaucracy also take precedence over religious custom. For example, due to environmental regulations in Britain, the body must be transported to the crematorium in a closed casket rather than, as is the custom in India, on a bier where the face of the deceased can be seen by the mourners.[10] As one of Firth's informants points out, "We are living in a culture where we are not in control" (Firth, 1997, p. 85). In the following, we will examine some of the main features of Hindu death rituals and note some of the compromises that have to be made outside of India. Bear in mind, however, that death rituals do not always conform to what may be considered correct according to the orthodox Brahmanic literature, but vary according to local, regional, and even family traditions and customs.

Among Hindus, at the moment of death, a person should ideally be at home, close to the earth, i.e., on the floor, surrounded by loving family, with the name of God on their lips. When a person is known to be dying, part of the preparation for death includes an "act of penance," i.e., the donation by family members of money or gifts to Brahmin priests or to charities; land may also be given by the wealthy. A small silver image of a cow is often given to signify the tradition of offering a cow – the Vaitarani cow, which gift is said to give the soul safe passage across the fearsome Vaitarani River that separates this world from Yama's kingdom (Firth, 1997, p. 62).

At the moment of death or immediately thereafter, water from the sacred Ganges River and a leaf of the sacred tulsi (basil) plant are placed in the mouth of the deceased. This is one of the most important services the family can perform for the deceased; in one case when it was prevented by hospital medical staff, the family were still distressed even 10 years later and felt that they would not be free of their responsibility for seven generations (Firth, 1997, pp. 117–118). Cremation should take place within 24 hours if possible, so in India, the body is washed and dressed in new clothes as soon as possible by members of the same sex and caste,[11] a gold or silver coin is placed in the mouth (to pay the ferryman), and the body is circumambulated by the mourners. From the moment of death throughout the mourning period, which varies according to caste and the relationship of the mourners to the deceased, the family is considered to be in a state of ritual impurity due to the pollution of death. Death is a dangerous period of transition for the soul that plunges the entire family into a liminal state. In their state of impurity, mourners may not visit the temple or the homes of friends or participate in any social or religious functions. Friends and relatives may visit the family to pay their condolences, but must ritually purify themselves upon leaving by bathing.

In India, the flower-bedecked body is transported on an open bier on foot carried by the men of the family or other male caste members. There are several stops along the way for offerings of rice balls (*pindas*) to be made. These offerings are intended as both nourishment and protection for the spirit (Firth, 1997, p. 75). At the cremation ground the eldest son (or in some cases the youngest son) lights the funeral pyre after circumambulating the body and sprinkling water around it.

> The circles of water purify the soul, enable it to rise upwards in the direction it is supposed to go, protect it from the dangers of the cremation ground, and create a boundary between the living and the dead, thus symbolizing both separation and farewell. (Firth, 1997, p. 77)

In order to finally release the soul, the skull is broken, either literally or symbolically through the breaking of a pot, which is thrown backward by the chief mourner who walks away without looking back. This ritual also appears to have the function of breaking the connection between the deceased and the chief mourner so that the spirit does not follow him back to the village.

In Britain, since the body is most often removed to a funeral home, the preparation of the body and cremation are more likely to take place up to a week or more after death. If the preparation of the body is done at the funeral home, then the coffin is taken by hearse to the family home for the funeral (or a simplified ceremony may be carried out at the funeral home). There, around the open coffin, the domestic rituals of decorating the body, circumambulating it, and offering the rice balls (here placed in the coffin) that would have been performed in India at the time of preparing the body and at the cremation ground are carried out. There is no ritual procession but the men of the family carry the coffin from the home to the hearse and into the chapel at the crematorium. After prayers are said, the chief mourner and male relatives go below to throw the switch that ignites the cremator. The ashes are gathered and dispersed in a river or ocean. The disposal of the ashes both in India and elsewhere often forms part of a longer pilgrimage to a holy river like the Ganges, but in the end as some suggest, all rivers run to the sea and wherever the ashes are scattered, faith is the most important thing.

The ceremonies that take place in the 10 or 11 days following death are called *shraddha*; they consist of three sets of rituals: (1) those that take place over the first ten days intended to create for the deceased a temporary body; (2) those that take place on the eleventh day intended to give the soul strength for its journey to the world of the fathers and assist the soul to negotiate the passage from disembodied spirit to ancestor; and (3) the *sapindikarana* ritual on the twelfth day that marks the final transformation of the deceased from a potentially wandering and dangerous spirit (*preta*) into a divine and benevolent ancestor spirit (*pitr*). Originally this process was intended to take 12 months of daily ritual activity. It now takes place in the 11 days after death and the *sapindikarana* ritual that establishes the deceased as an ancestor takes place on the twelfth day at the end of a symbolic year. The rituals of the first ten days are also often condensed into the ritual on the eleventh or twelfth day. In its most extended form, on the first day after death, the chief mourner forms a ball of rice (*pinda*) about the size of a tennis ball that represents the *preta* (the deceased's spirit) and pours over it a cup of water. This is the beginning of the creation of a new body, the head on the first day, the neck and shoulders the next, the heart and torso the next, and so on. Each day the cup of water is increased by one so that there are ten cups of water on the tenth day (Knipe, 1977, pp. 114–115). This concludes the period of extreme impurity and the family can now take a purifying bath and invite into the home the Brahmin priests who receive food and gifts on behalf of the deceased in order to fulfill all the needs of the soul in the coming 12-month journey. The climax of the *shraddha* rites is the *sapindikarana* ritual on the twelfth day in which the soul is transformed into an ancestor and united with the past generations of ancestors. This is shown concretely in the ritual by the cutting of the *pinda* that represents the deceased and mixing it with the *pindas* representing the past three generations, saying, "Go to your father (grandfather, great-grandfather)."

> Finally, the three are blended into one, and in *that moment* the deceased has passed from the preta [disembodied spirit] to the *pitr* [ancestor] stage and has joined the revered company of the ancestors at home in the three worlds... (Knipe, 1977, p. 121)

The *sapindikarana* ritual of the twelfth day brings to a close the funeral rituals and mourning period and the oil lamp that has been kept burning for the deceased throughout the mourning period can now be allowed to burn out. Every year, on the death anniversary, to ensure the well-being of the parents, whether as ancestors or in their next incarnation, sons are obliged to perform a *shraddha* ritual in which Brahmins are fed, given gifts, and alms distributed to the poor.

It should be noted that the final destination of the deceased soul would be further related to the person's spiritual practice in life, so, for example, the devotees of Vishnu would be expected to eventually reside in Vaikunta, the heaven of Vishnu, and a devotee of Shiva finds their way to Kailash. Yet, even this is not the end of the journey for most, because after a time, the soul would again be reincarnated according to its past karma to continue the cycle of birth and death until such time as liberation from rebirth is attained.

There is nothing definitive about such death rituals; they are in constant negotiation as the demands of culture, tradition, and orthodoxy are balanced with the needs of family, the pull of modernity, and the weight of custom. We can recognize in the rituals described above the cosmology of the ancient Vedic world and their concern with the welfare of the ancestors alongside beliefs in karma, transmigration, and liberation, as well as the fear of the spirits of the dead that is found in folk religions the world over, and finally, the hope of every devoted worshipper of God that he or she will dwell in God's presence.

A Conversation on Understanding Death

With Sudha and Harsha Dehejia

Sudha Dehejia is an Ottawa pediatrician who was born and raised in the Indian city of Mumbai. Along with her physician husband Harsha, she spent time in England and America before settling in Canada where they have lived for the last 43 years. Sudha's family spans the two worlds of India and Canada, with one son being born in India and one in Canada.

She remembers her first striking encounter with the death of a child in her profession back in Mumbai where she watched helplessly as a 9-year-old boy died from aplastic anemia brought about by the side effects of antibiotics. As a physician, she tells me, "You are not merely an onlooker, one must feel. To have compassion is

192

to be involved and to understand what the child and the parents are going through." When I ask what gives her comfort, she turns to the Hindu teachings of rebirth. "Death is not final; it is your body that leaves you. To speak of death, we say, *'dehant'* 'the end of the body.' Devotees of Vishnu would say the person is *'Vaikunth nivasi'* or those who worship Shiva would say *'Kailash nivasi'* meaning 'gone to dwell in the abode of Vishnu or Shiva.'" "A Hindu never dies," Harsha interjects, "death signifies a change in location, not a change in *atman*, one's essential state of being." Sudha reminds me of the *Bhagavad Gita*, which says, "Our bodies are known to end, but the embodied self [*atman*] is enduring, indestructible, and immeasurable." For Sudha, comfort is in the interconnections that are not severed at death. She notes that "it is because of the belief in rebirth that the death ceremonies are focused on helping the person to achieve a good continuation in their next life, as well as ritually finishing up the unfinished business of life so that the *atman* might be free to leave its associations with this life and go forward without the entanglements of unfulfilled desires and feelings."

Harsha is an art lover and storyteller, and he points out that "it is precisely through the medium of stories, television, and street plays that the Hindu philosophy that death is not the end of life but part of the ongoing cycle of birth and death is shared by street dwellers and elite alike." He stresses the circularity of existence, "whatever is born must die, and whatever dies is reborn," and notes that so many rituals of ordinary Hindus underscore this thought, "from the housewife who daily chalks a simple auspicious design (*rangoli*) on her doorstep and daily wipes it clean, to the worship of the goddess Savithri under a banyan tree at which the women pray to be reunited with their husbands for seven more lives."

When I ask Sudha about her own death and preparing for death, she comments that "perhaps when I was younger, it would have been harder because I would see all the unfinished business of my life, but now I feel that I have accomplished what I need to do." As far as preparing for death, she continues, "One lets go of one's own miseries by thinking of others, looking after society, learning to transform the particular into the universal – *Vasudhaiva kutumbakam*, 'the whole world is family.'" "Hinduism," she says, "honors every stage of life – as a student, as a householder, and in the end, renunciation of worldly life. I am now in the *vanaprastha* (literally, 'gone to the forest') stage and it is natural to turn one's mind from worldly things to spiritual thoughts."

Notes

1. Translation by Wendy Doniger in *The Rig Veda* (New York: Penguin Books, 1984), p. 52.
2. *Shraddhā* (faith) is cognate with the word *shrāddha*, the funeral ritual of making offerings to benefit the soul of an ancestor.
3. Soma also refers to the intoxicating drink of the gods, which was said to be contained in the moon. Here Soma refers to the moon itself, where the dead go after they leave the world of the fathers to become elixir for the gods, passing then into the sky, then into the wind, then into the rain, then into plants, which become food, which becomes semen, which becomes the child, which dies and rises up to the heavenly world of the fathers.
4. Translation by Raimundo Panikkar in *The Vedic Experience* (Pondicherry: All India Books, 1983), p. 555.
5. Ibid., p. 556.
6. Ibid., p. 538.
7. Ibid.
8. For example, among certain sects or for small children and *sannyasins* (renunciates who have already passed through a ritual death) or due to disease or disaster.
9. According to *The Illustrated Encyclopedia of Hinduism* (Lochtefeld, 2002), *sapinda* means "having a common body" in the sense of people who share a common ancestral line going back seven generations. Traditionally, marriage was prohibited between people who were in a *sapinda* relationship to each other. *Sapindikarana* is the ritual of uniting the spirit of the deceased with the ancestral spirits – making them of one body.

10. In 2006, mourners in India rioted at the procession of the South Indian film star Raj Kumar because they were unable to view the body as it was taken through the streets.
11. For men, it would be clothes they normally wear. If the deceased is a woman with a living husband, she would be dressed in her wedding sari; if a widow, in a white sari.

References and Further Reading

Chakrabarti, Arindam. "What Is It Like To Die? The Vedic Picture and Subsequent Indian Philosophical Debates Concerning Afterlife." In *Dying, Death, and Afterlife in Dharma Traditions and Western Religions*. Hampton, VA: Deepak Heritage Books, 2006, pp. 1–28.

Firth, Shirley. *Dying, Death and Bereavement in a British Hindu Community*. Leuven: Peeters, 1997.

Kaelber, Walter O. *Tapta Mārga: Asceticism and Initiation in Vedic India*. Albany: State University of New York Press, 1989.

Knipe, David M. "Sapiṇḍīkaraṇa: The Hindu Rite of Entry into Heaven." In Frank Waugh and Earlie Reynolds (eds.), *Religious Encounters with Death*. University Park: Pennsylvania University Press, 1977, pp. 111–124.

Lochtefeld, James G. *The Illustrated Encyclopedia of Hinduism*, Volume 2. New York: Rosen Publishing Group, 2002.

Olivelle, Patrick. *Upaniṣads*. Oxford: Oxford University Press, 1996.

Reat, N. Ross. *The Origins of Indian Psychology*. Berkeley, CA: Asian Humanities Press, 1990.

8

Buddhist Perspectives on Death

Buddhism arose in the socio-political and religious context of Brahmanic India. It accepted the Hindu worldview of intentional action (*karma*) leading to rebirth and redeath in the cycle of *samsara*. However, the Buddha rejected the orthodox belief of his time that the eternal soul (*atman*) transmigrated from life to life taking on new forms until it achieved final liberation. He claimed that no matter how much one searched, no unchanging, eternal component of the human personality could be found; human beings and, indeed, all other existing things were composed of ever-changing phenomena. His teaching on the subject, therefore, was that the human personality is without soul or unchanging essence (Skt: *anatman* / Pali: *anatta*). Buddhist doctrine regarding the soul-less or essence-less nature of all phenomena challenges notions of the individual self or soul shared by other religions and raises the question – who or what continues? This chapter will examine the life of the Buddha and discuss Buddhist beliefs regarding the continuation of the person over many

Understanding Death: An Introduction to Ideas of Self and the Afterlife in World Religions, First Edition. Angela Sumegi.
© 2014 Angela Sumegi. Published 2014 by Blackwell Publishing Ltd.

lives, the worlds of rebirth, and eventual liberation from the cycle of birth and death in relation to the teaching on "no-soul."

The Life and Death of the Buddha

Firm historical evidence for a biography of the Buddha is scarce. We cannot even establish with any certainty the exact dates of his birth and death. For a long time western scholars accepted the dates 566–486 or 583–483 BCE, but recent research suggests a later date of 490–410 or 480–400 BCE (Prebish and Keown, 2006, p. 27). Looking for the historical Buddha is much like looking for the historical Jesus – the textual sources that we rely on were written by those who were less interested in the facts of their lives and more interested in interpreting the meaning of their lives, sometimes for religious doctrinal purposes, sometimes to serve socio-political ends. In seeking out the events of the past, historians are aware that what may have been an historical event is most often embedded in layers of meaning that have been assigned to it, and vice versa; some events are "historical" because meaning requires it. It is not our task, however, in this book to disentangle history from pious legend; in order to discover the meanings that have been assigned to death and deathlessness in the founding days of Buddhism, we will explore the life of the Buddha as it has been traditionally recorded. One of the earliest biographies of the Buddha, called the *Buddhacarita* (Acts of the Buddha), was written by Asvaghosha in the second century CE. It presents us with the life story of the Buddha according to 12 archetypal acts or events. This biography is not merely concerned with the life history of one man; it intends to show the meaning of Buddhahood and how one arrives at that state. The story, therefore, is cast in a cosmic context in which karma and rebirth are operative.

In Asvaghosha's work, after many eons of lifetimes of meritorious action and training in the path of a *Bodhisattva* (Buddha-to-be), the first act in the career of a Buddha is for him to be born into the heaven world where he waits for the conditions to be right to enter into his last birth. Having decided on the time, the place, and the family into which he will be born, the second act is the descent of the *Bodhisattva* from the heaven world, and third, his entry into the womb. This is described in terms of a conception dream had by Maya, the mother of the present Buddha, who dreamed of a pure white elephant that entered her from the right side. The dream interpreters are called in and they proclaim that this dream means that she will give birth to a son who will be as great among men as the elephant is among beasts. The fourth act is birth. The Buddha is said to have been born from the right side of his mother and upon leaving the womb took seven steps, proclaimed himself supreme in heaven and earth, and prophesied that this would be his last birth. His birth is said to have taken place on the full moon of *Vesak* (April–May). Brahmin soothsayers examined the child and pronounced that if he left the palace for the life of a wondering ascetic (*samana*), he would become an Awakened One, a Buddha, but if he remained in the worldly life he would become a great king, a world ruler. Not surprisingly, his father, who was himself a great chieftain, wished for his son to be a world ruler rather than a wandering beggar. The young man was named Siddhartha, his clan name was Gautama, and he belonged to the Shakya tribe. He was born into wealth and privilege, the son of a tribal chief in the warrior/ruling (*kshatriya*) class of sixth-century BCE Brahmanic society. We are told that his father tried to shield him from the ugliness of the world by confining him to the luxury of the palaces and surrounding him with beauty; so the fifth act of a Buddha is to live the palace life of luxury and learning.

However, this was not his destiny and, as the story goes, despite his wealth and comfort, the young prince suffered from despondency. So, to raise his spirits, his father arranged a pleasure outing through the town, the streets of which were first completely beautified and cleared of all beggars, the sick, and aged. The gods, however, arranged for the prince to encounter the reality of the human condition in the form of four persons: a bent and aged man, a horribly diseased man, a corpse, and a wandering *samana* (one who has renounced the household life to seek for liberation). In the sixth act, then, the *Bodhisattva*, realizing the universal and inescapable nature of suffering, experiences disgust and disenchantment not only with

199

the frivolity of palace life, but with all that *samsara* has to offer. In the seventh act, at age 29, he renounces his life as a prince, leaves his parents, wife, and son behind, and becomes a wandering *samana*, seeking the truth that frees a person from suffering and death.

After studying with a number of teachers whose doctrines and practices he mastered, but which did not lead him to the liberating knowledge he was seeking, Gautama, as he was known to the *samana* community he joined, struck out on his own. In the eighth act, the *Bodhisattva* enters into six years of the most severe austerities that leave him completely emaciated and near death. After subjecting himself to years of severe ascetic practices, however, he realized that for what he was seeking, asceticism was also a dead end. Finally, he settled himself beside a river, under a pipal tree at a place called Bodhgaya, and embarked on the meditative path that led him to knowledge and insight, the liberation (*nirvana*) he was seeking. On the night of his liberation we are told that he was assailed by the demon Mara, who represents desire, death, and all the outer and inner obstacles to liberation. Mara tried to turn him from his course through argument, seduction, and fear, but he was unsuccessful; the ninth act, therefore, is the defeat of Mara, the defeat of death. Following the defeat of Mara is the tenth act: full awakening or *nirvana*. From this point on, Gautama becomes known as the Buddha, the Awakened One.

According to Buddhist legend, the Buddha was not at all sure that ordinary people who are driven by passions and prejudices would understand what he had experienced or the insights that he had gained; so, rather than go out and propagate any doctrine, his first inclination was to keep silent and simply enjoy the bliss of *nirvana*. However, the tradition says that one of the gods came to the Buddha and urged him to teach, saying that there were indeed some people with only a little dust in their eyes who would be able to understand the dharma that the Buddha taught. And so out of compassion and because he was asked, Gautama Buddha decided to teach. He made his way on foot from Bodhgaya to the Deer Park at Sarnath where he met up with five *samanas* who listened to his first teaching. And so the Buddha performed the eleventh act, called "setting in motion the wheel of dharma," by giving his first public sermon to these five who became the first members of the Buddhist monastic order called the *sangha*. For 45 years, the Buddha wandered all around the central Gangetic plain in the kingdom of Magadha, teaching in towns, parks, and villages, and ordaining those who wished to follow him as monks. When he was 80 years old he set out on his last journey. On that journey, it is said he ate a meal at the home of a low-caste blacksmith that made him ill with food poisoning. He continued on to the small and obscure village of Kushinagar (Kusinara) where he could not go further and, after giving his final instructions to his followers, passed away. Since one who has attained liberation is not reborn, the death of a Buddha is referred to as *parinirvana*, the attaining of *nirvana* with nothing remaining. The twelfth act of a Buddha, then, is attaining *parinirvana*.

The Buddha's death underscores one of the foremost elements in Buddhist doctrine – the impermanence of all compounded phenomena. According to the *Mahaparinibbana sutta*, the Buddha's last words to his disciples reminded them of this simple fact: "Decay is inherent in all component things! Work out your salvation with diligence!" (Coward et al., 1988, p. 140). The Buddha's body was cremated and his relics divided among the local rulers, who interred them in a special type of monument called a *stupa*. The *stupa* developed out of what was originally a burial mound; by the time of the Buddha, it had become a more elaborate structure intended to hold the relics and commemorate the death of a great ruler or spiritual leader. The preferred method of disposal of the body among Buddhists until today is cremation, and the relics of great Buddhist masters are still interred in *stupas*. They appear in many different cultural forms but in all Buddhist countries, *stupas* are revered as symbols that recall the Buddha's enlightenment and victory over death.

The Noble Truths

The Buddha's first teaching to a group of five *samanas* laid down the foundational insights that inform all Buddhist traditions. In it, he rejects the pursuit of sense pleasures as one extreme and that of self-mortification as another, both of which he had experienced. As the middle way, the Buddha puts forward what he calls the noble eightfold path leading to insight and liberation: right view, right intention, right speech, right action, right livelihood, right effort, right mindfulness, and right concentration. The eightfold path itself is set in the context of the four noble truths, all focused on the nature of suffering (*dukkha*).

1. The Noble Truth of Suffering
2. The Noble Truth of the Origin of Suffering
3. The Noble Truth of the Cessation of Suffering
4. The Noble Truth of the (eightfold) Path leading to the Cessation of Suffering

This teaching is based on, and expresses, the overarching principle of cause and effect, the doctrine of "dependent origination," according to which, whatever exists originates, and continues to exist, dependent on the specific causes and conditions that gave rise to it, and ceases when those causes and conditions cease.

In order to understand the Buddhist view of death and liberation from death, we must analyze this word, *dukkha*. It covers a wide range of meanings that are traditionally grouped under three headings: (1) ordinary *dukkha*; (2) *dukkha* based on impermanence and change; and (3) *dukkha* based on conditioned states. Ordinary *dukkha* refers to what we normally regard as pain, either physical or mental. From the merest feeling of discomfort to the severest suffering, it connotes dissatisfaction or dis-ease of any kind. *Dukkha* produced by change refers to the distress that arises due to the loss that we experience when things we desire end, whether that is the loss of a happy physical or mental state, a desirable object, or a beloved person. *Dukkha* produced by conditioned states refers to the observation that anything composite and conditioned, like the human personality, is subject to decay and destruction. So this is another meaning of *dukkha* – the inevitable decay, death, or destruction of anything and everything that exists dependent on causes and conditions.

In Buddhist theory, *dukkha* is one of the three characteristics exhibited by all phenomena:

(1) The characteristic of *impermanence* (*anicca*) – all phenomena exist in a state of constant flux and change. Although objects like chairs and tables may appear solid and unchanging, upon analysis, the reality is that from moment to moment the object is continually undergoing change. With regard to persons, whether we consider mental aspects such as thoughts, mind states, emotions, psychological states, or the physical body, every part and piece is changing at every moment, coming into being and passing away.

(2) The characteristic of *essencelessness* or no-soul (*anatta*). This concept correlates with the previous understanding of the radical impermanence of all states of existence. With regard to the human person, again, upon analysis, what is found is an ever-changing series of mental and physical factors arising and ceasing in dependence on the presence or absence of specific causes and conditions. Although it may seem that there is some unchanging core that is "me," that persists unchanged throughout my life and throughout all the changes that occur to me, Buddhist theory claims that such a feeling is exactly that, simply a feeling that arises dependent on the functioning of the various mental and physical factors that comprise the personality. The reality is that no part of the body–mind organism is unchanging; therefore, the human person, like all other existents, is without any permanent unchanging, eternal essence or soul.

(3) The characteristic of *suffering* (*dukkha*) follows on the impermanent, essenceless nature of existing things. We can consider this in two ways, physically and emotionally. Physically, whatever comes into existence dependent on changing causes and conditions is bound to cease, to be destroyed when the causes and conditions that support it change; therefore, since all things exist dependently on other factors, all things are subject to *dukkha* in the sense of

destruction. Mentally or emotionally, we are happy when things that we fear or things that we do not want to exist end, but we suffer when those things that we desire, or that we are attached to or want to continue, end, and since all states end, then there is no escape from the *dukkha* of loss so long as there is attachment to that which is impermanent.

The first noble truth expresses the observation that *dukkha* is present as an element in all human existence. The second noble truth proposes that the primary cause of *dukkha* is unquenchable thirst-like craving for self-satisfaction and attachment to whatever we perceive as providing such self-satisfaction. Based on the law of cause and effect, the third noble truth proposes that if self-oriented craving is removed, then the effect, *dukkha*, will cease to arise. However, it is acknowledged that it is not a simple matter for human beings to abandon their yearnings and attachments, and that to do so requires an entire retraining of the personality. The fourth noble truth, therefore, offers a path, a method by which the mind can be trained to generate positive mental states, to become still and peaceful, and finally to gain the knowledge and insight that liberate one from suffering and death.

Karma, Self, and the Wheel of Becoming

Since Buddhism accepts the doctrine of karma and rebirth, but not the doctrine of a transmigrating soul, the question to investigate is, who or what continues from birth to birth and how does that take place? There is no simple or definitive answer to this question, which has informed Buddhist philosophical discussion for centuries. However, we can aim to understand some of the main elements that any answer must address. To understand how the personality continues after death, it is first necessary to understand how Buddhism views the continuing person in life. According to one analysis accepted by all Buddhist schools, a person consists of five collections or aggregates called the five *skandhas*. *Skandha* means heap, like a heap of rice grains or wheat grains – it is often translated "aggregate" to indicate the idea of compositeness.

(1) The aggregate of *matter* or form (i.e., physical elements – solids, liquids, gases, and the element of heat represented in all ancient systems by earth, water, air, and fire). With regard to personality, this aggregate includes the five physical sense organs and their five corresponding objects – appearances, sounds, smells, tastes, tangibles. In Buddhist thought, the mind is also a sense organ or sense faculty of a kind; it senses or comes into contact with thoughts, ideas, and conceptions.

(2) The aggregate of *sensations* or feelings. Contact between any one of the six sense organs and its corresponding object results in some feeling or sensation, which can be pleasant, painful, or neutral.

(3) The aggregate of *perceptions* or cognition. Contact results not only in sensation but also in perception or recognition, which is also of six kinds based on the six senses. We can speak of perception/ cognition arising based on the activity of eyes coming into contact with visible objects, or ears contacting audible objects, and so on.

(4) The aggregate of *karmic formations* or mental habit patterns. The Theravada school identifies 52 possible mental states that come under this heading, such as attentiveness, courage, confidence, will, anger, hate, determination, energy, laziness, the idea of self. All these are considered intentional, that is to say, they direct the mind towards wholesome, unwholesome, or neutral activity that manifests in thought, speech, and action, producing effects. They are called karmic formations because they are formed by past karma and they inform present action, which will shape future mental states. This aggregate, then, is very important in the religious understanding of the person because karma (self-oriented intentional action) is the driving force in the cycle of birth and death; karma is the force that creates future conditions. It is understood that the present personality has been shaped or formed by such intentional acts that took place in the past, and also that the present person shapes their own future through their own present intentions and actions. Karma is, therefore, nothing but the energy of these mental habit patterns that replicate

themselves endlessly into the future, manifesting in actions of body, speech, and mind that create further mental habit patterns on and on. The crucial point is that intention or volition is not anything fated, decreed, or ultimate in any sense. Intention is directed by the mind and although mental habit patterns, like all habits, are difficult to break or change, still, they are nothing more than habitual tendencies that, with effort, can be redirected by the mind.

Those not raised in a culture that accepts the idea of rebirth often understand the principle of karma and the way past action conditions future experiences as it applies to a single lifetime. Accepting that the same principle extends over many lifetimes is much more difficult. Questions of just exactly how the individual continues from life to life so that it could be said that my present life conditions are a result of my own past actions fuel much debate in the Buddhist world, especially among western Buddhists, many of whom, like Stephen Batchelor (1997), adopt an agnostic approach. The twentieth-century German scholar-monk Nyanatiloka Mahathera uses the analogy of a wave to explain the Buddhist perspective on rebirth.

> *Nothing transmigrates* from this moment to the next, nothing from one life to another life. This process of continually producing and being produced may best be compared with a wave on the ocean. In the case of a wave there is not the smallest quantity of water that actually travels over the surface of the sea. The wave-structure that seems to hasten over the surface of the water, though creating the appearance of one and the same mass of water, is in reality nothing but a continued rising and falling of ever new masses of water. And the rising and falling is produced by the transmission of force originally generated by wind. Just so the Buddha did not teach that it is an ego-entity, or a soul, that hastens through the ocean of rebirth, but that it is in reality merely a life-wave which, according to its nature and activities, appears here as man, there as animal, and elsewhere as invisible being.[1]

For those who struggle with these concepts, it may be of some solace to know that even in the Buddha's time, this doctrine raised questions. In one conversation with an ascetic the Buddha is asked whether present suffering is self-created.[2] He answers, "Don't say that." In other words, that's not the way to put it. The ascetic continues his questioning, asking then if present suffering is created by another, by both self and other, or perhaps just arises by chance. In each case the Buddha answers, "Don't say that." Finally, the exasperated man suggests that perhaps the Buddha is trying to tell him that suffering simply does not exist, or perhaps the Buddha does not know or does not see suffering, but the Buddha affirms that indeed suffering exists and indeed he does know and see it. When pressed to explain himself, the Buddha points out that if he were to agree that "I" am now experiencing the results of "my" past action, that would be one kind of extreme; it would imply that the person continues essentially unchanged, that there is some permanent essence that persists from life to life that is "me." On the other hand, if he were to agree that my past actions have nothing to do with my experiences in the present, that would be another extreme; it would imply that there is no continuity of the person. The Buddha refuses to be drawn into questions of identity. He rejects both extremes, pointing out that both are dead ends that do not lead to the cessation of suffering. Finally, he offers his own teaching as the middle way between the extremes of "I am" and "I am not," the teaching of cause and effect. Instead of focusing on the identity of the person who suffers, the Buddha focuses on the experience of suffering and how that arises and ceases dependent on causes and conditions.

(5) The aggregate of *consciousness*. Consciousness here does not mean some kind of spirit or soul that is separable or distinct from the person as a holistic entity. It refers to awareness that arises and disappears, moment by moment, due to the contact of the sense faculties with the external world. As with perception above, there would be six kinds of consciousness based on the six sense faculties. More accurately speaking, however, these are not different types of consciousnesses; they simply refer to awareness arising due to different conditions. The Buddha compared it to a fire that is called a wood fire if its fuel is wood or a straw fire if its fuel is straw (Rahula, 1974, p. 24). Although consciousness

is understood to manifest dependent on certain conditions, Buddhism does not accept that what is immaterial (i.e., consciousness) can be produced solely through material processes. Therefore, consciousness is thought to be one of the preconditions necessary for the development of a human being in the womb, and upon death, it is thought that the gross material and mental aspects of the person are destroyed but the stream of consciousness is not. It is propelled through the subtle energy of the person's past karmic habit patterns into a so-called new birth. "So-called" because in reality, there is nothing but the movement of phenomena, like a wave traveling across the ocean, driven by the wind, the wind of karma. Therefore, the Pali tradition says, the person who is reborn is not the same as the person who died, but not different (Rahula, 1974, p. 34). The fifth-century commentator Buddhaghosa writes that although no single thing (like a soul) passes over from one stream of ever-changing aggregates to another, still, the present aggregates come into being with past karma as their condition, and when they break up at death, although no single thing passes into the future, other aggregates will be formed with the karma of this life-stream as their condition.[3] On the notion of the self that acts and experiences, he writes that it is merely convention, a figure of speech:

> ... the wise say "doer" when there is doing and "experiencer" when there is experiencing [of the results of doing] simply as a mode of common usage.
>   Hence the Ancients said:
> "There is no doer of a deed
> Or one who reaps the deed's result;
> Phenomena alone flow on – " (Nanamoli, 1991, p. 623)

None of the five aggregates operates in isolation. They function together in a web of mutual influence and conditionality – sensations are influenced by physical and mental factors; mental states conditioned by sensations and perceptions; perceptions colored by mental and physical factors. These five aggregates acting together give rise to the feeling "I am," and the idea of an ultimately separate individual self is a thought which Buddhist psychology simply lists as one of the possible mental states that arise due to the functioning of the five aggregates. In one of the more famous explanations of *anatta*, the monk Nagasena, in response to the questions of the Bactrian king Milinda, uses the simile of a chariot to explain the Buddhist view of personality. Just as no "chariot" is to be found apart from the wheels, the axle, the yoke, the reins, and so on, yet we use the name chariot to designate the collection of all these parts and pieces organized in a particular way. Similarly, he says, "Nagasena" is nothing more than a conventional name used to designate the five aggregates of form, feeling, perception, and so on. In itself, the name identifies nothing (Mendis, 2007, pp. 28–31).

In his first sermon, the Buddha identifies the entirety of the five aggregates as *dukkha*. The *dukkha*-infused aggregates arise, like everything else, according to the principle of dependent origination. To show how this takes place, Buddhism describes the wheel of birth and death as a circular chain of dependencies with 12 links. In this analysis, old age and death signify all the sufferings of *samsara*. Understanding the process begins with understanding death, the last link in the chain.

12. Death. Dependent on what does death and all suffering arise? The answer is:
11. Birth, which comes into being dependent on
10. "Becoming" (i.e., the orientation towards future goals, continuation, and existence), which arises dependent on
9. Clinging (attachment to desirable things and states), which arises dependent on
8. Craving (for the fulfillment of self-oriented desires), which arises dependent on
7. Feelings/Sensations (pleasurable feelings that inspire the desire for more of the same, and painful feelings that inspire the desire to escape them), which arise dependent on
6. Contact between the sense faculties and their objects, which arises dependent on
5. The six sense faculties, which arise dependent on

4. The body–mind organism, which arises dependent on
3. Consciousness, which arises dependent on
2. Karmic formations/mental habit patterns, which arise dependent on
1. Ignorance (of this very process, the way in which death and suffering arise and cease according to the principle of dependent origination).

Stopping the process begins with eliminating ignorance, the first link in the chain.

In the Buddhist context, any discussion of afterlife is really a discussion of this life – in the samsaric cycle of birth and death, this is the life after death. However, human life is not the only type of life recognized in Buddhism. The tradition accepts the existence of many other kinds of living beings, some that are available to ordinary human perception, like animals, and others that are not. According to karma, one takes birth in a world of our own making, so traditional Buddhist cosmology identifies six possible worlds into which beings can be born, each formed by certain mental habits: the realm of the gods; titans or anti-gods; humans; animals; hungry ghosts; and hell beings. In the Tibetan pictorial representation of these various worlds of rebirth as the Wheel of Becoming, the 12 links above are distributed around the periphery of the circle and the three forces that manipulate the personality are represented by three animals at the center of the wheel: a rooster symbolizing attraction, a serpent aversion, and a pig ego-delusion. The beings born into each world share certain common characteristics. The mental habits of those born into the realm of the gods are dominated by pride, the titans by jealousy and aggression, humans by desire, animals by ignorance, hungry ghosts by avarice and greed, and hell beings by hatred and anger. The worlds of the gods, the titans, and humans are called the three upper worlds, whereas the worlds of animals, hungry ghosts, and hell beings are called the three lower worlds. Beings cycle through these worlds, then, life after life, dwelling in one or the other according to the merit or demerit (good or bad karma) that they have generated in the past, and when the karma that has brought them to that birth is used up, then other karmic conditions come into play, and they continue their journey rising or falling in the wheel of life.

The religious goal of most ordinary Buddhists is to ensure that one's next rebirth is not in one of the three lower worlds, which are regarded as places of suffering. Of the three upper worlds, if one wishes to attain liberation, the best birth is said to be a human birth; the gods are said to live totally distracted by their lives of pleasure, and the beings of the lower realms are totally distracted by their suffering, but among humans there is the possibility to experience sufficient suffering to inspire renunciation of *samsara* and reorientation to *nirvana*, yet not so much as to make spiritual pursuits impossible. The accumulation of merit (good karma), then, becomes an important religious activity since it is merit that determines one's next birth. However, regardless of how much merit one is able to generate, regardless of where one is reborn, all worlds are impermanent and all beings must face suffering and death. The Buddha, however, claimed to have attained *nirvana* and put an end to his cycle of suffering and death. For such a person, the categories of birth and death no longer apply because, having seen clearly the nature of suffering, how it arises and how it ceases, one no longer generates the mental habit patterns that are the causes and conditions for the arising of *samsara*.

Nirvana: The Deathless

Nirvana, the ultimate spiritual goal set forth in the earliest Buddhist literature, is described through many synonyms: the uncompounded/unconditioned; cessation (of rebirth); extinction of thirst; absence of desire; the highest happiness; the deathless; freedom. The word means literally "blowing out" or "extinguishing" and although it is often portrayed as a state that one achieves, as Rupert Gethin points out, rather than "he or she attained *nirvana*," the word is more often used in the Pali texts as a verb – he or she *nirvana*-s or *parinirvana*-s (Gethin, 1998, p. 75). This expression points to an understanding of nirvana as action, the action or process of extinguishing – not the person's identity or self or soul, which in Buddhism is merely a convenient fiction, but what the tradition calls the "defilements" or the three "poisons" pictured at the center of the wheel of life: the *samsara*-perpetuating, *nirvana*-obstructing forces of greed/attraction, hatred/aversion, and delusion/ignorance. The mind-stream of the person who has experienced *nirvana* is free from these defilements, but in life, the other mental and physical constituents of the person remain functioning, so this is known as *nirvana* "with remainder." The aggregates that constitute such a person are, however, no longer "aggregates of clinging," which the Buddha defined as *dukkha*. The actions of such a person are no longer motivated by greed, aversion, or ego-delusion but by generosity, compassion, and wisdom. Furthermore, such a person no longer creates new karma (which is the result of actions motivated by the three poisons); therefore, upon death, when the aggregates (which are the result of past karma) break up, no conditions are present for rebirth – this is *nirvana* "without remainder" or *parinirvana*.

Gethin notes that nirvana is described in the Pali texts not only as the event of extinguishing the defilements, but also as the experience of a state that transcends the physical world of the elements as well as the highest states of meditation. Regarding that experience, the Buddha is reported to have said:

> There is, monks, a domain where there is no earth, no water, no fire, no wind, no sphere of infinite space, no sphere of nothingness, no sphere of infinite consciousness, no sphere of neither awareness nor non-awareness; there is not this world, there is not another world, there is no sun or moon. I do not call this coming or going, nor standing, nor dying, nor being reborn; it is without support, without occurrence, without object. Just this is the end of suffering. (Udana 80; quoted in Gethin, 1998, pp. 76–77)

With such descriptions we enter into a realm beyond language and concepts; a rarified state that ordinary people can hardly hope to relate to or understand. Yet, despite the accounts of *nirvana* as an extra-ordinary, transcendental state or experience, Buddhist scriptures also contain examples of the process of liberation that resonate with the simplest and most ordinary of experiences. In his explanation of the fruits of the spiritual life to the king of Magadha, the Buddha points out that one who attains *nirvana* does not enter into a state of trance or unconsciousness but is cognizant and aware that the mind is freed of the defilements. He says:

> It is as if, your majesty, there were a pool of water in a mountain valley – bright, clear, and still. A person standing on the bank would see, either moving about in it or remaining still, shellfish, sand and pebbles, and shoals of fish. He would think, "This is a pool of water – bright, clear, and still. Moving about in it or remaining still are shellfish, sand and pebbles, and shoals of fish." (Gethin, 2008, p. 35)

In the life of the Buddha, liberation is linked with victory over the forces of Mara, the mythological demon figure who symbolizes death and all that perpetuates death; but is this a present or a future victory? It is one thing to understand *nirvana* as victory over future death because the enlightened one is not reborn, but is there a sense in which *nirvana* can be said to be victory over death in the present, and what would that kind of deathlessness mean? In the *Samyutta Nikaya*, Mara is identified with clinging and attachment to the five aggregates. Where the body, feelings, perceptions, mental habit patterns, and consciousness are identified as "me" or "mine," there is the domain of "my" death. Where the aggregates are realized to be not only impermanent and subject to destruction but also self-less (*anatta*), then there is no me who dies. The Venerable Nyanatiloka sums up the relationship between *nirvana* and no-self in these words:

> One cannot too often and too emphatically stress the fact that not only for the actual realization of the goal of Nibbāna, but also for a theoretical understanding of it, it is an indispensable preliminary

condition to grasp fully the truth of Anattā, the egolessness and insubstantiality of all forms of existence, without such an understanding, one will necessarily misconceive Nibbāna – according to one's either materialistic or metaphysical leanings – either as annihilation of an ego, or as an eternal state of existence into which an Ego or Self enters or with which it merges. (Quoted in Walshe, 1995, p. 28)

The Buddha's response to one who wishes to avoid death is somewhat simpler:

Mogharaja: How does one view the world so as not to be seen by Death's king?

The Buddha: View the world, Mogharaja, as empty – always mindful to have removed any view about self. This way one is above and beyond death. This is how one views the world so as not to be seen by Death's king.[4]

Death, karma, and rebirth pertain to the being that perceives itself as persisting in some essential way. However, this is mere delusion. Phenomena change momentarily. According to the Pali commentaries, "When the Aggregates arise, decay, and die, O bhikkhu [monk], every moment you are born, decay, and die" (Rahula, 1974, p. 33). In other words, death is not merely a future state of the person but is an ongoing process throughout life. Similarly, deathlessness is not a future state to be attained but is the property of a mind for which every present moment is a moment of selfless, essenceless awareness.

Rituals of Departure

The various life-cycle rites of passage through which societies mark such occasions as birth, puberty, adulthood, marriage, and death have no specific doctrinal basis in Buddhism. They are considered worldly conventions; lay people follow the norms of their culture and community. Buddhist monks are usually invited to bring their blessings and provide religious instruction on such occasions; their presence also provides the opportunity for laity to gain merit by making offerings to them, but otherwise no monastic duties are incumbent on them with regard to social rituals.[5] That being said, Buddhist monks and priests of all types are recognized as experts in the intricacies of karma and how it impacts on the next life, the anxieties regarding which reach a peak at death, the point of transition. Therefore, although they are not a strong presence in other life-cycle rituals, funerals are quite another thing. Throughout Asian cultures, Buddhism came to have an enduring association with death rituals and has proved itself highly adaptive to the social customs and cultural needs of the countries in which it has been established. This flexibility allows for a great variety in funeral rituals and has allowed the lay populations to develop and adapt rituals to serve their needs. For example, over the last 50 years in Japan, *mizuko kuyo*, a ceremony for aborted, miscarried, or still-born children, has become increasingly popular. Although its roots are in Japanese folk religion with no foundation in Buddhist text or practice, the Bodhisattva Jizo is called on to comfort and protect the lost child. This ritual eases the distress of parents, allows for acknowledgment rather than denial, can function like a confession or memorial, and brings the child into the Buddhist and the social framework. Whereas abortion creates negative karma, this ritual creates merit.

In Buddhism, death is an inescapable and inevitable reality that befalls every living being, enlightened or not. The following verses are popularly chanted in the Theravada tradition at funeral ceremonies or death anniversaries or simply as an aspect of daily meditation.

> Like a flame blown out by the wind,
> This life-continuum goes to destruction;
> Recognizing one's similarities to others,
> One should develop mindfulness of death.

Just as people who have achieved
Great success in the world have died,
So too I must certainly die.
Death is harassing me.

Death always comes along
Together with birth,
Searching for an opportunity
Like a murderer out to kill.

Not the least bit stoppable,
Always going forward,
Life rushes towards its end
Like the rising sun to its setting.

Like lightning, a bubble, dewdrops,
Or a line drawn in water, life cannot last;
Death is like a murderer after his foe,
Completely unrestrainable.

Death slays those great in glory,
In strength, merit, powers, and wisdom,
And even the two kinds of conquerors;
No need to speak about one like me.

Due to a lack of the necessities of life,
To some inner or outer misfortune,
I who am dying moment after moment
Can die in the blink of an eye. (Gunaratana, 1999, pp. 50–51)

Such contemplation on the frailty of human life and the inevitability of death is not considered morbid, nor is it intended to foster depression or hopelessness. It is meant to inspire the meditator with a profound appreciation for the opportunity that life presents, the opportunity to liberate oneself from suffering and death. This chant belongs to a category of meditation called mindfulness of death (*maranassati*), which is one of ten subjects for recollection, each of which, when developed and pursued, it is said can lead to liberation.

> The Blessed One said, "Mindfulness of death, when developed and pursued, is of great fruit and great benefit. It gains a footing in the Deathless, has the Deathless as its final end. Therefore you should develop mindfulness of death." (AN 6.19)[6]

Mindfulness of death is promoted in order to emphasize the inevitability of death – to overcome the human tendency to deny or push death aside, and further, in order to emphasize the uncertainty of the time of death, at which point the only help that one can rely on for the future is one's own good karma (merit). It is the uncertainty of the time of death that underscores the immediate need for spiritual practice. In the Tibetan schools of Buddhism, there are many stories of their contemplatives who lived with the thought of death constantly in the forefront of their minds. Sogyal Rinpoche writes of the master Jikme Lingpa, who refused to allow his disciples to build a bridge over a pond near to his hermitage that daily gave him great trouble to cross, saying: "What's the use? Who knows if I'll even be alive to sleep here tomorrow night?" (Sogyal Rinpoche, 1994, p. 23). The implication being that the time spent in building the bridge would be better spent in spiritual practice. However, the lives of ordinary householders do not allow for such constant dedication to spiritual practice; for most, the goal of enlightenment is far off and Buddhist lay religious practice is generally focused on the accumulation of merit.

Merit is created through all positive acts of body, speech, and mind, but the greatest amount of merit is created through such positive actions dedicated to the benefit and support of the Buddha's teaching and the monastic community – so feeding the monastics, housing them, sponsoring their retreats, sponsoring the building of temples and *stupas* or the creation of sacred art or translation of sacred texts would all be considered acts of great merit. Although each person is thought to face death with their own store of merit and demerit leading to a future birth, Buddhism also has the equivalent of what would be known in the monotheistic religions as intercession. In this case, however, it is not a person or angel who intercedes to mitigate the future results for the dying or dead. In Buddhism, the same effect is achieved through the sharing of merit. In one way, the idea that good karma can somehow be transferred from one to another goes against the Buddhist teaching that our own actions create our own future. In another way, the idea of hanging on to one's own good karma serves only to support and increase ego-oriented mental states, so Buddhist rituals of all kinds generally end with the dedication of merit to the welfare of all beings. The sick, the dying, and the dead are thought to especially benefit from merit dedicated in their name. In all Buddhist communities, sharing merit is considered to be a win-win situation because it is an act of selfless giving; and since generosity is a prime source of merit, then not only do the recipients benefit, but the donors also create further merit for themselves. These ideas are founded on a worldview that understands that the way in which we live and die is primarily dependent on our own karma, but our thoughts and actions are not isolated. We are surrounded and influenced by the positive or negative actions of others – we benefit or falter also because of that and we benefit or harm others according to what we put into the world; hence the thought of sharing merit.

With these ideas in mind, then, let us examine some rituals of departure from the Tibetan Buddhist tradition. Tibetan Buddhism belongs to the historical development in Buddhist theory that began around the first century CE known as Mahayana (the Great Way). One of the biggest differences between Mahayana and earlier forms of Buddhism is the focus, alongside Gautama Buddha, on numerous celestial Buddhas and Bodhisattvas dwelling in their "Pure Land" paradises, to whom the faithful can appeal for spiritual guidance and assistance. Among these transcendent figures, the Buddha Amitabha dwelling in the western paradise called "Land of Great Bliss" (Tib. *Dewachen*) became the object of a widespread devotional cult that spread throughout Asia. His devotees pray that upon death, they will be reborn in his paradise. In the Tibetan tradition, the Pure

Land of Amitabha is the focus of the *powa* (consciousness transfer) ritual performed shortly after death.

In all schools of Tibetan Buddhism, there are numerous rituals intended to prolong life and avert untimely death due to negative karma. Among them is the practice of purchasing an animal destined for slaughter and releasing it. Around the world, on special days, Buddhists release fish, birds, goats, and all manner of creatures that would otherwise be killed for food. The merit gained from the act of saving a life is considered efficacious in prolonging one's own life and the life of those to whom the merit is dedicated. However, everyone has a natural lifespan and when that runs out, the Tibetans say it is like a lamp that has run out of oil – there is nothing to be done to avert death at that time. There is a firm belief that the state of mind of a person at death is one of the strongest influences in determining the conditions of the next life, so the most important thing at the time of death is to help the dying one to maintain a calm, clear mind focused only on Dharma and positive thoughts. Last thoughts of anger, regret, or hatred would lead to rebirth in the lower realms. Even after death, the family is discouraged from loud weeping or wailing so that the consciousness of the person that still lingers in the vicinity may not be disturbed. It is considered auspicious to die in the same way as the Buddha did, lying in what is called the "sleeping lion pose" on the right side with the head towards the north, so the dying one is often placed in this position shortly before or shortly after death.

In Tibetan Buddhism, the cessation of outer breath and physical functions does not signify death. The subtle inner consciousness is still associated with the body and the person is regarded as unconscious rather than dead. Death takes place when consciousness separates from the body. This is when decay sets in and the corpse can be cremated. The period of time that it takes consciousness to leave the body can range from immediately after the cessation of breath and heartbeat to a week or more in the case of high spiritual practitioners.[7] Three days is sometimes reported as the time that the body is kept before cremation, but Tibetans generally rely on the services of an astrologer to cast the death horoscope, which will determine the correct date and time for disposal, as well as provide various other indications such as the likely place of rebirth and what the family can do to improve the conditions of the deceased's rebirth (Gouin, 2010, p. 19 ff.). Before continuing, it is important to note that, like Buddhist death rituals elsewhere, Tibetan death rituals are as diverse as the communities that support them. As Margaret Gouin notes in the opening of her comprehensive study of this subject:

> The material studied shows clearly that there is no such thing as a "standard" form of funeral in the Buddhism of Tibet. There certainly are common elements, but these common elements are not always handled in the same (or even a similar) way, nor do all such elements always appear. (Gouin, 2010, p. 1)

What is being described here, then, are some of the elements that appear in the various constellations of rituals surrounding death in Tibetan Buddhism.

One of the first rituals to be performed after death would be *powa*, through which it is hoped that the person's consciousness would be transferred directly to Amitabha's Pure Land without having to journey through the intermediate state (*bardo*) between death and rebirth. This is usually performed in the presence of the body but can also be done without the body (Gouin, 2010, p. 16 ff.). As another way of assisting the deceased, a lama might be requested to read from various texts that remind the person of their spiritual instructions and that help guide the consciousness through the intermediate state to a good rebirth. One of those texts, called the *Bardo Thodol*, has become popularly known in translation as *The Tibetan Book of the Dead*; more accurately the title is translated as "Liberation Through Hearing in the Bardo." It is read preferably beginning in the presence of the body, and then continuing after cremation for a period of 49 days, at the end of which time it is understood that consciousness has found a new body and taken rebirth. The fourteenth Dalai Lama explains the continued existence of the person in the state between death and rebirth in terms of the strong attachment to a sense of self. He says:

At the time of death attitudes of long familiarity usually take precedence and direct the rebirth. For this same reason, strong attachment
is generated for the self, since one fears that one's self is becoming
non-existent. This attachment serves as the connecting link to the intermediate state between lives, the liking for a body in turn acts as a
cause establishing the body of the intermediate (bardo) being. (Sogyal
Rinpoche, 1994, p. 224)

The *bardo* state does not only refer to the period between lives. All of
life is also an intermediate state between birth and death, dreaming
is a *bardo* state, as are deep states of meditation. There are three *bardos*
associated with death: the intermediate state of the dying process
(*chikai bardo*), the state of "Reality-as-it-is" (*chonyid bardo*), and the
state of the rebirth process (*sipai bardo*).

The dying process has two phases: the dissolution of the outer
elements of the body and gross mental activity; and the inner dissolution, which is not so much dissolution as the appearance of
subtler and subtler levels of mind as the grosser levels fall away
(Sogyal Rinpoche, 1994, p. 247 ff.). When breath, heartbeat, and
mental activity come to a stop, the person is not considered dead –
consciousness is still associated with the body, there is still internal
subtle energy present that supports consciousness. At this point
successively subtle levels of mind begin to manifest in the following
order:

1. When conceptual thought ceases, the mind is flooded with white
   light.
2. When this mind dissolves then the mind is flooded with red
   light.
3. Then blackness.
4. Finally, the subtlest level of consciousness manifests, filling the
   mind with completely clear empty radiance.

This fourth level is called the Clear Light of Death. It is understood to
be a manifestation of Buddha mind, the absolute true nature of mind,
and if it is recognized as such, that is liberation. This is the mind
state of those high lamas and accomplished spiritual practitioners

who are said to be resting in *tukdam*, an honorific word meaning "meditation," specifically the meditation on the subtlest level of mind that arises at death. For most people, however, this moment passes instantly; there is nothing to see, nothing to be aware of, and so awareness itself goes unrecognized and the moment of death arrives in a state of unconsciousness. After a few days the person passes into the *chonyid bardo*, where he or she regains self-awareness in the form of a thought-body and can hear the words of the *Bardo Thodol* and perceive all that is going on. In the *chonyid bardo*, consciousness experiences all kinds of hallucinations, both beautiful and horrifying. The words of the *Bardo Thodol* encourage the person to recognize all these forms as nothing more than the display of one's own mind. At whatever point there is recognition, there is liberation, but if the person is unable to recognize their own mind, then they proceed on to the *sipai bardo*, where they experience the desire to rest from the interminable hallucinations of the *bardo*, the desire to have a material body. The *Bardo Thodol* urges caution at this stage lest the person find themselves in the womb of some wild animal. The person is told to let go of attraction for one place and aversion to another and put all their faith in their guru and the triple gem (the Buddha, Dharma, and Sangha).

When it comes to disposal of the corpse, many methods are practiced among Tibetan communities including disposal in earth, in water, in fire, and in air. Among the diaspora Tibetan community, cremation is practiced almost exclusively. High lamas are also always cremated and their relics interred in a *stupa*. In all cases, however, the disposal of the body is regarded as a compassionate act, creating merit for the deceased by offering the body as nourishment for other sentient life, whether worms or fish or birds. Cremation is considered a burnt offering in which not only the body is burnt but grains, oil, and various other substances, the scent of which is nourishment for wandering spirits (Gouin, 2010, p. 46 ff.). One of the more sensationalized Tibetan practices is the offering of the body to the vultures, sometimes called "sky burial," but which in Tibetan is called *jator*, "scattering to the birds." Again, this ritual is performed according to a number of different methods ranging from simply abandoning the body on a high place to ritualistic dismemberment by professional corpse-handlers (Gouin, 2010, pp. 64–65).

After the disposal of the body, according to the resources of the family, prayers, rituals, and acts of merit are performed throughout the 49 days for the purpose of benefiting the deceased and purifying his or her negative karma. Among the rituals to benefit the deceased is the burnt offering of food. It is believed that the spirit beings in the *bardo* are nourished by the scent that is carried on the smoke. Merit-making activity would include sponsoring religious art or construction, giving alms or food to the poor, and making monetary offerings to temples or the officiating lamas. The funeral rituals of purification generally make use of an effigy or picture of the deceased and a name-card. Gouin explains:

> The idea is that the consciousness of the deceased is easily distracted and flung about because of their disembodied state, so by giving them a "body" (in the form of the name-card), they are enabled to stay in one place and pay attention to the rituals being conducted for their benefit, until the officiating lama tells them to leave. (Gouin, 2010, p. 100)

The consciousness of the deceased is summoned into the name-card and the rituals performed in the presence of the person. Family members are in some cases required to serve as proxy for the deceased, for example, to offer the prostrations required as part of the ritual. At the end, the consciousness is released from the name-card, which is burned along with the picture, if there is one. The burning of the name-card represents the separation of the living relatives from the dead, the release of consciousness to find its way to its next birth, or the attainment of the Pure Land (Gouin, 2010, p. 102). A final ceremony marks the forty-ninth day and the end of the funeral rites.

The funeral rites are essentially dedicated to securing the future welfare of the person. There is little that deals with the comfort of those left behind except the knowledge that they have done all that could be done to benefit the deceased. There are, however, other rituals that are focused on the living – rituals of protection – and here is where pre-Buddhist Tibetan folk beliefs regarding the soul (*la*) are conjoined with Buddhist ideas of continuing consciousness. Similar to many other cultures, there is the belief that an unhappy or disturbed soul can linger around, bringing misfortune to the family and community. The rituals are intended to comfort the confused soul and persuade it that the body is gone, that it, too, should depart because there is no further place for it among the living. As Gouin notes, Tibetan funeral rites tend to cover all contingencies:

> In fact, it is quite likely that at one and the same time (for example, every seventh day after death), texts will be read to guide the deceased's *namshé* [consciousness] through the bardo while other rituals such as *powa* are performed to send their *namshé* directly to a pure land (or even to the state of enlightenment), at the same time as food and alms are being distributed to assist the deceased to a fortunate rebirth, but also food offerings are being made to [the soul of] the deceased at which they are told to eat up and leave because their continued presence is unwanted, and indeed feared. (Gouin, 2010, p. 118)

Nevertheless, despite what may appear as confusion, Tibetan death rituals are intended to achieve very clear goals related to the attainment of a good rebirth, the expression of compassion, and the realization of wisdom. Through meritorious acts and purification rituals, the living help the deceased to find the best rebirth possible; the motivation of compassion underlies the rituals of disposal in which the body is offered to nourish others; and in hearing the words of the *Bardo Thodol*, the deceased may recognize the clear light of death and awaken to his own true nature:

> O, Child of Buddha Nature, this radiant essence that is now your conscious awareness is a brilliant emptiness. It is beyond substance, beyond characteristics and beyond colour, completely empty of inherent existence in any respect whatsoever... The essence of your own conscious awareness is emptiness. Yet, this is not a vacuous or nihilistic emptiness; this, your very own conscious awareness, is unimpededly radiant, brilliant and vibrant... This intrinsic awareness, manifest in a great mass of light, in which radiance and emptiness are indivisible,

is the buddha [nature] of unchanging light, beyond birth or death. Just to recognize this is enough! If you recognize this brilliant essence of your own conscious awareness to be the buddha [nature], then to gaze into intrinsic awareness is to abide in the enlightened intention of all the buddhas. (Dorje, 2006, p. 231)

A Conversation on Understanding Death

With Izak Bouwer

Izak Bouwer is a retired professor of mathematics. He arrived in Canada from his native South Africa in 1958 as a doctoral student at the University of Toronto. At that time, he says, "I was a very up-tight person and extremely unhappy." However, Izak counts himself fortunate to have encountered the teachings of Zen Buddhism that were being popularized by writers of the time such as D.T. Suzuki,

225

R.H. Blyth, and others. During our conversation, Izak shows me three well-worn books that have guided his thoughts and life through the years: *The Zen Doctrine of No-Mind* and *Manual of Zen Buddhism*, both by D.T. Suzuki, and *The Supreme Doctrine* by Hubert Benoit. It is this last that Izak says "introduced me to the way Zen could resolve the important inner debate about one's self-worth." When I ask Izak to share his thoughts on death with me, he recounts a life-changing experience that resulted from his contemplation of the teachings in these books.

In his words: "It happened in the summer of 1961. I was studying late in Carruther's Hall, the old Math building of Queen's University in Kingston, Ontario. It must have been after midnight and I was alone in the cubicle area on the second floor. Besides mathematical papers, I had two books open on my desk: Benoit's *Supreme Doctrine* and Suzuki's *Doctrine of No-Mind*. Little green summer flies would fly up to the neon light, get their wings singed, and fall back dazed on my desk. I was at an absolutely critical stage trying to understand the Zen readings, and thought that either everything was nonsense, or it was true that everything was interconnected. I was looking at one little fly on my desk, and tried to imagine that it was part of myself looking at me. I tried to do this honestly and very hard. It seemed to me that I saw a spark of my own human intelligence in its eyes, and that was the trigger for a sudden and very profound experience. Over my right shoulder shone a brilliant light, and an oriental-looking man was sitting in my heart laughing. I experienced a tremendous sense of relief. For weeks after, I was in a state of euphoria. I was aware that I could perceive, with no intention of doing so, what people were thinking. Everyone around me was my brother or sister. This experience settled the debate about my self-worth, and still defines my attitude in all matters of life and death. Meditation and contemplation on Buddhist ideas of impermanence and emptiness helped me to realize that 'self' or 'soul' is a mental fabrication and has no independent existence otherwise."

Although he has practiced meditation and participated in many rituals, Izak does not look either to meditation or to ritual prayer to prepare him for death. As he puts it, "Life is the preparation for death. When life and death are a whole, then there is no need to separate them one from the other." When I asked what he thought happens after death, his humorous response was, "This is a subject on which I cannot form an informed opinion." In his view, "There was a time when I was not here, then I was, and then again there will be a time that I am not here." Izak's illness has made it more and more difficult for him to leave his home, but he makes it clear that this is not a reason for discontent. He closes our conversation with a quotation from Seccho, an eleventh-century Zen master:

> What life can compare with this?
> – Sitting alone quietly by the window,
> I observe the leaves fall, the flowers bloom
> as the seasons come and go. (Suzuki, 1960, p. 127)

I get the feeling that for Izak, dying will be much like the falling of a leaf, a natural and necessary part of living.[8]

Notes

1. Nyanatiloka Mahathera, "Fundamentals of Buddhism: Four Lectures," *Access to Insight*, June 16, 2011, http://www.accesstoinsight.org/lib/authors/nyanatiloka/wheel394.html, accessed March 26, 2013.
2. "Acela Sutta: To the Clothless Ascetic" (SN 12.17), translated from the Pali by Thanissaro Bhikkhu, *Access to Insight*, June 8, 2010, http://www.accesstoinsight.org/tipitaka/sn/sn12/sn12.017.than.html, accessed March 26, 2013.
3. *Visuddhimagga* XIX, 22.
4. "Mogharaja-manava-puccha: Mogharaja's Question" (Snp 5.15), translated from the Pali by Thanissaro Bhikkhu, *Access to Insight*, July 11, 2010, http://www.accesstoinsight.org/tipitaka/kn/snp/snp.5.15.than.html, accessed March 26, 2013.
5. Among western converts, however, who are accustomed to the religious celebration of such rituals as marriage, there is demand for "Buddhist" life-cycle rituals.
6. "Maranassati Sutta: Mindfulness of Death (1)" (AN 6.19), translated from the Pali by Thanissaro Bhikkhu, *Access to Insight*, July 4, 2010,

http://www.accesstoinsight.org/tipitaka/an/an06/an06.019.than.html, accessed March 26, 2013.

7. In such cases, the person during that time is considered to be in a meditative state called *tukdam*. He or she would not be disturbed so long as the body shows no signs of decay.

8. Izak Bouwer died in just such peaceful acceptance on December 18, 2012, some six weeks after granting me this interview.

References and Further Reading

Batchelor, Stephen. *Buddhism Without Beliefs*. New York: Riverhead Books, 1997.

Coward, Harold, Dargyay, Eva, and Neufeldt, Ronald. *Readings in Eastern Religions*. Waterloo, ON: Wilfrid Laurier University Press, 1988.

Dorje, Gyurme. (Trans.) *The Tibetan Book of the Dead*. New York: Viking Penguin, 2006.

Gethin, Rupert. *The Foundations of Buddhism*. Oxford: Oxford University Press, 1998.

Gethin, Rupert. (Trans.) *Sayings of the Buddha*. Oxford: Oxford University Press, 2008.

Gouin, Margaret. *Tibetan Rituals of Death: Buddhist Funerary Practices*. London: Routledge, 2010.

Gunaratana, Ven. Henepola. *Bhavana Devotions*. Bhavana Society, 1999.

Mendis, N.K.G. (ed.) *The Questions of King Milinda*. Kandy, Sri Lanka: Buddhist Publication Society, 2007.

Nanamoli, Bhikkhu. (Trans.) *Visuddhimagga: The Path of Purification by Buddhaghosa*. Seattle: BPS Pariyatti Editions, 1991.

Prebish, Charles and Keown, Damien. *Introducing Buddhism*. London: Routledge, 2006.

Rahula, Walpola. *What the Buddha Taught*. New York: Grove Press, 1974.

Sogyal Rinpoche. *The Tibetan Book of Living and Dying*. San Francisco: HarperSanFrancisco, 1994.

Suzuki, D.T. *Manual of Zen Buddhism*. New York: Grove Press, 1960.

Walshe, Maurice. *The Long Discourses of the Buddha*. Boston: Wisdom Publications, 1995.

Williams, Paul and Ladwig, Patrice (eds.) *Buddhist Funeral Cultures of Southeast Asia and China*. Cambridge University Press, 2012.

9

Daoist Perspectives on Death

Although this chapter will focus on Daoist approaches to death and afterlife, such views and practices are inextricably intermingled with other religious approaches that inform Chinese attitudes to death. For example, a Daoist priest conducting funeral rites may well share his official functions with a Buddhist priest or a local medium, as well as incorporate elements of Buddhist ritual, such as feeding the hungry ghosts, into the service. Beyond that, the Daoist priest may go so far as to take on the distinctive headdress of those other ritual experts and fulfill their functions himself (Schipper, 1974, p. 310). The so-called three great religious traditions of China are Confucianism, Daoism, and Buddhism. However, these religions are not mutually exclusive; their doctrines and practices draw on each other, and a person can participate in the practices and beliefs of all without necessarily belonging to any. One eccentric sixth-century CE scholar epitomized the overlap between these systems by going about dressed in a Daoist cap, Buddhist scarf, and Confucian shoes.

Understanding Death: An Introduction to Ideas of Self and the Afterlife in World Religions,
First Edition. Angela Sumegi.
© 2014 Angela Sumegi. Published 2014 by Blackwell Publishing Ltd.

When questioned by the emperor as to whether he was Buddhist, he pointed at his cap; when asked if he were Daoist, he pointed at his shoes; and when asked if he were Confucian, he pointed at his scarf (Moreman, 2008, p. 153). Buddhism, Daoism, and Confucianism belong to the cultural landscape of China, along with a host of other localized practices and beliefs that are rooted in the worldviews of Chinese antiquity. Therefore, before addressing specifically Daoist beliefs and practices, we will consider the broader cultural context pertaining to ancestors, death, and the soul that permeates all religious systems of China.

The Ancestors

The relationship between the living and the dead in Chinese culture is as binding, as complex, and as fraught with opportunity for discord as kin relationships are between the living members of a family. Ancestors refer not merely to one's own dead parents and grandparents, aunts and uncles; they are the branches that link a whole network of people together in a single extended family with the same surname, descended from a common ancestral founder. Each person occupies a particular position in the family tree and bears particular responsibilities according to that position. One's place in the family is often exemplified in mourning rituals; the closer the relationship, such as between child and parent or husband and wife, the more formal and elaborate the mourning (Thompson, 1996, p. 33). The close ancestors of a family were venerated at household altars in the form of wooden tablets representing the spirits of the ancestors; more distant ancestors were worshipped by the extended family in an ancestral temple, under the tablet of the founding ancestor. The Chinese word for religion, *zongjiao*, means literally "lineage-teaching," i.e., the transmission of doctrine or instruction from master to student in a direct line. *Zong*, however, also means blood lineage or ancestry, so the meaning of religion in China is in some way linked to the cult of the ancestors, evidence of which can be found in their earliest known records.

Archaeological findings hint at the beliefs, practices, and cosmology of early Chinese peoples. The famous oracle-bone inscriptions dating to the Shang era (*c.* 1766–1122 BCE)[1] provide evidence of scapulamancy (shoulder-bone divination), sacrifice, ecstatic religion, and above all, the importance of the ancestral cult and preservation of family lineage that has left its mark on Chinese religions until today.[2] Like many ancient cultures the Chinese conceived of a three-tiered universe: heaven above; the world of the dead below; and the middle world occupied by the living. Their spirit world included deceased ancestors, ghosts, nature spirits, and a supreme deity who ruled over all. The Shang rulers worshipped the supreme god as Di, meaning "Lord," also called Shangdi, "Lord-on-high." The fate of all the dead during this time was a place called the Yellow Springs where the shades of the dead dwelt. It was much like the Mesopotamian underworld or the Biblical Sheol, and, like Sheol, it sometimes referred simply to the grave under the earth. The Zhou who formed the next dynasty (1122–249 BCE) worshipped their own high god, Tian (Heaven). In time, Tian became the favored term for the supreme deity, but Tian is not to be taken as equivalent to the creator God of the monotheistic traditions. Tian has many connotations, both personal and impersonal: the vast blue sky above; the universe itself operating according to moral laws; the dwelling place of gods and ancestors; as well as the Supreme Ruler in heaven who oversees the affairs of men. As conquerors and overthrowers of the previous dynasty, the Zhou also introduced the concept of the "Mandate of Heaven." According to this idea, heaven is concerned with peace and order in human society, and requires kings and emperors to rule accordingly. Where virtue is lost and the ruler becomes corrupt and uncaring of the people, heaven withdraws its mandate, the ruler is overthrown, and the mandate passes to another. This concept implied that rulers had divine authority over their subjects. The fate of the aristocratic dead, therefore, should reflect their relationship with divinity. After death, then, the Zhou kings and noblemen did not share the commoners' anonymous destiny of the Yellow Springs; their souls rose to heaven. In a sense, the ancestors of the nobility were deified and worthy of worship.

Although the ancestral cult developed first among the families of the elite, it eventually included all family units and became the foremost method of instilling family pride, unity, and community cohesion (Moreman, 2008, p. 140). From the earliest times until today, Chinese religious practice has carried forward the notion that the living and the dead have distinctive roles and responsibilities with regard to each other. It is the task of the living family to ensure that the souls of the ancestors are given their due honor and attention, and it is the responsibility of the ancestors to promote the well-being and prosperity of the family. These values were enshrined in the enduring legacy of Confucius (*c.* 552–479 BCE), who promoted the rituals of ancestor veneration. He envisioned a moral order founded on principles of humaneness, virtue, duty, and reciprocity – expressed in an ideal social order in which children rendered honor and service to parents, wives to husbands, youth to elders, subjects to rulers, and the living to the dead. In return they received benevolent care, guidance, protection, and prosperity.

Chinese villages generally consist of one or more family lineages going back to a founding ancestor. The family founder and his descendants are collectively venerated in the village ancestral or lineage hall. Their presence is marked by inscribed wooden tablets or sometimes portraits. The closer generations are venerated in the home if the family has the economic means to have a special space set aside for ancestral tablets (Ahern, 1973, p. 133). In the secularized atmosphere of China today, the lineage halls are renamed "senior citizen" centers, but their contents and activity remain the same (Tam, 2011, p. 38). In village life, all major life-cycle celebrations such as births, weddings, the birthdays of venerable elders, and funerals take place at the lineage hall in the presence of the ancestors. Communal rituals to honor the ancestors take place on special days: the first and last days of the lunar year; in autumn on the ninth day of the ninth lunar month; and in spring at the Qingming festival:

> The ancestor veneration in the lineage hall will usually take place in the morning. It consists of offering incense, food, and wine to the ancestors and a reading of a memorial to the ancestors by an elder

member of the lineage. The ritual will be followed by a visit, known as "tomb sweeping," to the graveyards of the ancestors. The whole lineage will first visit the grave of the first settler and then break into groups according to lineage branches. The grave of the immediate ancestors will be visited last. (Tam, 2011, p. 41)

Ancestor veneration presents us with the benevolent face of the dead and positive relations between the living and the dead leading to family and communal prosperity. There is, however, another picture, one of illness, discord, and misfortune of all kinds that attends the death of those with no one to remember or venerate them, or those who died premature, violent, or accidental deaths. The spirits of such people have no place among the ancestors. They become wandering ghosts who are at best pitiful and at worst malevolent, bringing harm to the family and community. Whereas ancestors are kindly disposed spirits (*shen*) to be honored as family, ghosts or demons (*gui*) are despised, feared, and given handouts in the hope that they will move on. In the spiritual hierarchy they are the counterparts to homeless beggars, bandits, and other dangerous strangers. Further, the manner in which offerings are made indicates that concern for the dead takes place along a continuum, on one end of which are the direct lineage ancestors whose tablets are placed in the most honored position on the left of the domestic altar; on the right are other dependents of the family line who have no one else to care for them; somewhere in a corner of the kitchen or in a hallway are the tablets of non-family who contributed to the lineage; and on the far end are the offerings for ghosts placed outside the back door (Wolf, 1974, p. 147).

The souls of dead infants and small children are always ghosts. It is incumbent on children to care for their dead parents, but not the other way around. A young man who dies can expect to be worshipped by his children, but not by his parents. "On the contrary, his father will usually beat the coffin to punish his son for being so unfilial as to die before his parents" (Wolf, 1974, p. 148). The difference between ancestors and ghosts, however, is not as clear cut as it might seem. Wolf recounts the story of a young man who sees a ghost on his way home late at night: "a white thing floating across the fields." The sighting makes sense to him because the death anniversary of a neighbor's mother was coming up the next day, so the ghost would have been the mother on her way to the house to receive her ancestral death day offerings. As Wolf says, "One man's ancestor is another man's ghost." The distinction here is between family and stranger; reciprocal rights and responsibilities exist between family members, both living and dead. Ancestors are family; ghosts are strangers with neither rights nor duties (Wolf, 1974, p. 146). Ghosts are dealt with in different ways. Those who bring misfortune might be the subject of exorcist rituals, or the family may hire a medium to make contact and negotiate a peace. Some, however, are merely sad and pitiful and in need of attention, so the Ghost Festival that takes place on the fifteenth night of the seventh lunar month offers a communal opportunity to remember the neglected dead. Every family will set out food offerings and burn incense and replicas of money, clothes, houses – all that a homeless hungry ghost might need.

There is yet a further way to deal with a discontented ghost, and that is to bring it into the ancestral fold. In one case, a family lived constantly troubled by the ghost of a young man who was beheaded by the Japanese in World War II for smuggling, a violent death that would have doomed him to existence as a ghost. The man's brother and his wife blamed their recurring illnesses and lack of children on the jealousy of the malicious ghost. They tried everything to be rid of it – they burned offerings at the doorstep on every first and fifteenth of the lunar month, calling out, "We are giving you money and offerings; take them and be satisfied! Don't come back to bother our family!" They hired a famous Daoist priest to perform an exorcism to drive the ghost off. Finally, they thought to inscribe the brother's name on a silver plaque, put it in an urn, and provide a permanent tomb for the soul so that it could rest in peace, but during a village seance, the ghost spoke to them through a medium, saying, "It was not time for me to die. My head was severed by a Japanese sword. I am angry and lost because my bones are mixed with those of other people." Eventually, the ghost tells them that the silver plaque and the tomb are not necessary, that he will be happy if they simply write his name on a piece of silver paper and hang it beside the ancestral altar. "If you do this," the ghost said, "I will try to help you, my brother, and your wife to have good luck and many children" (Potter, 1974, pp. 208–209). The remedy in this case was to pacify the negative energy surrounding the ghost with ancestral reverence, and in so doing invoke reciprocal forces of benevolence.

Soul Theories

Oracle-bone inscriptions also provide the earliest record of Chinese theories of soul. They indicate that for ordinary people, upon death, the vital life-force departed from the body and lived on in the vicinity of the body as a ghost. When the body entirely disintegrated, the ghost would then descend to the underworld called the Yellow Springs, or continue to exist in the grave. As mentioned above, however, this common post-mortem existence gave way to the idea that individual souls could have a heavenly destiny. With regard to continuation after death, there were two aspects, the *hun* soul that became a powerful divine ancestor spirit (*shen*), and the *po* soul that became a ghost (*gui*).[3] The Confucian text called the Classic of Rites explains the two:

> The Master [i.e., Confucius] said, "The (intelligent) spirit is of the [*shen*] nature, and shows that in fullest measure; the animal soul is of the *kwei* nature, and shows that in fullest measure . . . " All the living must die, and dying, return to the ground; this is what is called *kwei*. The bones and flesh, moulder below, and, hidden away, become the earth of the fields. But the spirit [*shen*] issues forth, and is displayed on high in a condition of glorious brightness. (Quoted in Moreman, 2008, p. 143)

By the time of Confucius, soul concepts in Chinese thought are linked with a view of the phenomenal universe as arising from and functioning according to the dynamic interaction of two opposing but complementary forces – the forces of yin and yang. Yin is the energy of all that is soft, dark, moist, passive, contracting, sinking. Yang is the energy of all that is hard, bright, dry, active, expanding, rising. From the interplay of these two forces, the five basic elements (*xing*) of existence arise – metal, water, fire, wood, earth. Just as the forces of yin and yang are in a state of continuous flux and interchange, so the five elements are to be understood in an active dynamic sense; and from the combinations of the five elements all the phenomena of existence arise. All things, then, can be understood in the bipolar terms of yin and yang. Among humans, the female manifests primarily yin energy, and males, yang energy. In nature, the earth is yin and the sky yang. It should be noted that there is nothing that is pure yin or pure yang; each contains the seed of the other and they are best described as "definable phases in a ceaseless flow of change" (Thompson, 1996, p. 2). For example, the height of winter would be primarily yin and the height of summer primarily yang, but each gives way to the other, like the coming and going of day and night. Yin and yang are not moral forces; where they are in proper balance, either in the individual, in society, or in nature, then the situation is harmonious, healthy, and positive; where there is an imbalance, the situation is one of discord, ill health, negativity.

The soul or spiritual dimension of a human being, then, is to be understood in the same terms, as a balance of yin and yang. In life, the yin force that supports the material body and the yang force that supports consciousness are not differentiated, but upon death, they separate into two aspects. The yang force is manifest in the *hun* soul that rises to heaven and becomes a *shen* (benevolent spirit). It also has its seat in the ancestral spirit tablet in front of which the family makes offerings. The yin force is manifest in the *po* soul that descends into the earthly grave and becomes a *gui* (ghost), which can remain at peace but, if not buried or cared for properly, can become a troublesome roaming ghost bringing harm to the family and community – this happens also to those who die a violent death. The *hun* soul is associated with the breath of life and with conscious intelligence. Death is the permanent departure of the *hun* soul from the body. It is possible, however, for it to return, for the person who appears dead to revive, so it became a common custom upon death to carry out the ritual of "calling back the soul," i.e., to take a piece of the deceased's clothing outside or onto the rooftop and there to hold it up in all directions, calling the soul to return. If there was no revival, then preparations for burial could begin.

The Nameless Way

The idea of yin and yang forces combining in a ceaseless flow of change brings us to the concept of the Dao, one of the more difficult of Chinese religious concepts to define, yet it is used in every school of Chinese thought. The word is usually translated "way" or path, in the ordinary sense of a route that is followed by humans or planets or birds, or the flowing course of a stream. It has the sense of the "natural way," the way of constant change, the progression of the seasons, the ebb and flow of the tide. Dao also has connotations of truth, teaching, or doctrine – the right way to go along, the true way, the way of virtue. It also has a more metaphysical meaning; one could speak of the Dao as ineffable Ultimate Reality: the underlying, governing principle of the universe; that which is immanent in all things, the source of all things, and to which all things return. No language can circumscribe this ultimate meaning of Dao, as the opening words of the *Dao-de-jing*, the classic work of Daoist philosophy traditionally attributed to the sixth-century BCE sage Laozi, make clear:[4]

> The way that can be spoken of
> Is not the constant way;
> The name that can be named
> Is not the constant name.
> The nameless was the beginning of heaven
> and earth;
> The named was the mother of the myriad
> creatures. (Lau, 1963, p. 57)

In this context, the Dao is the effortless way of nature that is the way of virtue, the good that should be the model for human behavior. In the *Dao-de-jing*, this good is compared to water:

> Highest good is like water. Because water excels in benefiting the myriad creatures without contending with them and settles where none would like to be, it comes close to the way. (Lau, 1963, p. 64)

By following the Dao, one participates in virtue and in its power, a power that comes about naturally, effortlessly.

> Without stirring abroad
> One can know the whole world;
> Without looking out of the window
> One can see the way of heaven.
> The further one goes
> The less one knows.
> Therefore the Sage knows without having to stir,
> Identifies without having to see,
> Accomplishes without having to act.
> (Lau, 1963, p. 108)

There are numerous Daoist schools and the term "Daoism" can imply models of mysticism and philosophy, or models of self-cultivation and longevity practices, or models of ritual and liturgy. No religion consists of a singular body of doctrine and practice, but in the case of Daoism, the internal variation is best understood not only in terms of sectarian differences but also as overlapping constellations of belief and practice that appear differently in different historical periods and societies. In his revisionist work on Daoism, Russell Kirkland examines the intersections and interconnections between these various constellations to show the shared concerns and assumptions that result in a Daoist approach to life, which he characterizes as consisting of "*a holistic worldview* and an ethos centred upon a *holistic transformation* of self, [and] society . . . through a variety of interrelated *moral activities and religious practices"* (Kirkland, 2004, p. 215).

With regard to death, there are a number of approaches to be found in Daoism. The philosophical approach in classical texts such as the *Dao-de-jing* and the *Zhuangzi* emphasizes acceptance of death as an integral part of the ever-changing processes of existence, the return to the eternal Dao. However, Daoism also includes esoteric methods of inner alchemy that are intended to transform the person from a mortal into an immortal being, as well as elaborate liturgical death rituals carried out to ensure the passage of the soul from hell to heaven.

Transformations of the Self

In the following conversations recounted by Zhuangzi, we see the philosophical approach to death (Hoffman, 1986, pp. 69–70). The conversations take place among four wise old friends visiting each other when ill. In the first, the visitor asks how his friend is doing and is told:

> "My back is as crooked as a hunchback's and my organs are all topsy-turvy. My chin sticks in my navel, my shoulders rise up above my head and my pigtail points to the sky. The elements of nature must be all confused."
>
> "Does it upset you?" asks the visitor.
>
> "Why should it? . . . I was born when it was time to be born, and I shall die when it is time to die. If we are in peace with time and follow the order of things, neither sorrow nor joy will move us. The ancients called this 'freedom from bondage.' Those who are entangled with the appearance of things cannot free themselves. But nothing can overcome the order of nature. Why should I be upset?"

In another conversation Master Li, who is visiting his dying friend, says to him:

> "Great is the Maker of Things! What will become of you now? Where will he send you? Will you be the liver of a rat or the leg of an insect?"

His dying friend responds that he will happily go wherever he is sent:

> "If life is good, death is good also. If an ironsmith were casting metal and the metal were to jump up and say, 'Make me into the best of all swords!' the ironsmith would regard it as a bad omen. Now that my human form is decomposing, were I to say, 'I want to be a man! Nothing but a man!' the Maker of Things would think me most unworthy. Heaven and earth are a great forge and the Maker of Things is a master ironsmith. Can the place he is sending me be the wrong place?"

In these passages, there is no sense of a soul ascending to heaven or of a ghost descending to the grave. Change and transformation brought about through the interplay of yin and yang forces are responsible for the beginnings and the endings of things. The human state is merely a phase in the ongoing processes of transformation that reflect the power of nature. One accepts death as one accepts life, understanding both to belong to the eternal flow that is the Dao. This is the point of the famous story of the death of Zhuangzi's wife.

> Chuang Tzu's wife died. When Hui Tzu went to convey his condolences, he found Chuang Tzu sitting with his legs sprawled out, pounding on a tub and singing. "You lived with her, she brought up your children and grew old," said Hui Tzu. "It should be enough simply not to weep at her death. But pounding on a tub and singing – this is going too far, isn't it?" Chuang Tzu said, "You're wrong. When she first died, do you think I didn't grieve like anyone else? But I looked back to her beginning and the time before she was born. Not only the time before she was born, but the time before she had a body. Not only the time before she had a body, but the time before she had a spirit. In the midst of the jumble of wonder and mystery a change took place and she had a spirit. Another change and she had a body. Another change and she was born. Now there's been another change and she's dead. It's just like the progression of the four seasons, spring, summer, fall and winter.

Now she's going to lie down peacefully in a vast room [the universe]. If I were to follow after her bawling and sobbing, it would show that I don't understand anything about fate [the inevitable way of nature]. So I stopped." (Hoffman, 1986, pp. 69–70)

In life the Daoist sage aims to model himself on the Dao, the natural way, the effortless flowing way, contending with no one, doing nothing, and thereby accomplishing everything. Death, in this view, is a return to the source, the nameless that is naturally so. There is nothing more to be said or to be done.

> Man models himself on earth,
> Earth on Heaven,
> Heaven on the way,
> And the way on that which is naturally so.
> (Lau, 1963, p. 82)

In this approach to death, immortality could be conceived of as the realization that no one is lost to the Dao, which is the matrix, the substance, and the unending totality of things. As Zhuangzi says:

In the universe, all things are one. For him who can but realize his indissoluble unity with the whole, the parts of his body mean no more than so much dust and dirt, and death and life, end and beginning, are no more to him than the succession of day and night. They are powerless to disturb his tranquillity. (Creel, 1970, p. 3)

However, to recognize one's unity with the whole is to abandon the desire for the continuation of individual identity. This is a significantly different kind of immortality than that found in other constellations of Daoism, in which personal immortality is the goal, and death, if not possible to be avoided, is to be transcended. The notion of humans who become immortal through their esoteric knowledge and various methods of self-transformation can be traced as far back as the late fourth century BCE and became an enduring element in the Chinese cultural landscape.

The Search for Immortality

The bronze inscriptions of the Western Zhou period (1122–771 BCE) record prayers to the ancestors or to heaven for longevity and prolonged life; there is no hint that death can be avoided, but around the eighth century BCE, prayers for "no-death" appear (Yü, 1964–1965, p. 87). In his article entitled "Life and Immortality in the Mind of Han China," Yü notes a number of Chinese terms that are associated with immortality. He translates them as: "long-life"; "no-death"; "preservation of the body"; "transcending the world"; "ascending to the distant place"; "becoming immortal." The first three, he suggests, reflect an intensification of the desire for continued life in this world, but the latter three indicate a different level of immortality – an other-worldly immortality. According to Yü, "This is the immortality of the immortality cult . . . To achieve this new immortality was not to live permanently on earth as a man but rather to leave this world as a *hsien* or immortal" (Yü, 1964–1965, pp. 88–89). Zhuangzi gives the earliest description of such an immortal:

> Far away on the mountain of Ku I there lived a spiritual man. His flesh and skin were like ice and snow. His manner was elegant and graceful as that of a maiden. He did not eat any of the five grains, but inhaled the wind and drank the dew. He rode on clouds, drove along the flying dragons, and thus rambled beyond the four seas. (Yü, 1964–1965, p. 91)

Princes and emperors, however, were not interested in this kind of rarified transcendent immortality; they wanted a worldly life with all their palaces and pleasures. And so Yü notes that what he calls "other-worldly" immortality became conflated with worldly physical immortality. The search for the substance that would bring this about gained its strongest impetus with the first emperor of China, Qin Shi Huangdi (d. 210 BCE), and continued with the subsequent Han emperors. The immortals were said to dwell on the mythical island mountain of Penglai in the eastern sea or on the Kunlun mountains to the far west where:

> The houses are made of gold and silver. The birds and animals are all white. The pearl and coral trees grow there in great profusion. The flowers and seeds all have a sweet flavour. Those who eat them do not grow old nor die. There they drink of the fountain of life and live in ease and pleasure. (Quoted in Overmyer, 1974, p. 217)

With all the power and resources of the state at their disposal, the Han emperors sent men east to the sea and west to the mountains in search of the immortals and the "drug of no death." Around 133 BCE, in the court of the Emperor Wu Ti, the reputed founder of Chinese alchemy Li Shao-chun convinced his ruler to fund the transmuting of cinnabar into gold as an aspect of creating the elixir of immortality. Many experiments were carried out, none of which were success-ful, but which, nevertheless, fueled belief in such possibilities. Li Shao-chun claimed to be an immortal himself who had lived for centuries, but when he died, instead of being shocked, the emperor explained that his death was merely a show, so as not to disturb ordinary people. In reality, he had simply transformed himself and departed. If the graves of such people were to be examined, no phys-ical body would be found, only clothes left behind (Moreman, 2008, p. 149). As the immortality cult grew in popularity, people believed that it could be achieved through any number of methods: through religious sacrifices, through immortality drugs, through ingesting gold and gems, eating the flowers of a certain plant, abstaining from grains, regulating the breath, or even by transforming the body into a bird (Yü, 1964–1965, p. 110).

Eventually, however, the search for the elixir of immortality turned from external experiments and geographical explorations to internal methods involving practices of yoga and breathing ex-ercises. Just as the alchemist combined and refined various mineral substances to produce a new substance, so the Daoist practitioner gathers the energies of the body, mind, and cosmos and refines them in the furnace of the body to produce health and immortality. Daoist longevity techniques are based on an understanding of *qi* as the primordial energy of the universe. They focus on balancing the yin and yang forces in the body so as to recover and suffuse the body with *qi*. This means the retention of all outflow of *qi* in the form of breath, blood, and semen. David Palmer describes the process in three stages:

> The first stage involves techniques for ending seminal emissions (for men) and menstrual flows (for women), thereby preventing the dissipation of vital essence. Through meditation [and breathing] techniques, the essence is circulated and transformed into vital energy (*qi*). The next stage involves, through other procedures, turning *qi* into spirit, and from thence, from the realm of the spirit, to return to the void. The process is thus one of transmuting the essential substance of the body, turning it into something increasingly ethereal, until it can no longer be affected by the processes of decay and death. Indeed, it is said to reverse the process of aging, returning to a state of infancy and even beyond, to a state of pure energy that has not yet condensed itself into the physical form of the human body. (Palmer, 2011, p. 92)

Among the esoteric practices involved in the process described above is "embryonic breathing," which is intended to imitate the closed-circuit breathing (i.e., circulation of *qi*) of the embryo in the womb. The breath is held within the body for as long as possible, mentally circulating throughout the body and being collected in the belly below the abdomen, the area called "Sea of Breath." Slowly, like an embryo, a new spiritual self forms, which is of the nature of *qi*, and at death is released from the body to exist in the paradise of the immortals (Overmyer, 1974, p. 210). There were many methods of self-transformation promoted in the history of Daoism and it is difficult to determine in many cases whether the goal of immortality was to avoid death or to transcend death. It is likely that both existed side by side. One ninth-century text relates immortality to the cultivation of mind:

> To cultivate the mind is to cultivate the Tao. Now, the mind is the residence of spirit [*shen*] within the human body. When the mind remains empty and in non-action, then it will, after some time, begin to radiate with the Tao . . . Guard emptiness, non-being, and the spontaneous flow of life, let your body and spirit become one with the Tao, and you can live forever as an immortal [*hsien*]. (Quoted in Kirkland, 2004, p. 197)

However, whether they seek longevity or immortality, physical or spiritual, and by whatever means they seek it, from the ancient Han emperors to the groups of elderly practitioners doing their *taiji* and *qigong* exercises in a present-day Beijing park, the core of Daoist practice is, as Kirkland summarizes, "a practice of self-cultivation within a cosmos comprised of subtly linked forces" (Kirkland, 2004, p. 192).

Rituals of Departure

The afterlife in Chinese culture is a complicated tapestry made more complicated by the advent of Buddhism in the first century CE. Notions of where people go after death have been influenced by: (a) the mystical return to nature of the early Daoists; (b) visions of the paradises of the immortals; (c) the pragmatic approach of Confucius, who preferred the pursuit of virtue in life to speculation on the afterlife; (d) the Buddhist hierarchy of heavens and hells, which became in the Chinese version an other-worldly replica of the imperial bureaucracy, its courts and palaces, officers and administrators, judges, prisons, and torture chambers – in the context of Buddhist belief also, the paradises of the immortals gave way to the western Pure Land of Buddha Amitabha where devotees could live sorrowless until final enlightenment; and finally, (e) the beliefs of localized folk religions that include a pantheon of gods and ancestors inhabiting celestial regions, the underworld with its ghostly inhabitants, as well as beliefs in the efficacy of Amitabha to rescue souls from hell and take them to his "Western Paradise."

There is no systematization of beliefs or practices, but in his study *Religion in Chinese Society*, C.K. Yang identifies the following purposes and components of Chinese death rituals: (a) for the benefit and salvation of the soul: burning paper effigies of houses, horses, cars, boats to accompany the dead, sponsoring religious services for 49 days to assist and guide the dead through the underworld to arrive safely in heaven; (b) for protection of the living from the dead: the corpse would be placed with the feet facing the door so that the ghost could walk away from the home, mourners could not enter other people's homes, divination was needed to determine the auspicious time for burial so that evil forces would not be aroused, the burning of mourning garments; (c) for the expression of grief: loud wailing, whether ritualistic or genuine, wearing mourning garments made of cheapest sackcloth or hemp; (d) for reasserting the family status weakened by death: gathering a large group of extended family and friends to participate in the funeral procession and funeral feast, constructing elaborate mourning arches and funeral decorations, spending lavishly on the coffin and the funeral procession that might include banners and marching bands (Yang, 1961, p. 31 ff.).

Many of these elements are still present in the traditional Daoist rites that constitute the most common funeral rituals in present-day Hong Kong. However, China's move towards urbanization and secularization has brought about some significant changes. Cremation, which used to be reserved for Buddhist monks, has been encouraged by the Chinese state since the 1930s as a way of promoting secularism and freeing up arable land (Palmer, 2011, p. 92). Land being scarce and expensive, cremation is now the norm in most Chinese cities. There is still resistance to the practice in the villages as it goes against the Chinese traditional concern for a proper burial so that the soul might be at peace. Other changes are related to the fast pace of modern city life; Daoist funerary services that may have lasted over several days and nights in the past are now completed in half a day, and formal mourning often ends at the gravesite when the chief mourner removes his mourning clothes (Cheung et al., 2006, pp. 76, 91). However, whether performed in the village or in the city, funerals performed by Daoist priests have as their focus the ritual called the "attack on hell." Other important parts of the funeral service include "rites of bathing and dressing," "crossing the bridge," and "untying the knots." The Daoist death liturgy is a way for the family to help the deceased to pay debts and expiate sins.

In essence, the "attack on hell" enacts the dramatic rescue of the soul from hell, which can then journey to the world of the blessed. It is highly theatrical and involves the family members as participants in the transformation of the soul from beleaguered ghost to divine ancestor. In a description of the ritual in Hong Kong, the eldest son carries a tablet with the deceased's name and a banner to show the spirit the way. Behind him are other family members who wish to accompany the descent to the underworld and assist in the rescue. The priest leads the procession using his ceremonial sword to break nine pieces of clay representing the nine gates of hell. The priest then takes the tablet and jumps over a container holding fire to symbolize the purification of all bad karma and the release of the soul from hell. All this takes place to the accompaniment of cymbals and other musical instruments (Cheung et al., 2006, pp. 74–75). Subsequently, the eldest son carrying the tablet and the banner follows the priest to a symbolic bridge over the river that separates the living from the dead. This is the final moment of farewell at the "Bridge of Sighs." The living must turn back and the soul continue on to heaven.

The "rites of bathing and dressing" is a purification ritual during which the soul is symbolically cleansed in the waters of the heavenly river. In one Hong Kong ceremony, the eldest son is sent with a wet towel to the cold room at the back of the hall, where the body is kept, to cleanse the face of his parent. The soul is then ready to enter the heavenly world. "Untying the knots" refers to debts or entanglements in worldly affairs that may hinder the soul from a smooth journey. The priest mixes 49 coins with 49 buttons and then separates them, symbolizing the separation of the deceased from all the knots of existence (Cheung et al., 2006, p. 73).

Traditional mourning periods, especially for parents, last up to three years, but in modern Hong Kong, more people consider the mourning complete after 49 days. Prayers and liturgies said for the dead are usually repeated on every seventh day after death for seven weeks. The forty-ninth day, called "the breaking of seven," focuses on the living with prayers being said for their repentance and the purification of the house of mourning. People then burn the mourning clothes and return to normal life. In a more condensed version, however, the mourning is finished at the graveyard immediately after burial – mourners are asked to wash their hands and cross over a pool of fire to cleanse themselves of death, and the chief mourner burns his mourning clothes in a ritual called "the hero's shedding of mourning clothes." The family then invites all participants to a longevity meal called "wine that washes away the unclean," a seven-course meal that usually takes place at a Chinese restaurant (Cheung et al., 2006, pp. 76–77). A final service might be had at the family home to drive away the last vestiges of the negativity of death and welcome the deceased as an ancestor. This is not thought to be part of the funeral rituals proper and is called the "good service."

Daoist death rituals vary in their details according to where they are performed and by whom. In her description of a funeral in a Taiwanese village, where there is perhaps more space, more time, and more taste for funeral drama, Emily Ahern gives another picture of the "attack on hell" (Ahern, 1973, p. 221 ff.). A paper figure representing the deceased forms the focus of the ritual and is moved around according to the events taking place. To the sound of horns and drums, the priest and his acolytes dressed in yellow or purple holding the paper figure and a figure of a horse enact the journey of the soul to the underworld by racing in and out and around an elevated table until they are exhausted. They are replaced by acrobats tumbling from the table and performing stunts with spinning torches to the delight of the crowd. Finally, when the soul arrives at the gates of hell, in order to identify the soul to the officials of the underworld, the priest recites from a document the name and address of the deceased and the names of the close family. This appears to be also part of a liturgical purification as it marks the point in the ceremony when all the soul's sins are erased.

In the next stage of the ritual, two tables are set apart and a length of cloth stretched between them. The soul effigy is placed at one end. Next the earth god makes his appearance – one of the assistants dressed as an old man. After wandering around the crowd making the children laugh, he leads a line of the deceased's direct descendants around the "bridge," telling them that it will be very difficult for the soul to cross safely without his assistance because monsters and demons wait to snatch up the soul should it fall. Everyone knows that the god must be paid for this service and each time they circle the bridge they throw coins into a bowl under the cloth until the god is satisfied. The soul effigy is then slid across the cloth to the other side, the descendants kneel in front of it, and the eldest son throws two coins until they both land face up to indicate that the soul has arrived safely in the underworld.

Finally, the descendants take piles of special funeral paper money to an open area to be burnt – they join hands in a circle around the fire and must remain and watch over it until all is burnt to ashes so that ghosts may not snatch the money intended for their relative. During the next 49 days the family continues to carry out ritual weeping and make offerings for the well-being of the deceased, in terms of both providing them with all the necessities (in the form of symbolic paper effigies) for their new dwelling place and offering money to the judges of hell in the hopes that their judgment will be light. Sometime during the 49 days, a moving-in party is held for the soul that is to take up residence in a new house in the underworld. On the forty-ninth day, the soul is believed to be finally through all its hardships and the grand paper effigy of the soul's house is burned, signifying the end of the mourning period.

Whether prolonged or contracted, Chinese funeral rituals reflect a history of intense involvement with the dead that is still felt in the modern metropolises of China today. The reciprocal care and responsibilities of family do not end at death. The peace, comfort, and well-being of the living are intimately related to the experiences of the dead. No living person is useless; the dead have always need of them.

A Conversation on Understanding Death

With Jim Nicholson

Jim is a Calgary-born Canadian, currently based in Vancouver, who, in his early twenties, found himself drawn to the practice of Tai Chi as a form of physical training. For this purpose, he joined the Taoist Tai Chi Society (TTCS), but as he says, "I always felt something deeper behind the mere physical exercises." That "something deeper" eventually led Jim on to explore Daoism in his university career, to train with Moy Lin-shin, the founder of the society, to adopt Daoism as a personal spiritual path, and to join in the lay leadership of the TTCS and its temple affiliate, Fung Loy Kok (Islands of the Immortals) Institute of Taoism.[5]

Throughout our conversation, Jim emphasizes the permeable boundaries of the categories that we discuss – body and mind, religious ritual and silent meditation, Tai Chi exercise and temple ceremony. "In Taoism, physical cultivation," he points out, "goes with the cultivation of the whole person." Jim's approach to death, then, takes into account the way in which the category of death merges with the category of life. In this, he says, "I was inspired by the opportunity that I had to be near Master Moy as he passed away." "I learned from him that what we do with our life each day can lead to a transformation, a return to a state of harmony and equilibrium that results in a better life and death." "Comfort in the face of death comes from doing our best to help others, to be positive, and to be part of a community with whom one can remember those that have passed on."

Although Jim describes his engagement with Daoism as less of a belief system and more of a way of life, nevertheless, he says, "I enjoy the rituals, they are effective in helping us to deal with change, helping us to find ways of keeping composure and dealing with loss." "A prominent and important feature of the larger FLK temples," he tells me, "is the memorial hall where one can find pictures and plaques installed by families in memory of their ancestors and deceased loved ones." "The 'All Souls' festival sometimes known as the 'Festival of Ghosts' is the most important religious ceremony that takes place every year in the seventh lunar month; at this time all the departed souls are remembered, including those who at other times have no one to remember or care for them." Jim admits that perhaps such rituals that imply the continuation of the soul may appear contradictory to the idea expressed by Master Moy that all that is left after death is one's deeds, but again, the notion of permeable and overlapping boundaries allows him to give these thoughts each their own space. He points out that "both form equally important parts of the teachings he left us, so even though they appear contradictory on some level, they very much form part of the same system of spiritual training, which encourages his students to try to understand and even embrace the benefits of both." Jim continues: "When I perform the rituals then I must engage with them authentically; at other times, one needs to be willing to appreciate other perspectives and not be pulled around by one's own narrow ideas." "Interestingly, the rituals and the chanting also have a profound effect on both body and mind, it changes the way you think, gives you more energy and the ability to see things clearly."

As far as preparing for death, he says, "If you are engaged in the training, which involves being a vehicle for good deeds, performing the rituals, and practicing the art of inner alchemy or internal cultivation, then one's whole life is a preparation." Jim points again to the example of Master Moy, whom he says "completely accepted his own death, and even embraced it with the same equanimity he showed throughout the time we knew him, taking every opportunity to teach us how to care for someone who was dying – in other words, living his life as a teacher up to the very end." "This is why we cannot discount community, we need each other to reflect back our strengths and weaknesses; we learn from others how to let go of individual concerns, how we are part of something bigger, that there is no difference between helping ourselves and helping others." It is something you build in yourself, a transformation that changes the quality of who you are, that goes beyond the surface personality."

Our conversation ranges widely from the mystical philosophy of the *Dao-de-jing* to the burning of "dragon tickets" and "dharma treasures" during funeral rites, but for Jim, my questions about death are essentially answered by the Daoist phrase that he quotes, "walking, standing, sitting, sleeping," a reference to the importance of training in every moment, training that is both outer and inner, individual and communal, dedicated to harmony and the transformation from personal mortality to the immortality of the natural way.

Notes

1. Different chronologies yield different dates falling between the sixteenth and eleventh centuries BCE.

2. The oracle-bones were tortoiseshell or cattle scapula used by diviners to answer questions put by rulers to their dead ancestors. Hollows were scraped out in the bone, which would then be touched by a burning hot poker and the resulting cracks interpreted in answer to the question. Later, inscriptions were added that identified the question and the result, and sometimes the verification, i.e., whether or not the divination proved correct.
3. In Daoist developments, the dichotomy evolved into a complex system of three *hun* souls and seven *po* souls associated with the person.
4. Laozi is a figure of legend who may or may not have been a historical person. Recent scholarship shows that the *Dao-de-jing* was not the work of a single author but more likely a collection of oral wisdom that passed through many hands, eventually evolving into the text we have today that was fixed around the third century CE (Kirkland, 2004, p. 53).
5. The International Taoist Tai Chi Society together with the Fung Loy Kok Institute of Taoism, founded in Canada in 1970 by Moy Lin-shin, currently constitute one of the most prominent and widespread Daoist organizations in the western hemisphere with some 40,000 members in 26 countries.

References and Further Reading

Ahern, Emily M. *The Cult of the Dead in a Chinese Village*. Stanford, CA: Stanford University Press, 1973.

Cheung, Peter Ka Hing, Cecelia Lai Wai Chan, Wai Fu, Li Yawen, and Grace Yee Kam Pau Cheung. "'Letting Go' and 'Holding On': Grieving and Traditional Death Rituals in Hong Kong." In Cecelia Lai Wai Chan and Amy Yin Man Chow (eds.), *Death, Dying and Bereavement: A Hong Kong Chinese Experience*. Hong Kong: Hong Kong University Press, 2006, pp. 65–86.

Creel, Herrlee G. *What is Taoism? and Other Studies in Chinese Cultural History*. Chicago: University of Chicago Press, 1970.

Hoffman, Yoel. *Japanese Death Poems*. Rutland, VT: Charles E. Tuttle Company, 1986.

Kirkland, Russell. *Taoism: The Enduring Tradition*. New York: Routledge, 2004.

Lau, D.C. *Lao Tzu: Tao Te Ching*. London: Penguin, 1963.

Moreman, Christopher M. *Beyond the Threshold*. Lanham, MD: Rowman and Littlefield, 2008.

Overmyer, D.T. "China." In Frederick H. Holck (ed.), *Death and Eastern Thought*. Nashville: Abingdon Press, 1974, pp. 198–225.

Palmer, David A. "The Body: Health, Nation, and Transcendence." In David A. Palmer, Glenn Shive, and Philip L. Wickeri (eds.), *Chinese Religious Life*. Oxford: Oxford University Press, 2011, pp. 87–106.

Potter, Jack M. "Cantonese Shamanism." In Arthur P. Wolf (ed.), *Religion and Ritual in Chinese Society*. Stanford, CA: Stanford University Press, 1974, pp. 207–231.

Schipper, Kristofer M. "The Written Memorial in Daoist Ceremonies." In Arthur P. Wolf (ed.), *Religion and Ritual in Chinese Society*. Stanford, CA: Stanford University Press, 1974, pp. 309–324.

Tam, Wai Lun. "Communal Worship and Festivals in Chinese Villages." In David A. Palmer, Glenn Shive, and Philip L. Wickeri (eds.), *Chinese Religious Life*. Oxford: Oxford University Press, 2011, pp. 30–49.

Thompson, Laurence G. *Chinese Religion*. Belmont, CA: Wadsworth, 1996.

Wolf, Arthur P. "Gods, Ghosts, and Ancestors." In Arthur P. Wolf (ed.), *Religion and Ritual in Chinese Society*. Stanford, CA: Stanford University Press, 1974, pp. 131–182.

Yang, C.K. *Religion in Chinese Society*. Berkeley, CA: University of California Press, 1961.

Yü, Ying-shih. "Life and Immortality in the Mind of Han China." *Harvard Journal of Asiatic Studies*, 25 (1964–1965): 80–122.

Index

Understanding Death: An Introduction to Ideas of Self and the Afterlife in World Religions,
First Edition. Angela Sumegi.
© 2014 Angela Sumegi. Published 2014 by Blackwell Publishing Ltd.

Index

Index

Index